Cookery

An Illustrated
Teach Yourself book

Ann Kendall

Illustrated
Teach Yourself
Cookery

TREASURE PRESS

First published in Great Britain by Brockhampton Press
(now Hodder & Stoughton Children's Books)

This edition published in 1983 by Treasure Press
59 Grosvenor Street
London W1

© 1974 Hodder & Stoughton Ltd

ISBN 0 907812 41 4

Printed in Singapore

The Publishers gratefully acknowledge the help given by the following companies in supplying colour photographs for use throughout the book:

cover: top and page 53, The White Fish Kitchen; bottom left and page 45, British Meat Service, Meat and Livestock Commission; bottom right and page 65, Wall's Ice Cream

frontispiece and page 42: Angostura Aromatic Bitters

page 7: Brown and Poulson

page 11: top, Angostura Aromatic Bitters; foot, Danish Food Centre, London

page 31: Rice Information Service

page 34: left, Lawry's Foods International Inc.; right, Angostura Aromatic Bitters

page 39: Angel Studio, London

page 43: Lawry's Foods International Inc.

pages 48, 57: Quaker Oats Limited

page 49: British Bacon Curers Federation

page 52: Danish Food Centre, London

page 56: top and foot, Quaker Oats Limited

page 61: top, Young's Seafoods Limited; foot, Potato Marketing Board

page 64: The Stork Cookery Service, Van den Berghs

page 68: Angel Studio, London

page 69: Australia House

page 72: Brown and Poulson

page 73: Quaker Oats Limited

page 76: top, The Stork Cookery Service, Van den Berghs; foot, Tate and Lyle

Contents

Metric and Imperial Measures

The United Kingdom Federation for Education in Home Economics recommends that, for simple recipes, 25gm should be taken as the equivalent of 1 oz and 500ml as the equivalent of 1 pint.

Full and accurate conversion tables are given below. PLEASE NOTE that when following a recipe you should use either metric measures or imperial measures but not a mixture of both because they are not interchangeable.

MASS
1 oz = 28.35 gm
2 oz = 56.7 gm
4 oz = 113.4 gm
8 oz = 226.8 gm
12 oz = 340.2 gm
16 oz = 453.6 gm
1 kilogram = 2.2 lb

CAPACITY
¼ pint = 142 ml
½ pint = 284 ml
1 pint = 568 ml
½ litre = 0.88 pint
1 litre = 1.76 pints

LENGTH
1 inch = 2.54 cm
6 inches = 15.2 cm
100 cm = 1 metre =
    39.37 inches

TEMPERATURE
32°F =   0°Celsius
212°F = 100°C
225°F = 107°C
250°F = 121°C
275°F = 135°C
300°F = 149°C
325°F = 163°C
350°F = 177°C
375°F = 190°C
400°F = 204°C
425°F = 218°C
450°F = 232°C

1 Introduction

There is nothing difficult or alarming about cooking. To the beginner who sees an experienced cook flinging handfuls of this and that into the pot, apparently haphazardly, it may look like magic, but by starting the right way, weighing and measuring the ingredients carefully and understanding the processes involved, everybody can learn to turn raw materials into appetising meals. As your experience grows, you can allow yourself more freedom in adapting recipes and methods, but to begin with, follow these simple rules:

1 Study the recipe before you start and make sure you understand all the processes.
2 Collect all the ingredients, utensils and dishes you will need.
3 If you will be using the oven, turn it on and arrange the shelves.
4 Follow the recipe exactly, weighing and measuring all ingredients.
5 Do not leave prepared dishes standing before cooking.
6 Don't keep hot food waiting. Serve it as soon as it is cooked.

Quantities   All the recipes in this book give enough for 4 people unless otherwise stated. Many people do not always cook for this number so here are some hints on altering the recipes for different numbers :

1 All recipes based on individual servings, e.g. chops, steaks, vegetables, fish fillets, can be adjusted by adding or subtracting portions as necessary. Cook for the time given but vary the size of the cooking utensil if necessary.

2 Sauces, soups and stuffing recipes can be altered easily by halving or doubling quantities. Cook for the time given but adjust the size of the pan for larger or smaller amounts of sauces and soups.

3 Do not alter recipes for pastry, cakes and made-up meat and fish dishes and puddings until you are experienced. The cooking times and utensils will vary for different amounts. If necessary, make more than you want and keep the leftovers in the fridge for the next day. If you want larger quantities, make up two separate dishes, each using the given amounts of ingredients. Remember when re-heating made-up meat dishes like stews that they must simmer for at least 15 minutes, for safety reasons.

Entertaining   'Entertaining' doesn't necessarily mean having an enormous party with lots of food and drink – two or three friends in for a simple meal is often just as much fun and far easier on you and your purse.

Occasionally you may like to throw a big party. In this book there are recipes which are suitable for parties of this sort – recipes which can easily be doubled, such as soups, salads, Baked Chicken Joints (served cold with salads) or Scotch Eggs. For a sweet make several Fruit Gâteaux or a big bowl of fruit salad, and don't forget that bowls of crisps, nuts and cheesy biscuits are always popular.

Some cooking processes described   BAKING : cooking in the oven using dry heat. Used for cakes, biscuits, bread and pastry.

BOILING : cooking in liquid at boiling point. Used for vegetables, rice and pasta.

Egg Mayonnaise

Shallow frying

Deep frying

FRYING : cooking in hot fat. There are two methods of frying :
Shallow Using a little fat in a frying pan. Used for fish, chops, steaks, sausages and fish cakes. For thin pieces of food, use only enough fat to prevent the food sticking to the pan. For thicker things, like fish cakes, use enough fat to form a layer ½-inch thick.
Deep Using a special pan with a wire basket. Used for chips, fish in batter and Scotch Eggs. Place enough fat in the pan to come about halfway up the pan. Heat until the right temperature is obtained (see below), then place the food in the basket and lower gently into the fat. Cook as directed, reheating the fat between each batch. Do not overfill the basket as this will lower the temperature of the fat. Food in batter is better lowered into the fat on a slotted spoon, rather than in the basket.
Fat for frying Any kind of fat or oil may be used for frying, but in practice, oil (vegetable, groundnut or corn oil), lard or butter are the most common. The cost of butter and the fact that it quickly burns means that it is only used for shallow frying. Lard or oil used for deep frying can be used over and over again if it is strained after use and stored in a basin or bottle in a cool, dark place.
Frying temperatures Until experienced, most cooks find a kitchen thermometer a good investment for perfect frying results. Recommended temperatures are given in the individual recipes.

GRILLING : cooking under or over a direct heat. Only suitable for tender food.
Used for steaks, chops, bacon, sausages, tomatoes, mushrooms, fish.
Preheat the grill before using.

ROASTING : formerly cooking on a turning spit before an open fire; now usually means cooking in fat in the oven.
Used for meat, poultry, vegetables. Meat and poultry should be of good quality for roasting.

SIMMERING : cooking in liquid just below boiling point. The liquid is brought to the boil and the heat then lowered, so that the surface is just moving.
Used for stews and fish.

STEAMING: cooking in a special perforated steamer, placed over a saucepan of boiling water. Top up the saucepan with more boiling water from time to time during the cooking. Used for sponge puddings, fish, some vegetables.

STEWING: slow cooking in a saucepan or casserole with close-fitting lid. Can be done on top of the stove or in the oven. Used for cheaper cuts of meat, boiling fowls.

Steaming

Cooking terms

Beat

ALUMINIUM FOIL: it is sensible to stock a roll of aluminium foil for wrapping food to be stored in the refrigerator, and for wrapping meat to be roasted. If you wrap joints or chicken in foil before cooking, you will find that there is less mess in the oven and the juices are conserved. However, the joint will tend to have a rather 'boiled' appearance so it is recommended that you open the foil for the last 30 minutes of cooking so that the food can become appetizingly browned.

BEAT: to mix together vigorously, using a circular movement to incorporate air. A term often used when making cakes or a batter.

BLEND: to mix two or more ingredients smoothly together. Used in making sauces and soups.

BOUQUET GARNI: a small bunch of herbs cooked with the food for flavouring, but thrown away before serving. It usually consists of parsley, thyme and bayleaf, but can include other herbs. Dried bouquet garni can be bought in small muslin bags.

BREADCRUMBS: *Fresh* Made by rubbing cubes of white bread against a grater or through a coarse sieve, or by using a liquidizer. Keep for 24 hours.
Used for stuffings, bread sauce and as an ingredient in some dishes.
Browned Made by drying off crusts and slices of bread in a cool oven until lightly coloured. They are then crushed or put through a mincer. Keep for several months in a cool, dry place. Used for coating food which is to be fried, for adding a crisp topping to savoury dishes.

CREAM: to beat fat and sugar together until pale and fluffy. Used in cake making.

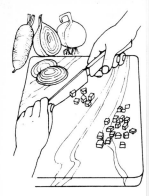

DICE : to cut into even-sized cubes.
Used for vegetables and for stewing meats.

FOLD IN : to mix a dry ingredient into a creamed or beaten mixture, or to add beaten egg whites to a mixture by stirring in very gently, using a metal spoon or a plastic spatula. Folding is a delicate process as everything must be completely mixed together, but too much beating will cause a fluffy mixture to sink.

PIPE : to force a soft mixture through a plain or patterned nozzle.
Used to make éclairs and to decorate cakes, pastries and sweets. A large nozzle can be used to pipe mashed potato round a meat dish.

RUB IN : to mix fat and dry ingredients by rubbing together gently with the fingertips until the mixture resembles fine breadcrumbs.
Used in pastry and some cakes.

SEASONED FLOUR : Flour mixed with a little salt and pepper.
Used to coat foods before they are cooked.

SHRED : to cut into narrow strips.
Used for vegetables.

SIEVE : to press cooked vegetables or fruit through a sieve to make a purée.
Used for soups, sauces and fruit creams.

SIFT : to put flour and other dry ingredients through a fine sieve.
Used to eliminate lumps and aerate the flour for cake making.

Dice

Pipe

Rub in

Shred

Opposite: **Cream of Tomato Soup**
Shellfish Cocktail

WHIP or WHISK : to introduce air by vigorous beating.
Used for egg whites or cream and in some gelatine dishes.
A special rotary beater or electric mixer can be used.

Using an electric mixer

An electric mixer can be used in many of these recipes. It is best to follow the times, settings and suggestions given in the manufacturers' instruction booklet.

Recipes in this book for which a mixer can be used include : batter for Yorkshire Pudding, Mayonnaise, Baked Custard, Baked Jam Sponge, Victoria Sandwich and Sponge Sandwich.

Whip or whisk

2 Soups and starters

A special-occasion meal always includes a soup or starter, but there is no reason why they should not be served more often. Soup is economical and delicious, and some soups are so filling that they almost make a meal in themselves.

Stocks The basis of most soups is a well-flavoured stock. Choose chicken-flavoured stock cubes for light-coloured soups and beef for darker ones. Make up the stock cubes as directed on the packet, remembering that they are strongly flavoured so amounts of salt, pepper and herbs may have to be adjusted. When you have time it is well worthwhile to make your own stock:

BROWN STOCK

Shin of beef, 1 lb/400 gm
Marrow bones, 1 lb/400 gm
Mixed vegetables (onion, carrot, leek, celery), 1 lb/400 gm
Water, 3 pints/1500 ml
Bouquet garni
Salt

1 Ask the butcher to chop the bones for you. Place them and the chopped meat in a flat oven-proof dish in the oven until browned.
2 Prepare vegetables as described in chapter 8.
3 Place browned meat and bones in a large saucepan with the vegetables and the rest of the ingredients. Cover, and simmer for 4 hours.
4 Strain into a bowl and cool. When set, skim off fat and use as desired. Unused stock will keep in the refrigerator for 2–3 days.

WHITE STOCK

Knuckle of veal, or veal bones, 2 lb/800 gm
Mixed vegetables (onion, carrot, leek, celery), 1 lb/400 gm
Water, 4 pints/2000 ml
Bouquet garni
Salt

1 Ask the butcher to chop the bones for you. Place them in a large saucepan with the prepared vegetables and the remaining ingredients.
2 Continue as for Brown Stock.

CHICKEN STOCK may be made as above by substituting chicken carcase and giblets for the knuckle of veal.

FRENCH ONION SOUP

Onions, ¾ lb/300 gm
Butter, 1 oz/25 gm
Flour, 1 oz/25 gm
Brown stock, 1½ pints/750 ml
Salt and pepper

1 Skin onions and slice thinly.
2 Melt butter in a large saucepan and fry onions, stirring, until evenly browned.
3 Stir in flour, add stock gradually, season with salt and pepper and simmer, covered, for 30 minutes.

Traditionally this soup is served with slices of French bread, topped with cheese, and browned. They can either be floated on top of the soup tureen or placed in the individual soup bowls and the soup poured over them.

MINESTRONE

Onion, 1
Carrot, 1
Leek, 1
Turnip, 1
Celery, 1 stick
White cabbage, quarter, small
Bacon, 2 rashers
Butter, 1 oz/25 gm
Macaroni, 1 oz/25 gm
Brown stock, 1¾ pints/875 ml
Tomato purée, 2 teaspoons
Salt and pepper
Garlic (optional), 1 clove
Grated Parmesan or Cheddar cheese

1 Prepare vegetables as described in chapter 8 and slice thinly.
2 Rind and dice bacon.
3 Melt butter in large saucepan, add bacon and vegetables and fry gently for 3–4 minutes, stirring, until beginning to soften.
4 Break up macaroni and add with stock, tomato purée, salt and pepper, and crushed garlic if used.
5 Simmer, covered, for 30 minutes. Re-season if necessary and serve sprinkled with cheese.

Add the stock and macaroni

Cream soups Cream soups consist of a purée of vegetables or meat, thickened with flour. Eggs or cream can also be used for thickening, but are more tricky and, of course, expensive.

CREAM OF TOMATO SOUP

Illustrated on page 11

Onion, 1
Carrot, 1
Tomatoes, 1½ lb/600 gm
Bacon, 2 rashers
Butter, 1 oz/25 gm
Flour, 1 oz/25 gm
White or chicken stock, 1 pint/500 ml
Bouquet garni
Salt and pepper
Cream or top-milk, 3 tablespoons
Sugar

1 Skin onion, peel and chop carrot; chop tomatoes.
2 Rind and dice bacon.
3 Melt butter in large saucepan and fry onion, carrot and bacon for 3–4 minutes without colouring.
4 Add tomatoes and sprinkle with flour. Stir and gradually pour in the stock.
5 Bring to the boil, stirring, add bouquet garni and salt and pepper. Simmer, covered, for 30 minutes.
6 Sieve and reheat. Stir in cream, re-season, adding a little sugar, and heat until not quite boiling. Serve with croûtons (see below), or sprinkle with chopped parsley.
If the soup seems too pale, stir in 1–2 tablespoons tomato purée with the cream.
Variation: Use a can of tomatoes (1 lb 12 oz/700 gm). Drain and make the juice up to 1 pint/500 ml with stock, instead of using all the stock as above.

Soup garnishes Any kind of soup, bought or home-made, looks better served in an attractive mug or bowl, with an appetizing garnish. Some garnishes merely look pretty, while others, such as pasta and croûtons, are more substantial and turn a snack into a filling meal.

CROÛTONS: particularly good with cream soups, where they add a different texture.
1 *Fried croûtons* Dice bread into ½-inch cubes and fry in butter, lard or dripping until browned. Drain on kitchen paper and serve immediately.
2 *Toasted croûtons* Toast ½-inch thick slices of bread, and dice evenly.

PASTA: often added to thin soups. Special soup pastas are made, though broken macaroni or noodles can be used. Cook in the soup for the time recommended on the packet.

VEGETABLE GARNISHES: finely sliced or diced vegetables are an attractive garnish to any soup. Cook by boiling in salted water until tender, or by frying gently in a little fat. Mixed diced vegetables are good with potato soup and fried, sliced leeks with cream of tomato.

Grated cheese, chopped parsley or chives or a spoonful of cream (swirled over the top of a bowl of tomato soup) are all easy garnishes that add colour and interest.

Canned and packet soups

Make up as directed on the can or packet, but add extra touches like your own garnish, or use milk or home-made stock instead of water. A spoonful of cream or top of the milk improves cream soups if added just before serving. Stir a spoonful of sherry or wine into clear soups. Combine two types of soup to give an unusual flavour.

Try: Oxtail with onion
  Tomato with minestrone
  Green pea with mushroom
  Chicken and rice with celery

Condensed canned soups, used undiluted, make excellent sauces for main course dishes.

Try: Mushroom with fish or chicken
  Tomato with meat loaf or sausages

Starters

It is sometimes easier to serve a cold starter than a soup, since it is generally possible to prepare it in advance. Choose the starter to complement the other courses – do not, for instance, have a fish cocktail before a fish main dish, or a fruit cocktail when you are serving fruit salad as a sweet.

MELON

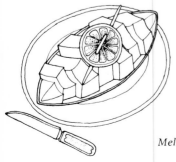

1 Chill for 1–2 hours, then slice into even, wedge-shaped pieces, removing seeds and membranes.
2 With a sharp knife, cut round the flesh just inside the skin and then cut the flesh into pieces.
3 Decorate with a cherry or a slice of orange on a cocktail stick.

Serve with caster sugar and ground ginger in separate small bowls.

Melon garnished with orange slice

GRAPEFRUIT

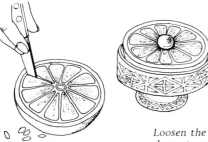

1 Cut fruit in half crosswise and loosen the flesh from the skin and membranes with a grapefruit knife or sharp, serrated knife.
2 Discard pips, membranes and centre core.
3 Decorate with a cherry or a sprig of mint and hand sugar separately.
Grapefruit are better if served chilled.

*Loosen the grapefruit flesh;
decorate with a cherry*

TOMATO JUICE COCKTAIL

Pour the contents of a 19 oz/475 gm can of tomato juice into a jug with a dash of Worcestershire sauce, the juice of ½ lemon, salt and pepper. Stir, chill and serve in glasses topped with a lemon wedge and a sprig of mint.

*Top with lemon wedge
and a sprig of mint*

Special starters   A little more elaborate and tricky, but they make a wonderful beginning for a special meal.

HORS D'OEUVRES VARIÉS

Lettuce, 4 leaves
Potato salad (page 69) or
   7 oz/175 gm can
Sardines in oil, 4¼ oz/106 gm can
Thinly sliced salami or
   garlic sausage, 4 oz/100 gm
Tomatoes, 4 large
Cooked beetroot, 2 small
Lemon juice, 2 tablespoons
Oil, 4 tablespoons
Salt and pepper
Chopped chives or parsley

1 Arrange the lettuce on 4 plates with the potato salad.
2 Drain oil from the sardines and arrange on the plates with the salami.
3 Slice tomatoes thinly, dice beetroot and divide on the plates.
4 Beat the lemon juice with the oil and seasoning. Pour over tomatoes.
5 Garnish with chopped chives or parsley.

SHELLFISH COCKTAIL

Illustrated on page 11

Prepared shrimps or prawns (fresh,
 frozen or canned), 8 oz/200 gm
Lettuce, 1 small
Mayonnaise or salad cream,
 3 tablespoons
Cream or top-milk, 2 tablespoons
Tomato ketchup, 2 tablespoons
Worcestershire sauce
Salt and pepper
Lemon wedges

1 Thaw frozen fish or drain canned fish if used.
2 Shred lettuce finely and divide between four
sundae dishes or stemmed glasses. Top with fish,
reserving a few for garnish.
3 Mix mayonnaise, cream and ketchup, and
season with a dash of Worcestershire sauce, salt
and pepper. Spoon over fish.
4 Chill and serve garnished with the reserved fish
and lemon wedges, and perhaps a sprig of parsley.
Canned or fresh lobster or crab can be used
instead of shrimps or prawns.

*Arrange ingredients in layers;
garnish with lemon wedges and
one or two of the fish*

EGG MAYONNAISE

Illustrated on page 7

Eggs, 4
Lettuce, 1 small
Mayonnaise or salad cream,
 ¼ pint/125 ml
Lemon juice or milk
Anchovy fillets, 4
Capers or stuffed olives
Tomato, 1 (optional)
Green pepper, shredded

1 Hardboil the eggs (see page 71). Drain and cool
under running water. Shell and halve lengthwise.
Place on a rack over a plate.
2 Divide the lettuce between four small plates,
or arrange on a serving dish.
3 If the mayonnaise is very thick, mix with a
little lemon juice or milk, and spoon over the
eggs so that they are thickly coated, or serve
separately.
4 Carefully transfer eggs on to the lettuce leaves
and garnish with halved anchovy fillets, capers
or halved stuffed olives, or green pepper. Cut the
tomato, if used, into 4 slices, cut each in half and
arrange beside the eggs.

*Decorate with anchovy fillets
and stuffed olives*

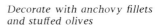

3 Fish

Skinning fish

Fish is a very useful source of protein; fresh, frozen or canned fish can be bought everywhere, so plan to have one or two fish meals every week.

Most fresh fish bought from the fishmonger is, in fact, frozen within a very few hours of catching and kept in this state until it is placed on the slab. This means that it is in prime condition when sold, but use it straight away as it will not keep for more than 12 hours in the refrigerator. Frozen packeted fish should be kept in the frozen food compartment of the refrigerator until cooked as directed on the packet.

Buy fresh fish when it is in season; choose fish with firm flesh, bright scales and no 'fishy' smell.

The fishmonger will generally clean the fish for you and bone and fillet it if necessary. However, you may want to remove the skin, particularly the dark skin from plaice fillets. To do this, lay the fillet skin side downwards and grip the tail end securely with the fingers. Using a sawing motion, use a sharp knife to divide the flesh from the skin.

Before cooking the fish, wash well in running cold water and wipe dry with kitchen paper.

Types of fish –
a brief list

This can be divided into *white fish* (sea or freshwater), *oily fish* and *shellfish*.

White fish

COD: a large, white-fleshed fish generally sold in fillets or steaks. It has very little flavour, so a tasty stuffing or sauce is added. It can be baked, fried, grilled or poached.
Cheap and available all the year round.

HADDOCK: also has firm white flesh, but with a better flavour than cod and used in the same ways.
In season September to February.

HAKE: another firm, white-fleshed fish with a good flavour.
Used as cod.
In season June to January.

HALIBUT: an expensive, white-fleshed fish with a good flavour, generally sold in steaks.
Used as cod, but mostly baked or grilled.
In season August to April.

PLAICE: a white-fleshed flat fish with a good flavour.
Can be filleted or cooked whole.
In season all the year round.

SOLE: an expensive flat fish with an excellent flavour.
Can be filleted or cooked whole.
In season all the year round.

TURBOT: another high quality flat fish with a good flavour, generally sold cut into steaks.
In season March to August.

Oily fish HERRING: a cheap and extremely nourishing fish.
Can be fried, grilled or soused.
Available all the year round.
Other types of herring are available, including kippers (split open before smoking), bloaters (smoked whole) and salt herring.

MACKEREL: larger and rather more delicate flesh than herring; they must be eaten very fresh.
Cook as herring.
Available all the year round.

SALMON: a freshwater fish, either fresh or imported (frozen or chilled).
Poach or grill. Can be served hot or cold.
Available all the year round.

TROUT: another freshwater fish with a very delicate flavour.
Good grilled or fried.
At their best April to August.

Shellfish CRAB: choose a medium-sized crab (4–6 lb/1 kg 600 gm – 2 kg 400 gm) as the shell is heavy.
Serve as salad or hot as a savoury.
In season April to October. Also canned and frozen.

OYSTERS: very expensive.
Eaten raw with lemon juice.
In season September to April.

LOBSTER: served hot or cold. A very expensive fish.
In season June to September.

SCALLOPS: delicate flavour.
Can be cooked in sauce or fried and are usually served in their own shells.
In season October to March.

SCAMPI: large prawns.
Often served fried or in a fish cocktail.
Can be bought frozen but are expensive.

SHRIMPS AND PRAWNS: delicately flavoured small shellfish. Prawns are slightly larger than shrimps and more expensive. Usually sold already cooked.
Used in salads, fish cocktails, sauces and garnishes.
Can be bought frozen or canned.

Canned fish Canned fish is a useful store-cupboard buy as all varieties form the basis of a substantial snack and some are essential items of certain dishes.
Salmon: use in made-up dishes, in salads or in sandwiches.
Crab: use in made-up dishes, seafood cocktails, sandwiches and salads.
Shrimps and prawns: use as for crab and as a garnish for fish dishes. Use in shrimp or prawn sauce to serve with Baked Fish.
Tuna: use in salads, made-up dishes and sandwiches.
Pilchards and sardines: use in salads, sandwiches and on toast as a snack.
Anchovies: use as a garnish for Egg Mayonnaise and with Scrambled Eggs as a snack.

To fry fish Coat the fish so that the fat does not penetrate and make the food greasy.
Use: seasoned flour (for shallow frying only), see recipe for Sole Meunière
egg and breadcrumbs (shallow or deep frying), see recipe for Egg and Breadcrumbed Plaice
batter (deep frying only), see recipe for Batter-coated Cod
oatmeal (shallow frying of oily fish), see recipe for Fried Herrings

Shallow fry: thin, even pieces of fish like fillets of plaice, sole, herrings and mackerel.
Deep fry: fillets of plaice and thicker pieces of fish like cod and haddock fillets.

To grill fish 1 Season fish and sprinkle with lemon juice. Brush with melted butter (except for oily fish).
2 Place in grill pan under heated grill; cook from 3 to 10 minutes each side, depending on thickness.

To poach fish Simmer very gently in milk, stock (made with the fish trimmings) or water. It is often difficult to avoid breaking the fish when taking it out.

To bake fish Most types of fish can be baked in an ovenproof dish, often with stuffings, garnishings or vegetables such as tomatoes and onion.

EGG AND BREADCRUMBED PLAICE (using frying pan)

Illustrated on page 61

Fillets of plaice, 4 large or
  8 small
Egg, 1
Fresh white breadcrumbs
Fat for frying
Lemon wedges

1 Wash and dry fillets. Beat egg on a plate and place breadcrumbs on a piece of kitchen paper.
2 Coat fillets with egg, using a brush, and dip in breadcrumbs, patting well in and coating fillets evenly.
3 Heat a little fat in the pan and fry fillets, two at a time, for 3–5 minutes on each side, turning once. Re-heat fat, adding extra if necessary, between each frying.
4 Drain on kitchen paper and keep warm in a low oven.
Serve quickly with lemon wedges, parsley sauce (page 86), potatoes and peas, or with a green salad and chipped potatoes.
Cook sole, thin fillets of cod and haddock in the same way.

Coating fillets with egg

BATTER-COATED COD (deep pan with wire basket)

Illustrated on page 53

Cod fillets, 4, each 6 oz/150 gm
For the batter:
Plain flour, 4 oz/100 gm
Salt and pepper
Egg, 1
Milk, ¼ pint/125 ml
Fat for frying
Lemon wedges

1 Follow directions on page 50 for making the batter.
2 Heat the fat in the pan to 350°–370°F (177°–188°C) or until it will brown a cube of bread in 60 seconds.
3 Wash and dry the cod, dip in the batter and lower gently into the hot fat. Cook, two at a time, for 5–7 minutes until golden. Re-heat the fat and fry the remaining fish. Serve quickly, with lemon wedges, chipped potatoes, tomatoes and peas. Garnish with watercress.
Cook plaice and fillets of haddock in the same way.

Dipping cod in batter

BAKED COD STEAKS

Cod steaks, 4, each about 6 oz/150 gm
Salt and pepper
Butter, 2 oz/50 gm
Fresh white breadcrumbs, 2 oz/50 gm
Chopped parsley, 1 teaspoon
Dried mixed herbs, a pinch
Lemon wedges

Ovenproof dish for cooking and serving
Oven temperature : moderate (350°F,
  177°C, Mark 4)

1 With a sharp knife remove central bone from each cod steak. Trim fins, wash, wipe dry, season with salt and pepper and arrange in buttered dish..
2 Melt half the butter and stir in breadcrumbs, parsley, herbs and seasoning. Stuff the hole in the middle of each steak with this mixture.
3 Dot steaks with remaining butter and bake in centre of oven for 15–20 minutes.
Serve with lemon wedges.
Cook halibut steaks in the same way.

VARIATION
Mix 2 peeled, chopped tomatoes
    2 oz/50 gm cooked rice
    2 oz/50 gm grated cheese
    salt and pepper
Use in the same way to stuff the steaks.

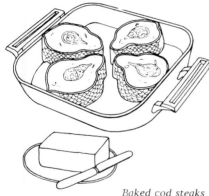

Baked cod steaks

SOLE MEUNIÈRE

Sole, 4, filleted
Seasoned flour
Butter, 4 oz/100 gm
Lemon, juice of one
Parsley, 3 tablespoons
Lemon wedges

Use a shallow frying pan

1 Wash and dry fillets and coat with seasoned flour.
2 Melt half the butter in the pan and fry the fish (in two stages if the pan will not hold all the fillets at once) for 3–4 minutes on each side, turning once. Lift out carefully; drain on kitchen paper. Arrange on serving dish and keep warm.
3 Wipe out pan with kitchen paper, add remaining butter, lemon juice and parsley. Heat, but do not allow it to colour. Pour over the fish and serve immediately with lemon wedges.
Cook whole sole (allow 5 minutes cooking time each side) or filleted or whole plaice in the same way.

PLAICE WITH SOUR CREAM

Plaice, 8 fillets
Butter, ½ oz/12 gm
Onion, 1 small
Green pepper, 1 small
Tomatoes, 2
Salt and pepper
Sour cream or yoghurt, 5 oz/125 gm
  carton
Paprika, level teaspoon

Use shallow ovenproof dish
Oven temperature: moderate (350°F,
  177°C, Mark 4)

1 Skin fillets (see page 19) and grease dish with the butter.
2 Peel and chop the onion finely. Halve the pepper and remove seeds and white pith. Put onion and pepper in the dish, cover with tomato cut into slices, season with salt and pepper.
3 Roll up the plaice fillets and arrange on the tomatoes. Stir paprika into the cream and pour over the fish.
4 Cook, covered, in the centre of the oven and serve from the dish.

*Rolled fillets of plaice
on tomato slices*

FISH PIE

Cod fillet, 1 lb/400 gm
Milk
Bay leaf, ½ leaf
Onion, 1 slice
Salt and pepper
Mashed potatoes (page 83),
  2 lb/800 gm
Butter, 1 oz/25 gm
Flour, 1 oz/25 gm
Chopped parsley, 1 tablespoon

Use an ovenproof dish
Oven temperature: fairly hot (400°F,
  204°C, Mark 6)

1 Wash the fish and place in a saucepan with ¼ pint/125 ml milk, the piece of bay leaf, onion slice, salt and pepper. Bring to the boil, cover and simmer for 5–10 minutes or until the fish flakes easily. Drain off the liquid and make up to ½ pint/250 ml with more milk.
2 Flake the fish, removing bones, skin and the bay leaf and onion.
3 Melt the butter and stir in the flour. Cook for 1–2 minutes. Remove from the heat and stir in most of the fish liquor. Bring to the boil, stirring, and cook for 2–3 minutes. Add the flaked fish, parsley, extra seasoning and reserved fish liquor. Pour into the dish.
4 Pile the potatoes evenly on the fish mixture, marking the top with a fork (see opposite page). Bake at the top of the oven for 25–30 minutes until the pie is heated through and the top is golden brown.

VARIATIONS
1 Add 1–2 chopped, hardboiled eggs, or 2 oz/50 gm fresh, frozen or canned prawns to the sauce.
2 Sprinkle the top of the potato with dried breadcrumbs, crushed crisps or grated cheese before baking.
Use haddock, fresh or smoked, or smoked cod fillet in the same way.

FRIED HERRINGS

Herrings, 4
Salt and pepper
Oatmeal
Fat for frying
Vinegar, or mustard sauce

Use a frying pan

1 Wash and dry herrings. Sprinkle with salt and pepper and roll in oatmeal, pressing well in all over.
2 Heat fat in frying pan and shallow fry herrings for about 8–10 minutes, turning once, until browned and cooked through.
Drain on kitchen paper and serve with salt and vinegar or mustard sauce (page 87).
Filleted herrings and mackerel may be cooked in the same way.

GRILLED MACKEREL

Mackerel, cleaned, 4
Salt and pepper
Melted butter

1 Wash and dry mackerel, sprinkle inside and out with salt and pepper and brush with melted butter. With a sharp knife make 3–4 slashes on each side, cutting down to the bone. This allows heat to penetrate evenly.
2 Heat grill and place fish on the grid. Cook under a medium heat for about 12–15 minutes, turning once, until lightly browned and cooked through.
Serve with mustard sauce (page 87).
Cook herrings in the same way.

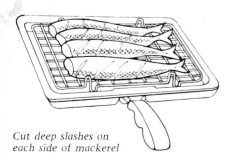

Cut deep slashes on each side of mackerel

SOUSED HERRINGS

Herrings, boned, 8 small
Salt and pepper
Bay leaves, 2
Onion, 1 slice
Black peppercorns, 6
Water and malt vinegar, mixed
  ½ pint/250 ml

Use shallow ovenproof dish
Oven temperature: moderate (350°F,
  177°C, Mark 4)

1 Wash herrings, remove heads and trim fins. Season with salt and pepper. Place a small piece of bay leaf in each fish and roll up from the head. Place in a single layer in the dish, tails upward.

2 Divide onion slice into rings and scatter over the dish with the peppercorns. Pour in enough liquid almost to cover the fish. Cover and cook in centre of oven for 35–40 minutes. Cool in the liquor and serve as a starter or with salad as a main course.

Cook mackerel in the same way.

Scatter onion rings over fish

Salmon Fresh or frozen salmon is bought whole, in a large piece or in steaks. It tends to break up when poached, so large pieces are most successful baked in the oven. Steaks can be baked or grilled.

Fresh salmon is delicately flavoured but very expensive.

Frozen or chilled salmon has a good flavour, but dries out quickly when grilled; bake the fish for the best results.

Canned salmon has a completely different flavour but is a useful store-cupboard standby for all types of made-up fish dishes, salads and sandwiches. Drain thoroughly, flake the flesh and remove bones before using.

Smoked salmon is sold thinly sliced and used as a starter. Serve with thin brown bread and butter and lemon wedges. Allow 1½–2 oz/40–50 gm per person.

BAKED SALMON

Salmon, 2–3 lb/800 gm–1 kg 200 gm
 piece
Butter
Salt and pepper
Lemon juice

Oven temperature: cool (300°F, 149°C,
 Mark 1–2)

1 Wipe salmon, butter a large piece of foil and place fish in the centre. Season with salt, pepper and lemon juice. Wrap loosely.

2 Place on baking tray in centre of oven and cook for 30 minutes per lb/400 gm.

3 Remove from oven and fold back foil. If skin can easily be peeled from the flesh, the fish is cooked. If not, return to the oven for a further 10–15 minutes.

To serve hot Remove foil and transfer fish to a serving dish. Serve garnished with lemon wedges, accompanied by new potatoes, and peas or cucumber salad (page 70).

To serve cold Allow to cool in the foil, remove foil and skin and transfer to a serving dish. Garnish with cucumber slices and serve with green salad (page 67), new potatoes and mayonnaise (page 91).

For a special occasion, remove central bone before serving, to simplify serving.

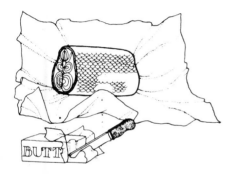

Cook salmon in foil

GRILLED SALMON STEAKS

Salmon steaks, 4
Salt and pepper
Lemon juice
Melted butter

1 Wipe the salmon steaks, season with salt, pepper and lemon juice.

2 Brush the grill grid and the steaks with melted butter and arrange the steaks on the grid. Grill under a medium heat, turning once, for about 15 minutes.

3 Serve with lemon wedges and the same vegetables as for Baked Salmon.

Here is a recipe for a 'special' dish made with shellfish. Quantities are for a main course for 2, or a starter for 4. Crab, lobster or prawns can be used in place of the scampi.

SCAMPI PROVENÇAL

Onion, 1 large, peeled and chopped
Butter, 1 oz/25 gm
Tomatoes, 15 oz/375 gm can
Salt and pepper
White wine or dry sherry, 2–3 tablespoons
Mixed herbs, a pinch
Clove of garlic, crushed (optional)
Frozen scampi, 8 oz/200 gm, thawed and drained
Parsley to garnish

1 Peel and chop the onion and fry in the butter until soft. Stir in the tomatoes, salt, pepper, wine, herbs and garlic. Bring to the boil and simmer for 10–15 minutes until thick.

2 Add the scampi and simmer for a further 3–5 minutes.

3 Serve with boiled rice, garnished with parsley.

Frozen fish For many people the most convenient way of buying fish is to buy it frozen in packets. There is no waste as all bones, skin, etc., are removed before packaging and in most cases the portions are separately packed so, with care, it is possible to remove what you need and return the rest to your frozen food compartment. The packet will indicate the length of time you can safely keep fish in your particular type of frozen food compartment.

Follow the directions on the packet for thawing and cooking times, though as a rule these are the same as for fresh fish. Several types of frozen fish are better cooked from the frozen state.

Here are a few notes on what is available:

White fish: cod, plaice, haddock – fillets and steaks. These can be cooked in all the usual ways, baking, frying, grilling or used in made-up dishes like fish pie.

Cured fish: smoked haddock, kippers – useful for breakfasts, snacks and made-up fish dishes.

Fancy fishes: trout, prawns, scampi, shrimps, crab. These are expensive but worthwhile for a special occasion. A few prawns are a nice addition to a fish pie or as a garnish to a fish salad. Both prawns, shrimps and crab can be used in Shellfish Cocktails. Potted shrimps are a ready-made starter which only need thawing and serving with lemon wedges and brown bread and butter.

Made-up fish items: fish fingers, fish cakes, etc. Useful for quick snacks and children's meals. Cook as directed on the packet, but serve with an interesting sauce or garnish.

4 Meat

Meat contains proteins, vitamins, minerals and fats, which are all essential to a balanced diet. High quality meat, always more expensive, is the basis of simple meals like roasts and grills. The cheaper cuts, which are just as nutritious, need long, slow cooking as stews, casseroles and made-up dishes.

Buying and storing meat

Buy meat from a clean shop which has a good turnover. In a supermarket, look for packs which do not have discoloured wrappings, indicating that the meat may have been packed the day before and not kept in the best conditions.

Most imported frozen meat is thawed out by the butcher before sale. Some supermarkets sell frozen packs – these can be taken home quickly and kept for a limited time in the freezer compartment of your refrigerator, but as a rule aim to cook meat within 3 days and offal and mince within 24 hours of purchase.

Thaw *frozen meats* completely before cooking. Some small, commercially packed items like beefburgers can be cooked from the frozen state, but follow the directions on the packet. Small pieces of meat take 1–2 hours to thaw at room temperature; joints should be left, covered, overnight in a cool place.

Store *fresh or cooked meat* in a refrigerator or very cool larder, lightly covered. Take cooked meats out of the refrigerator 30 minutes before using, or they will be hard and tasteless.

Portions: how much will you need?

Roasting joints

As most people aim to have enough left over for at least one cold meal from a joint, it is better to buy too large a joint than too small. Joints do shrink on cooking, so allow about 8 oz/200 gm per person of a joint without bone and about 12 oz/300 gm for a joint with bone. For a family of four you will need a 3½–4 lb/1 kg 400 gm–1 kg 600 gm joint for one hot and one cold meal.

Fried and grilled meat

Allow one large chop or escalope or two small ones per person. A steak of 6–8 oz/150–200 gm is a good size; steaks of up to 12 oz/300 gm are for hearty appetites.

Made-up dishes

Stews, casseroles and offal dishes are generally based on a serving of 6 oz/150 gm meat per person. Allow about 1½ lb/600 gm of stewing steak for a casserole for four.

Stuffed joints   Most joints contain bones, which make them rather difficult to carve, so a butcher often removes them and ties the joint into a neat shape. In the following pages you will find recipes for such boned and rolled or boned, stuffed and rolled joints, in which the bone cavity is filled with herb (page 90) or sage and onion (page 89) stuffing and the joint is then tied into a neat shape. Stuffing adds extra bulk to the joint, making it go further; it also adds extra flavour. Stuff and tie the joint loosely, as stuffing expands on cooking. Calculate the cooking time on the total weight of the joint plus stuffing. Remove the strings before serving.

Remember to ask the butcher to let you have the bones, which will make a basis for stock (page 13) which can be used for gravy or soup.

Roasting in foil   As mentioned on page 9, joints to be roasted may be wrapped in foil to minimize oven cleaning. However, it is essential to fold back or remove the foil for the last 30 minutes of cooking, to allow the joint to brown.

See-through roasting wrap is available on roll and as made-up bags. The meat browns through the wrap. Use as directed by the manufacturers.

Fold back the foil to enable joint to brown

Beef   Good quality beef is bright red in colour, with creamy-coloured fat. Fat should also be 'marbled' through the lean, as this keeps the joint moist during cooking.

Some of the most usual cuts are:

SIRLOIN: a good quality roasting joint, sold on the bone, or boned and rolled.

RIBS: another roasting joint sold on or off the bone.

TOPSIDE: a cheaper, lean roasting or braising joint. Needs extra fat.

SILVERSIDE: a lean cut sometimes sold salted. Suitable for boiling.

CHUCK OR SHOULDER STEAK: a cheaper cut for stews and pies.

STEWING STEAK: cheaper, tougher meat from the leg or shin, used only for stewing. It needs long cooking and careful removal of the fatty parts and gristle for the best results.

Beef Curry with rice

STEAK: for grilling or frying. There are various different cuts; the most common are *rump*, which comes near the sirloin and includes some fat, and *fillet*, lean, high quality and very expensive, often cut into small rounds called Tournedos.

MINCE: offcuts and pieces of stewing steak are sold ready minced by most butchers. Good mince should be fine and lean.

BRISKET: a cheap cut sold on or off the bone. It is rather fatty and can be slow roasted or used in casseroles. It is also sold salted for boiling.

32

Cooking times and temperatures for Roast Beef

JOINT	PREPARATION	OVEN TEMP.	COOKING TIME	FINISH
Sirloin Ribs	On the bone	Hot (425°F, 218°C, Mark 7)	15 min. per lb/ 400 gm plus 15 min.	Rare
Sirloin Ribs	Boned and rolled	As above	20 min. per lb/ 400 gm plus 20 min.	Medium
Sirloin Ribs	On the bone	Fairly hot (375°F, 191°C, Mark 5)	25 min. per lb/ 400 gm plus 25 min.	Rare–medium
Sirloin Ribs Topside	Boned and rolled	As above	30 min. per lb/ 400 gm	Rare–medium
Brisket	On or off the bone	Warm (325°F, 163°C, Mark 3)	40 min. per lb/ 400 gm	Medium–well done

ROAST BEEF

A roasting joint
Lard or dripping

1 Wipe the joint, place in a roasting tin, fat side uppermost, and dot some lard or dripping on the top if the meat is very lean.
2 Roast in the centre of the oven as shown above. Most people like beef rare rather than medium cooked, though cheaper cuts like brisket must be medium to well done, otherwise they will be tough.
Serve with thin gravy (page 87), roast potatoes (page 84), Yorkshire pudding (see below) and a green vegetable. Parsnips, baked round the joint (page 79), are good with beef.

YORKSHIRE PUDDING

Plain flour, 4 oz/100 gm
Salt, a pinch
Egg, 1
Milk and water, mixed, ½ pint/250 ml
Fat or dripping, 2 tablespoons

Use a 7-inch square cake tin
Oven temperature: fairly hot (400°F, 204°C, Mark 6)

1 Sift the flour and salt into a bowl. Add the egg and some of the liquid.
2 Beat until smooth then stir in the remaining liquid.
3 Place the dripping in the tin and heat at the top of the oven for 5 minutes.
4 Remove the tin from the oven, pour in the batter and return to the top of the oven. Cook until risen and golden – about 30–35 minutes.
Serve immediately, cut into squares, with Roast Beef.

BEEF CURRY

Illustrated on page 31

Stewing steak, 1½ lb/600 gm
Ground ginger, ½ level teaspoon
Turmeric, 1 level teaspoon
Ground coriander, 1½ level teaspoon
Ground cumin seed, 1 level teaspoon
Chili powder, ½ level teaspoon
Ground cinnamon, a pinch
Salt, 2 level teaspoons
Onions, 2 large
Tomatoes, 6
Oil, 2 tablespoons
Flour, 1 level tablespoon
Stock, ¼ pint/125 ml

1. Trim the meat and cut into even-sized chunks. Mix the spices with the salt. Peel and slice the onions, peel and quarter the tomatoes.

2 Heat the oil in a saucepan and add the spices. Fry for about two minutes, stirring all the time, then add the meat and cook slowly, stirring until browned all over.

3 Remove the meat and add the onions to the pan. Fry, stirring, until lightly browned. Add the flour and cook for 2–3 minutes.

4 Remove from the heat and stir in the stock and tomatoes. Return to the heat, add the meat and bring to the boil.

5 Cover and leave to simmer gently for about 2 hours or until the meat is tender and the sauce is reduced to a thick gravy.

Serve with boiled rice and some of the accompaniments mentioned below.

Note: Cooking instructions for rice are on page 94.

VARIATIONS

1 For a Chicken Curry – use 4 chicken joints. Trim and halve. Fry with the spices and then cook in the same way for 1 hour.

2 For a less hot curry the amount of chili powder may be halved. Two cloves of garlic, crushed, may be added with the onions.

3 If commercially blended curry powder is used, instead of the spices in this recipe, you will need 1½ level tablespoons.

ACCOMPANIMENTS

Although it is not essential, you could serve accompaniments with a curry – choose two or three from the following list:

Mango chutney

Sliced banana sprinkled with lemon juice

Tomato and onion salad – very thinly sliced raw onion and peeled, sliced tomatoes mixed together with a little French dressing

Pineapple – chunks or slices

Desiccated or grated fresh coconut

Ground almonds

Hamburger

BROWN STEW

Stewing steak, 1½ lb/600 gm
Flour, 2 level tablespoons
Salt and pepper
Onions, 2
Carrots, 2
Turnip, 1 (optional)
Stock, ½ pint/250 ml
Mixed dried herbs, a pinch
Bay leaf, 1

Use an ovenproof casserole
Oven temperature: moderate (350°F,
177°C, Mark 4)

Shepherd's Pie

1 Cut the stewing steak into 1-inch cubes, removing skin and fat. Mix the flour with plenty of salt and pepper and use to coat the meat. Peel the onions, carrots and turnip, if used, and slice.
2 Melt the dripping in a saucepan and fry the onions until lightly browned. Add the meat and fry, stirring, until browned. Transfer to an ovenproof casserole.
3 Stir the remaining flour into the fat and cook, stirring, until evenly browned. Remove from the heat and gradually stir in the stock.
4 Return to the heat and bring to the boil. Add the mixed herbs and bay leaf and pour over the meat in the casserole. Add the carrots and turnip.
5 Cover and cook in the centre of the oven for about 2 hours. Remove the bay leaf before serving. A flameproof casserole can be used for both the preliminary frying and the cooking.
Serve Brown Stew with potatoes in their jackets, mashed potatoes or rice and a green vegetable.

VARIATIONS
1 Add a drained can of tomatoes – use the juice in place of some of the stock.
2 Add crushed garlic, or fresh herbs, mushrooms, a little sliced green pepper.
3 Add 4 oz/100 gm diced kidney to the meat.

Mince Good quality fresh beef mince is a very economical buy and can also be the basis of many appetizing meals. It can also be used for Spaghetti with meat sauce (see page 93).

HAMBURGERS

Illustrated on page 34

Lean minced beef, 1 lb/400 gm
Onion, 1 small
Garlic, 1 clove (optional)
Seasoned salt, seasoned pepper
Flour for shaping
Oil or lard for frying

Ask the butcher to mince the meat finely.
1 Peel and very finely chop or grate the onion. Crush the garlic if used. Mix the onion, garlic, salt and pepper with the meat.
2 Divide into four portions and shape each into a round flat cake about 1 inch thick using a little flour.
3 Melt the oil or lard and shallow fry the hamburgers, turning once, for about 5–8 minutes in all.
4 Drain and serve with fried onions, mashed potatoes and fried tomatoes. Or use in a soft roll as a snack. Serve a selection of mustards and relishes.

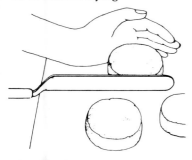

Shape into rounds about 1-inch thick

SHEPHERD'S PIE

Illustrated on page 34

Lean minced beef, 1 lb/400 gm
Onion, 1
Dripping, 1 oz/25 gm
Flour, 1 oz/25 gm
Stock, 4 tablespoons
Mixed herbs, a pinch
Gravy browning
Mashed potatoes, 1½ lb/600 gm

Use an ovenproof dish
Oven temperature: fairly hot (375°F, 191°C, Mark 5)

1 Peel and slice the onion and fry in the hot dripping until lightly coloured. Add the beef and cook, stirring, until browned all over – about 5 minutes. Pour out and discard any excess fat.
2 Add the flour and cook, stirring, for 1–2 minutes. Add the stock and herbs and stir well. Colour with a few drops of gravy browning if very pale. Pour into a greased ovenproof dish.
3 Cover the meat with the potatoes. Smooth the top and mark with a fork into a pattern. Bake at the top of the oven for about 30 minutes or until golden brown and heated through.
Serve with a green vegetable.

VARIATIONS
1 Flavour with Worcestershire sauce, tomato purée, crushed garlic or other herbs.
2 Cook chopped mushrooms with the onions.

Steak Steak is expensive but is easy to cook and serve and has an excellent flavour, so is a popular choice for a special meal. There are many cuts of steaks and ways of serving them but here are details of the more usual cuts and ways of cooking them.

RUMP: the most common cut with a good flavour; the tenderness varies.

SIRLOIN: another cut with a good flavour which comes from the joint next to the rump.

FILLET: the most expensive cut, very tender but with less flavour than rump.

Cooking and serving steak Steak is cooked by grilling or frying. It is usual to cut the meat into portions before cooking and to trim any excess fat. The surface of the meat can be seasoned before cooking by sprinkling with salt and pepper, or a cut clove of garlic may be rubbed on the meat.

The cooking time depends on how the eater likes it served – either 'rare', which means really red in the middle, 'medium' – pink but not bloody, or 'well done' – really cooked through.

Steaks do not keep warm so it is important to have the accompaniments ready and to cook the meat at the last minute.

Serve steak with chipped potatoes or baked potatoes in their jackets, tomatoes, mushrooms and peas. It is normal to garnish the dish with watercress. All vegetables can be omitted and a simple green salad served instead.

GRILLED STEAK

Steak, 4 pieces, each about 6 oz/150 gm
Butter or oil

Prepare the steak and brush on both sides with melted butter or oil. Place on a greased grill grid and cook under a high heat for 1 minute on each side. Lower the heat to medium and cook, turning once, for the remaining time.

FRIED STEAK

Steak, 4 pieces, each about 6 oz/150 gm
Oil

Prepare the steak. Melt a little oil in a large frying pan and cook the steaks for 1 minute on each side over a high heat. Lower the heat to medium and continue to cook, turning once, for the remaining time.

Cooking times for steak (total time in minutes)	THICKNESS	RARE	MEDIUM	WELL DONE
	½ inch	4	8–10	12–15
	1 inch	6–8	10–12	15–18
	1½ inch	8–10	12–15	18–20

BŒUF BOURGUIGNONNE

Illustrated on page 43

Topside of beef, 1½ lb/600 gm
Streaky bacon, in one piece, 4 oz/ 100 gm
Oil, 1 tablespoon
Flour, 1 level tablespoon
Red wine, 6 tablespoons
Stock, ¼ pint/125 ml
Seasoned salt, seasoned pepper
Mixed dried herbs, a pinch
Bay leaf, a piece
Onions, 8 small
Butter, ½ oz/12 gm

Use a large casserole
Oven temperature: warm (325°F, 163°C, Mark 3)

1 Cut the meat into cubes. Rind and dice the bacon.
2 Heat the oil and fry the bacon until lightly coloured. Drain and place in a large casserole.
3 Fry the meat in the remaining fat, turning, until browned all over. Drain and place in the casserole.
4 Sprinkle the flour into the remaining fat and cook, stirring, until lightly browned. Remove from the heat and add the wine and stock, stirring.
5 Return to the heat and bring to the boil. Season with the salt, pepper, herbs and bay leaf. Pour over the meat.
6 Cover the casserole and cook in the centre of the oven for about 2½ hours.
7 Meanwhile peel the onions and fry, whole, in the butter until evenly browned. Add to the casserole for the last 30 minutes of cooking time. Garnish with chopped parsley; serve with mashed potatoes or boiled rice.
This is a good choice for a party as the quantities are easily increased. Serve the Bœuf Bourguignonne with fluffy boiled rice and green salad, and follow with a fruit sweet.

Pork Pork should be pale pink in colour with a layer of firm white fat and a thin skin. Joints for roasting usually have the skin left on and this should be scored by the butcher, so that it will roast to a crisp crackling.
Some of the most usual cuts are:

LEG: a good quality roasting joint which is sold either whole or halved, as a half leg and a fillet joint. It can be boned, stuffed and rolled.

FILLET: as well as being sold as a roasting joint, fillet is also sold thinly sliced, with no bone. These slices are generally casseroled or prepared and cooked in the same way as veal escalopes.

LOIN: a good quality roasting joint which is also cut into chops for frying, grilling or baking. Loin chops often include a portion of kidney.

BELLY: a cheaper cut that is rather fatty, but can be cut into strips and grilled or used in stews.

HAND AND SPRING: an awkwardly-shaped roasting joint which is generally fairly cheap. It can also be used in stews and pies.

SPARE RIB: a cheaper joint which can be roasted.

Pork chops tend to be rather fatty, so are best grilled or baked.

ROAST PORK

Illustrated on page 39

A roasting joint
Oil
Salt

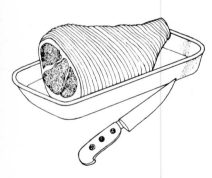

Score the rind of the joint by cutting down in thin strips

1 Wipe the joint. If the butcher has not already scored the rind, cut down in thin strips with a sharp knife. Weigh the joint and calculate the cooking time, allowing 25 minutes per lb/400 gm plus 25 minutes.

2 It is important not to serve pork underdone, so make sure the joint is completely cooked. Roast the joint in the centre of a hot oven (425°F, 218°C, Mark 7). If it is very fatty, place it on a rack or trivet in the roasting tin; this prevents the cooked joint absorbing more fat. Brush the scored rind with oil and sprinkle thickly with salt.

Serve Roast Pork with thick brown gravy, apple sauce (page 88), baked onions (page 79), roast potatoes (page 84) and a green vegetable. Sage and onion stuffing (page 89) can also be served as stuffing balls.

Note: Most roasting joints can be boned, stuffed and rolled before cooking. Use sage and onion to stuff the bone cavity. Tie into a neat shape and score the rind as above. Cook on a rack in the centre of a fairly hot oven (375°F, 191°C, Mark 5) for 35 minutes per lb/400 gm plus 35 minutes.

Roast Pork and
Grilled Pork Chops

GRILLED PORK CHOPS

Illustrated on page 39

Pork chops, 4
Salt and pepper
Melted butter and oil

1 Trim the chops. Season on both sides with salt and pepper.
2 Place on a greased grill grid and brush lightly with melted butter or oil. Grill under a high heat for 1 minute on each side. Then lower grill to medium heat and continue to cook, turning once, until tender and browned – about 15–20 minutes in all.
Serve with mashed potatoes and a green vegetable; grilled tomatoes and mushrooms, lemon slices or apple make a good garnish.

BAKED PORK CHOPS

Pork chops, 4
Salt and pepper

Use a shallow ovenproof dish
Oven temperature: fairly hot (375°F, 191°C, Mark 5)

1 Trim the chops and season well.
2 Place in a single layer in a shallow ovenproof dish and bake in the centre of the oven for about 45 minutes.
3 Drain and serve with apple sauce, mashed potatoes and a green vegetable.

VARIATION
A drained, canned pineapple ring may be placed on top of each chop before cooking.

Lamb Imported frozen lamb is cheaper than English, home-bred meat, which generally has a rather better flavour. English lamb should have firm white fat and pale pink flesh if it is young, darker red flesh if it comes from an older animal. Imported meat has firm white fat with medium red meat.

Some of the most usual cuts are:

LEG: a roasting joint which is sometimes cut in half to give a half leg and a fillet joint.

SHOULDER: a more fatty roasting joint with a good flavour. It can be boned, stuffed and rolled.

CHOPS: cut from the loin or top of the leg (when they are known as *chump* chops); these can be fried, grilled or baked.

BREAST: a cheap cut which is rather fatty but is excellent boned, stuffed and rolled and then slow-roasted.

BEST END OF NECK: sometimes roasted whole or cut into cutlets, which can be cooked as chops.

LOIN: generally divided into chops but sometimes roasted whole.

MIDDLE AND SCRAG END: stewing cuts containing a lot of bone and fat, but cooked in dishes where they are fried initially, so that some of the excess fat can be removed, and then cooked slowly. Alternatively, the stew can be made the day before it is needed, then cooled and the fat skimmed off before re-heating.

ROAST LAMB

A roasting joint
Dripping or lard

Oven temperature: moderate (350°F, 177°C, Mark 4)

1 Wipe the joint and weigh to calculate the cooking time, allowing 27 minutes per lb/400 gm plus 27 minutes.
2 Place in the roasting tin, with the thickest layer of fat uppermost. Add some dripping or lard if the meat is very lean.
Serve Roast Lamb with thick gravy, mint sauce (page 88), roast or new potatoes and a green vegetable. For joints from an older animal, a sharp flavoured jelly like red currant is often served in place of the mint sauce.
Note: Some joints of lamb are also served boned and rolled, or boned, stuffed and rolled. Use Herb Stuffing (page 90) and cook as above allowing 35 minutes per lb/400 gm plus 35 minutes.

GRILLED LAMB CHOPS

Lamb chops, 4
Salt and pepper
Melted butter or oil

1 Trim the chops. Season on both sides with salt and pepper.
2 Place on a greased grill grid and brush with melted butter or oil. Cook under hot grill for 1 minute on each side, then reduce the heat to medium and cook for a further 10–15 minutes, turning once. Drain on kitchen paper and serve with fried tomatoes, mushrooms, mashed potatoes and a green vegetable.
Note: Lamb chops may also be served as part of a Mixed Grill (illustrated on page 45) – allow 1 small lamb chop, 2 chipolata sausages, 1 rasher back bacon, 1 tomato and a few mushrooms per head. Kidneys and steak can also be included. Prepare and grill as described under the separate recipes, keeping the quicker cooking items warm in a slow oven while the remainder are cooked. Serve with chipped potatoes and a green vegetable or salad.

LAMB HOTPOT

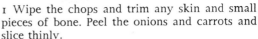

Illustrated frontis. and below

Middle neck or scrag end of neck
  chops, 8
Onions, 2
Carrots, 2
Lard, 1 oz/25 gm
Salt and pepper
Mixed herbs, a pinch
Bay leaf, 1
Potatoes, 3–4 large
Stock, ½ pint/250 ml
Tomatoes, 8 oz/200 gm (optional)

Use an ovenproof casserole
Oven temperature : moderate (350°F,
  177°C, Mark 4)

*Arrange Lamb Hotpot
ingredients in layers*

1 Wipe the chops and trim any skin and small pieces of bone. Peel the onions and carrots and slice thinly.
2 Melt the lard and fry the onion until transparent and lightly coloured. Drain and place in the base of an ovenproof casserole. Fry the chops in the remaining fat until browned all over. Drain and place on top of the onions. Cover with the carrots. Season well with the salt, pepper and mixed herbs.
3 Peel and thinly slice the potatoes; peel and chop tomatoes if used. Arrange over the carrots in an even layer. Pour over enough stock to come halfway up the casserole.
4 Cover and cook in the centre of the oven for about 1½ hours, removing the lid after 1 hour to allow the potatoes to brown.
Alternatively, omit the potatoes in the recipe but layer the other ingredients. Cover and cook for 1 hour. Stir and serve with a green vegetable.

Opposite: **Chicken Casserole**
Bœuf Bourguignonne
and below, **Lamb Hotpot**

Veal   Veal is the meat of the calf, and since it comes from a young animal should always be pale in colour with very little firm, pink or cream-coloured fat. There tends to be a lot of bone and tissue in veal and this makes excellent jellied stock. Veal is sometimes difficult to find, but we include a recipe for Veal Escalopes which are thin slices taken from the fillet.

FRIED VEAL ESCALOPES

Veal escalopes, 4, each about 4–6 oz/100–150 gm
Egg, 1
Fresh white breadcrumbs
Butter, 2 oz/50 gm
Lemon wedges

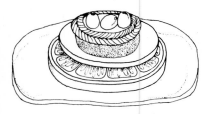

Garnished for a party meal

1 Ask the butcher to beat the escalopes, or do this yourself with a steak hammer or rolling pin.
2 Beat the egg and place the breadcrumbs on a plate. Brush the escalopes all over with the egg and coat with the breadcrumbs, pressing them in well.
3 Heat the butter and fry the escalopes, two at a time, turning once, until browned on both sides – about 6 minutes in all. Drain on kitchen paper and keep warm while frying remaining escalopes. Serve immediately with lemon wedges, a green, salad and rice or mashed potatoes.
For a party, garnish with a slice of lemon, topped with a slice of hardboiled egg, a curled anchovy fillet and a few capers.
Fried Veal Escalopes are also delicious served with buttered spaghetti and a tomato sauce.

Ham, bacon and gammon   These meats all come from pigs, but are differently cured and preserved and can be served in many ways.

HAM is the thigh of a pig which is removed before curing. It is sold as whole joints which are boiled, or smaller pieces which can be boiled or baked. Cooked ham, sold on or off the bone, is useful for made-up dishes, salads and sandwiches.

BACON is the cured sides and back of the pig, sold either 'green' (unsmoked) or 'smoked', when the rind darkens in colour and the bacon has a more pronounced flavour. Bacon is sold as joints which are boiled and baked, and in slices which are grilled or fried.
Here are some of the more popular cuts:
Back: sliced bacon from the back with a good proportion of lean to fat. The most expensive sliced bacon.
Streaky: a cheaper sliced bacon with fat and lean alternately streaked.

Mixed Grill

Collar: wider sliced bacon, also sold as joints for boiling and baking. A good choice for an economical joint as there is no bone.

Forehock: a cheaper joint, including the bone and knuckle. Good boiled for made-up dishes.

GAMMON : the thigh of the pig, cured and smoked in the same way as bacon. It is either sold in joints which are boiled or baked, or sliced into thick rashers, which can be fried or grilled.

PACKAGED BACON : ready-sliced back or streaky bacon sold in vacuum packs. It tends to be more expensive than ready-sliced bacon sold loose.

BOIL-IN-THE-BAG BACON : joints of bacon packed in special polythene bags in which the bacon is cooked. Follow the directions on the label for the exact cooking time. These joints have a rather mild flavour, but the bag keeps the joint in good shape and retains the juices.

Soaking a bacon or ham joint

Bacon can be very salty (ask the grocer about this when buying) and most people like to soak the joint for 2–3 hours or overnight in cold water to remove some of this excess salt.

Mild cured hams do not need soaking but most smoked joints are better for soaking.

BOILED BACON, HAM OR GAMMON JOINT

Illustrated on page 52

1 Weigh the joint and calculate the cooking time, allowing 20 minutes per lb/400 gm plus 20 minutes. Soak the joint if necessary.
2 Drain and place skin side downwards in a large pan. Cover with cold water and bring to the boil. Remove scum, cover and simmer gently for the required time.
To serve hot: after the cooking time, remove the joint from the pan and peel off the rind. Cut into thick slices and serve with parsley sauce and vegetables for a main course. Or serve with roast poultry.
To serve cold: cool the joint in the water for 2–3 hours then remove and slice or pull off the rind. Coat the fat with browned breadcrumbs, pressing them well in. Serve sliced with salads, or in sandwiches.

BAKED BACON, HAM OR GAMMON

A bacon, ham or gammon joint
Fat for basting
Cloves
Demerara sugar, 4 tablespoons
Canned pineapple rings

Oven temperature : moderate (350°F,
    177°C, Mark 4)

Ready for final baking

1 Weigh the joint and calculate the cooking time as for Boiled Ham. Soak if necessary then boil as described above for half the cooking time.
2 Drain and place in a roasting tin, with a little fat. Bake in the centre of the oven until 20 minutes before the cooking time is complete. Baste two or three times.
3 Remove from the oven, slice off the rind and score the fat into diamonds. Stud the fat with the cloves and sprinkle with the sugar. Drain the pineapple rings and arrange in the fat. Turn the oven to hot (425°F, 218°C, Mark 7) and bake the joint on the top shelf until the cooking time is complete.
Serve the joint surrounded by the drained pineapple rings. Make a gravy (see page 87) using some of the pineapple juice in place of stock. Serve with mashed or roast potatoes and a green vegetable.
The sugar gives a glazed, crisp finish to the fat.

VARIATIONS
1 The fat can be brushed with honey instead of sprinkled with sugar.
2 The pineapple rings may be replaced by canned halved apricots or peaches.
3 The gravy may be made with cider instead of pineapple juice.

GRILLED BACON

1 Rind the bacon and arrange on the grill grid.
2 Cook under a medium heat until the fat is transparent and the bacon lightly browned.
Drain and serve as for Fried Bacon.

FRIED BACON

Illustrated on page 49

1 Remove the rind of the bacon with scissors.
2 Heat a frying pan and arrange the bacon rashers in a single layer with no extra fat.
3 Cook gently, turning once, until the fat is transparent and the bacon beginning to brown. Serve with fried eggs, mushrooms, etc., for breakfasts or snacks.
For crisp bacon, cook until the bacon is browned, then drain well before serving.

Gammon Rashers with spaghetti ring

GAMMON RASHERS

Illustrated above

Choose gammon rashers about ¼–½ -inch thick, allowing 4–6 oz/100–150 gm per head.

Snip the fat at intervals

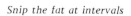

1 Trim the rind and snip the fat at intervals.
2 Place on a greased grill grid, brush the lean with melted fat or oil and grill under a medium heat for 5–10 minutes. Turn, brush the second side with fat or oil and cook for a further 5–10 minutes.
3 Drain and serve with fried eggs, mushrooms, vegetables, salad or pasta. Or serve surrounded by a ring of spaghetti and garnished with mixed vegetables.

A pineapple ring is an excellent accompaniment to gammon rashers. Drain canned pineapple and place the rings on the grill grid with the gammon. Brush with fat or oil and cook, turning once, until heated and lightly browned. Allow 1–2 rings per portion.

Fried Bacon

BACON ROLLS

Used as garnish for roast poultry or veal.
Choose thinly sliced streaky bacon.

1 Rind and cut each rasher into pieces about 2 inches long.
2 Roll up and thread on a skewer.
3 Fry until crisp (about 10 minutes), or grill under a medium heat (about 10 minutes), or cook with the joint (about 20 minutes).

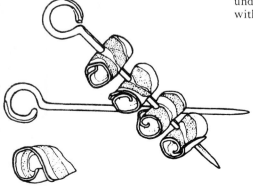

Sausages There is a big choice of sausages – 'branded' makes as well as butchers' own. Pork sausages are milder than beef. It is worth trying different types to find which you like best.

Both pork and beef sausages are generally sold large (8 to the lb/400 gm) or as chipolatas (16 to the lb/400 gm), which are thinner. Both are cooked in the same way, though the chipolatas obviously take a shorter time to cook. In some places tiny cocktail sausages (generally pork) are available. These are about half the size of chipolatas and are useful for parties.

Pork and beef sausages are fried, grilled or baked and can be served hot for breakfasts, snacks and main meals or cold in salads, in sandwiches and for picnic meals.

Pork and beef sausagemeat is also available – it is exactly the same mixture as the sausages of the same brand, but is useful for stuffings or Scotch Eggs (page 75).

TOAD IN THE HOLE

Chipolata sausages, 8 oz/200 gm
For the batter:
Plain flour, 4 oz/100 gm
Salt, a pinch
Egg, 1
Milk, ½ pint/250 ml

Use a shallow ovenproof dish
Oven temperature : hot (425°F, 218°C, Mark 7)

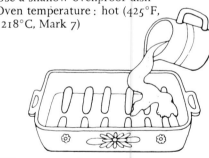

1 *To make the batter:*
Mix the flour and salt. Make a well in the centre and add the egg. Add half of the milk and beat until smooth. Beat in the remaining liquid.

2 Arrange the sausages in a greased shallow baking tin or ovenproof dish. Pour the batter over them and bake at the top of the oven for 35–40 minutes or until the batter is risen and browned.

Serve immediately with a green vegetable and a thick gravy if desired.

FRIED SAUSAGES

Heat a little lard in a frying pan, add the sausages and fry gently, turning from time to time until browned and cooked through – about 12–15 minutes for chipolatas and 18–20 minutes for large sausages.

GRILLED SAUSAGES

Heat the grill and grease the grid. Arrange the sausages on the grid and cook under a medium heat, turning once, for the same times as for Fried Sausages.

BAKED SAUSAGES

Oven temperature: fairly hot (400°F, 204°C, Mark 6)

Place the sausages in a baking tin with a little lard, and cook at the top of a fairly hot oven for 25–35 minutes. Turn halfway through the cooking time.

CONTINENTAL SAUSAGES

Most Continental sausages are sold ready cooked and sliced and are eaten with salads or in sandwiches. However, Frankfurters and 'boiling rings' are served hot with rolls as 'Hot Dogs' or with vegetables. Follow the directions on the packets for exact times. As a rule, Frankfurters should be placed in a pan of cold water, brought slowly to the boil and then left covered, off the heat, for 5 minutes before serving.

Offal This is the term given to the edible internal parts of animals. Offal is generally not too expensive and is very nutritious, so is a good choice for family meals, though some recipes, like the Kidneys in Raisin Sauce (on page 54) make excellent party dishes.

There are many types of offal and the names and cuts differ in various parts of the country. Here are some notes on the most common varieties:

LIVER: types – calves', lambs', sheep's, ox and pigs' liver. Calves' and lambs' livers are the most tender and delicate and so are generally fried and used for special dishes. Ox and sheep's livers are coarser and are better for made-up dishes with long, slow cooking. Pigs' liver has a strong and distinctive flavour and is generally used for spiced dishes like pâtés.

KIDNEY: types – as liver.
Lambs' and sheep's kidneys are grilled, fried or used in quick-cooked, made-up dishes. Ox kidney is an essential ingredient in made-up dishes like steak and kidney pie, which needs long, slow cooking.

HEARTS: types – sheep's and ox. These are generally stuffed and served casseroled or roast. Small hearts are served whole, but ox hearts are sliced.

OXTAIL: delicious, but tends to be rather fatty. It needs long, slow cooking.

TONGUE: types – sheep's, calves', ox and pigs'.
Butchers often sell pickled ox-tongues. They are simmered slowly until the small bones fall out, then served hot with a sauce, or pressed under a weight until cold, and served sliced with salads or in sandwiches. Small tongues are delicious casseroled in a spicy sauce.

Gammon Joint

FRIED LIVER AND ONIONS

Calves' or lambs' liver, 1 lb/400 gm
Flour
Salt and pepper
Onions, 2 large
Rashers of bacon, 4
Fat for frying

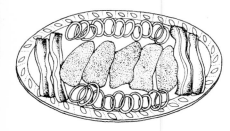

*Arrange the liver, onions and
bacon on a dish*

1 Wash and dry the liver. Cut into thin, even slices.

2 Mix about 2 tablespoons flour with the salt and pepper and use to coat the liver slices.

3 Peel and thinly slice the onions. Rind the bacon and cut each rasher in half.

4 Melt a little fat in a frying pan and fry the bacon, turning once, for about 5 minutes, or until cooked, and beginning to brown. Drain and keep hot in a low oven.

5 Add the onions to the fat and fry gently, stirring, until transparent and beginning to brown. Add more fat if the onions tend to stick.

6 Add the liver slices and cook gently, turning once, until browned and tender – about 7–10 minutes in all.

7 Drain the onions and liver slices and transfer to a serving dish. Add the bacon and serve with mashed potatoes and a green vegetable.

Batter-coated Cod

KIDNEYS IN RAISIN SAUCE

Lambs' kidneys, 8
Flour
Onion, 1
Mushrooms, 4 oz/100 gm
Butter, 1 oz/25 gm
Stock, ½ pint/250 ml
Raisins, 2 oz/50 gm
Mixed dried herbs, a pinch
Chopped parsley

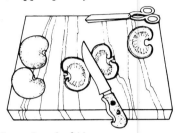

Preparing the kidneys

1 Halve the kidneys, removing skin and fat. Snip out the cores using kitchen scissors. Place about 1 tablespoon flour on a plate and roll the prepared kidneys in this until evenly coated.
2 Peel and slice the onion. Wipe and slice the mushrooms.
3 Melt the butter in a frying pan and fry the onions until browned.
4 Add the mushrooms, stock, raisins, salt, pepper and herbs and bring to the boil.
5 Cover and simmer for about 25 minutes, until the kidneys are tender and the sauce reduced. Dish up and sprinkle with chopped parsley. Serve with plain boiled rice or mashed potatoes and a green vegetable or a simple salad.

VARIATIONS
The mushrooms in this dish may be omitted or replaced by 2 tomatoes, peeled and quartered.
Two tablespoons dry sherry or red wine may be substituted for some of the stock.

OXTAIL CASSEROLE

Oxtail, 1
Lard or dripping, 1 oz/25 gm
Onions, 2
Carrots, 2
Turnips, 2 small
Dried mixed herbs, a pinch
Bay leaf, 1
Beef stock, ¾ pint/375 ml
Salt and pepper
Flour, 1 oz/25 gm

Use a large casserole
Oven temperature : warm (325°F, 163°C, Mark 3)

1 Ask the butcher to chop the oxtail into 2-inch chunks. Wash and dry. Melt the lard in a frying pan and fry the oxtail pieces, a few at a time.
2 Peel the onions, carrots and turnips. Slice the onions and halve the carrots and turnips.
3 When the meat is browned remove from the pan and drain on kitchen paper. Add the onions to the pan and fry until browned. Place in the casserole with the meat, carrots, turnips, herbs, bay leaf, stock, salt and pepper.
4 Cover and cook in the centre of the oven for about 4 hours or until the meat comes away from the bones easily.
5 Blend the flour with a little water to a smooth paste, stir into the casserole and return to the oven for 10 minutes, until thickened. Serve with mashed potatoes.
As this dish is rather greasy, it is a good idea to make it the day before you need it. Cook it for 3½ hours, then cool quickly and place in the refrigerator overnight. The next day, skim off the layer of fat that will have risen to the surface and turn the meat, etc., into a large saucepan. Bring to the boil, cover and leave to simmer for about 30 minutes, adding the blended flour 10 minutes before the end of cooking time.

Canned and frozen meats Every supermarket shelf has a bewildering display of canned meats and every shop freezer has several types of packeted convenience meats. Though it would be expensive to base your daily menus on these, they are useful and it is a good idea to have some canned meats in the store-cupboard for emergencies.

Here are some notes on types you may find in your shops:

CORNED BEEF: useful for salads, sandwiches and for made-up dishes – see recipe for Corned Beef Hash (below).

LUNCHEON MEAT: useful for salads, sandwiches and for made-up dishes.

STEWED STEAK: use for quick main meals with vegetables; for pie fillings; over spaghetti or rice for quick snacks. Heat the contents of the can, adding extra flavourings, such as mixed dried herbs, crushed garlic, tomato purée or cooked canned or frozen vegetables.

HAM, CHOPPED HAM: use sliced in salads, sandwiches or in made-up dishes.

HAMBURGERS, BEEFBURGERS (FROZEN): cook as directed on the packet and serve with potatoes, rice, spaghetti or vegetables for main meals or snacks. Use also in rolls for quick snacks. Chop and use instead of minced beef in spaghetti sauces.

CORNED BEEF HASH

Potatoes, 2 lb/800 gm
Corned beef, a 12 oz/300 gm can
Onion, 1 small
Fat for frying
Salt and pepper
Worcestershire sauce, 1 tablespoon

1 Peel the potatoes, cut into even-sized pieces and cook in boiling salted water until tender. Drain and mash.

2 Meanwhile open the can of corned beef and cut the meat into ½-inch chunks. Peel and dice the onion.

3 Melt a little fat in a frying pan and fry the onion until cooked and lightly coloured. Drain and turn into a basin. Add the potatoes, corned beef, salt, pepper and Worcestershire sauce. Mix well.

4 Heat a little more fat in the pan, add the corned beef mixture and press down into an even layer. Cook over a gentle heat until well heated and golden brown on the underside – about 20 minutes. Turn on to a heated serving dish, cut into wedges and serve immediately with fried tomatoes.

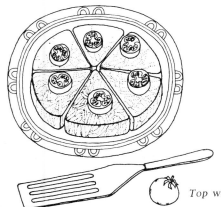

Top with fried tomatoes

Above: **Plain Omelette**
Top left: **Roast Chicken with stuffing balls**
Bottom left: **Scotch Eggs**

5 Poultry

A high proportion of the chickens and turkeys we buy are frozen, and are therefore available all the year round. Fresh (free-range) poultry is, of course, still available at somewhat higher prices, which many people are prepared to pay as these birds have so much more flavour than the 'battery' type.

Chickens　POUSSINS: very small chickens, weighing only about 2 lb/800 gm each. Can be bought fresh or frozen and are generally halved and grilled, or fried. Allow one half poussin per person.

BROILERS: medium-sized birds (generally 3–4 lb/1 kg 200 gm–1 kg 600 gm), can be either fresh or frozen. One broiler serves 3–4 people. Broilers can be roasted, casseroled, fried or grilled.

LARGE ROASTERS (over 4 lb/1 kg 600 gm): these are usually fresh. Allow about 12 oz/300 gm per portion.

CAPONS: large roasters specially treated to produce a bird with plenty of white meat. A capon of 6 lb/2 kg 400 gm serves 6–8 portions.

BOILING FOWLS: older chickens, varying in size and generally fresh, which need slow cooking and are boiled and used in fricassées, pies and casseroles.

CHICKEN JOINTS: frozen and ready packed or sold separately by the butcher. They are generally about 12 oz/300 gm in weight and come from broilers. Allow one per head. Chicken joints can be fried, grilled, baked or used in casseroles.

Turkeys　They vary in size from 6 lb/2 kg 400 gm up to 20 lb/8 kg plus. Allow 12 oz/300 gm per portion. A 10 lb/4 kg bird serves 12–14 portions and an 18 lb/7 kg 200 gm bird serves about 25.

Cooking frozen poultry　It is important to thaw poultry slowly and completely before cooking in order to obtain the best flavour. Leave the frozen bird in its original wrapping in a cool place until completely thawed – an average broiler takes 12 hours to thaw and a large turkey up to 48 hours. In an emergency, the defrosting process can be speeded up by placing the unopened package in a large basin of cold water or in a sink of running cold water. A thawed bird will come to no harm if it is stored for up to 24 hours in a refrigerator after defrosting, provided the bag of giblets is removed. Wash and dry the bird thoroughly before cooking.

The giblets Both fresh and frozen poultry are sold with the giblets (heart, liver, gizzard and neck) either in a polythene bag inside the bird or separately wrapped. Cook the giblets by simmering in salted water with a sliced onion until tender. Use the stock for gravy or in dishes requiring chicken stock. The chicken liver can be chopped and added to stuffings. Chicken livers can also be bought by the pound from some butchers and supermarkets and used in pâtés or risottos.

ROAST TURKEY

Turkey, 1
Herb stuffing
Sausagemeat, 1–2 lb/400–800 gm
Salt and pepper
Lard or butter
Watercress to garnish

Oven temperature : see chart on
  page 60

1 Wash and dry the turkey inside and out and weigh to calculate the cooking time – see chart on page 60.
2 Make up the herb stuffing (page 90) and use to stuff the neck end. Fold the wing tips over to secure the skin, or stitch or skewer in position. Season the sausagemeat with plenty of salt and pepper and use to stuff the body cavity of the turkey. Tie or skewer the legs together.
3a For the quick method of cooking, place the turkey on a large piece of foil and spread the breast with softened lard or butter. Wrap the foil loosely round the bird, sealing the edges with a double fold. Place the package on a roasting tin and cook at the bottom of the oven for the required time. Turn the bird halfway through cooking, and fold back the foil about 30 minutes before the end of cooking time so that the breast browns.
3b For the slow method, do not use foil to wrap the bird – this slows the cooking time and gives a steamed appearance. Place on a roasting tin and spread the breast and legs with softened lard or butter. Cook at the bottom of the oven for the required time. Baste every 30 minutes and turn the bird round halfway through cooking. If the legs start to get too brown, wrap in foil to prevent overcooking.
4 Serve with roast potatoes, a green vegetable, bread sauce (page 88) and thick brown gravy and garnish with watercress. Bacon rolls and chipolata sausages are sometimes served; also cranberry sauce or jelly. Buy cranberry sauce or jelly or make in the same way as apple sauce (page 88) by stewing fresh cranberries until soft. Note : It is usual to stuff turkeys with two different stuffings though this is not essential. For a turkey over 14 lb/5 kg 600 gm, use the larger quantity of sausagemeat and double the recipe given on page 90 for herb stuffing.

Cooking times for Roast Turkey

WEIGHT	FAST METHOD, WITH FOIL 450°F, 232°C, Mark 8	SLOW METHOD, NO FOIL 325°F, 163°C, Mark 3
6–8 lb/2 kg 400 gm–3 kg 200 gm	2¼ hours	3½ hours
8–10 lb/3 kg 200 gm–4 kg	2½ hours	3¾ hours
10–12 lb/4 kg–4 kg 800 gm	2¾ hours	4 hours
12–14 lb/4 kg 800 gm–5 kg 600 gm	3 hours	4¼ hours
14–16 lb/5 kg 600 gm–6 kg 400 gm	3¼ hours	4½ hours
16–18 lb/6 kg 400 gm–7 kg 200 gm	3½ hours	4¾ hours

ROAST CHICKEN

Illustrated on page 56

A roasting chicken
Herb stuffing (optional)
Streaky bacon rashers
  or oil or melted butter

Use a roasting tin
Oven temperature: fairly hot (400°F, 204°C, Mark 6)

Ready for roasting

1 Wash and dry the chicken inside and out and weigh to calculate the cooking time, allowing 15 minutes per lb/400 gm plus 15 minutes.
2 Make up the stuffing (page 90) and use to stuff the neck end. Fold the skin over and fold the wing tips to secure the skin, and skewer the legs together.
3 Place the chicken in a roasting tin and cover the breast with streaky bacon rashers, or brush the bird all over with melted butter or oil. Place some oil or lard in the tin.
4 Cook in the centre of the oven for the required cooking time. Remove the bacon and baste the chicken with the fat in the tin about 20 minutes before the end of cooking, to allow the breast to brown. Remove the skewers before serving.
Serve with thick gravy, roast potatoes, bread sauce (page 88) and a green vegetable. Bacon rolls and chipolata sausages are also served as accompaniments and stuffing balls can be made if the bird is not stuffed.
Serve cold Roast Chicken with salads and mashed potato, or baked potatoes in their jackets.

Opposite: **Egg and Breadcrumbed Plaice Chipped Potatoes**

62

Chicken joints Chicken joints can be prepared and cooked in many ways. Here are some simple recipes.

CHICKEN CASSEROLE

Illustrated on page 43

Chicken joints, 4
Onions, 2
Carrots, 2
Celery, 2 sticks (optional)
Streaky bacon, 2 rashers
Butter, 1 oz/25 gm
Flour, 1 oz/25 gm
Tomatoes, 15 oz/375 gm can
Mushrooms, 2 oz/50 gm
Salt and pepper
Chicken stock, ½ pint/250 ml
Mixed herbs, a pinch
Chopped parsley

Use an ovenproof casserole
Oven temperature: moderate (350°F, 177°C, Mark 4)

1 Wipe the joints and trim. Peel and slice the onions and carrots. Chop the celery if used. Rind and dice the bacon.
2 Fry the bacon in the butter until lightly coloured. Add the chicken joints and fry, turning, until coloured. Drain and remove from the pan. Add the onions, carrots, mushrooms and celery and cook for about 5 minutes. Sprinkle with the flour and cook for 3 minutes, stirring continuously.
3 Drain the tomatoes and add the juice to the vegetables with the salt, pepper, stock and mixed herbs. Stir well and bring to the boil.
4 Pour into the casserole, add the tomatoes and chicken. Cover and cook in the centre of the oven for about 45 minutes or until the chicken is tender.
5 Sprinkle with chopped parsley. Serve with potatoes baked in their jackets, mashed potatoes, rice or toast. Peas or beans or a green salad make a good accompaniment.

VARIATIONS
1 Add a small packet of frozen or dehydrated peas about 15 minutes before the end of cooking.
2 Substitute 2–3 tablespoons red wine for some of the stock.

BAKED CHICKEN JOINTS

Chicken joints, 4
Eggs, 2
Fresh white breadcrumbs or browned breadcrumbs
Lard, 2 oz/50 gm

Use a shallow roasting tin or ovenproof dish
Oven temperature: fairly hot (400°F, 204°C, Mark 6)

1 Trim the joints and wipe. Beat the eggs lightly and place the breadcrumbs on a plate. Brush the chicken joints with the egg and coat with the breadcrumbs, pressing them in well.
2 Heat the lard in the tin, or dish, in the oven for 5 minutes. Remove from the oven, add the chicken joints and turn them in the fat.
3 Return to the top of the oven and cook for about 40 minutes or until the chicken is tender and browned.
4 Drain and serve with mashed potatoes, rice or pasta, with a green salad or a green vegetable. The breadcrumbs may be replaced by crushed cornflakes or crushed crisps.

FRIED CHICKEN JOINTS

Chicken joints, 4
Eggs, 2
Fresh white breadcrumbs
Fat for frying

1 Prepare the chicken as described for Baked Chicken Joints.
2 Heat about 1 inch of fat in a frying pan and cook the joints, turning once, for about 20 minutes in all, or heat a deep-fat pan half full of fat and cook the joints for about 10–12 minutes.
3 Drain on kitchen paper and serve immediately with mashed potatoes or baked potatoes and a green salad.

Ducks

Most birds sold nowadays are frozen though fresh ducks may be available from specialist butchers. Allow about 1 lb/400 gm per person.

ROAST DUCK

Duck, 1
Sage and onion stuffing
  or Onion, 1
Salt and pepper
Watercress to garnish

Use a roasting tin
Oven temperature: fairly hot (400°F, 204°C, Mark 6)

1 Wash and dry the duck inside and out. Weigh to calculate the cooking time, allowing 20 minutes per lb/400 gm.
2 Make the stuffing (page 89) and use to stuff the tail end. Tie or skewer the legs together. If not using stuffing, peel the onion and place in the body for extra flavour.
3 Place the duck in a roasting tin and sprinkle with salt and pepper. If very fatty, prick all over with a fine skewer or darning needle.
4 Cook in the centre of the oven for the required cooking time. Baste 2–3 times during cooking.
Serve, garnished with watercress, with roast or new potatoes, thin gravy, apple sauce and a green salad or vegetable. A salad of sliced oranges is a traditional accompaniment, or the rind and juice of an orange may be added to the gravy.

Baked Jam Sponge *and opposite,* **Baked Alaska**

6 Salads

Salads are served as an accompaniment to a variety of main courses, hot and cold, as starters and as complete meals. In this chapter there are recipes for each kind.

Accompaniment salads are served with or instead of a hot vegetable with a main course. Often a simple dressed green salad is the best partner to a rich main course – it can be prepared well in advance and dressed and tossed just before serving. Some main courses have a traditional salad accompaniment, such as Cucumber Salad with Baked Salmon. Salads are the obvious accompaniment to cold meats of every type with perhaps boiled new potatoes, baked potatoes or crusty rolls. As a general rule, accompaniment salads are simply served and simply garnished.

A salad can also be served with a snack to add variety and vitamins to what otherwise might be a rather stodgy meal. For instance, a small mixed salad is pleasant with a toasted sandwich and a salad with a slice of cold meat makes a quick, well-balanced meal.

Main course salads are complete meals needing only the addition of a crusty roll or potatoes to add bulk. They always contain some form of protein. Some main course salads make excellent starter salads when served in smaller portions.

Preparation of salad vegetables

Wash all salad ingredients

Wash all salad ingredients when you bring them home from the shops – store them in the salad compartment in your refrigerator or in a plastic box or polythene bag in the bottom of the refrigerator.

BEETROOT: this is generally bought cooked, though directions for cooking are given on page 8o. Rub off the skins and slice thinly or dice into a bowl. Some people like their beetroot served covered with vinegar. Beetroot is used in mixed salads but it is best to add it at the last moment as the red colour stains the other ingredients.

CELERY: divide into sticks and scrub each one carefully, trimming the leaves and removing any stringy parts.

CHICORY: remove any discoloured outer leaves and wash. Do not cut until needed.

CUCUMBER: wipe but do not peel or slice until needed.

ENDIVE: divide into leaves, removing any discoloured parts. Tear into smaller pieces. Wash.

GREEN PEPPER: chopped or thin slices of green pepper add 'crunch' to salads. To prepare, wipe and cut in half. Remove seeds and white pith, then chop or slice as needed.

LETTUCE: divide into leaves and wash very carefully. Place in a salad shaker or tea towel and shake to remove excess moisture. Tear the leaves into smaller pieces if necessary when serving.

MUSTARD AND CRESS: cut off the leaves and place in a sieve. Wash under cold running water, removing any seeds.

RADISHES: trim the leaves and roots. Wash well.

SPRING ONIONS: trim off the root and most of the green leaves. Remove the outer skin. Wash.

TOMATOES: wipe, removing any stem. To peel tomatoes, nick the skin and place in a bowl of boiling water for 1–2 minutes, when they will peel easily.

WATERCRESS: wash, removing any discoloured leaves and tough stalks.

Salad garnishes

Celery curls

Salad garnishes are used to decorate salad dishes as well as other dishes like cold meats. The simplest garnish is chopped parsley, but try some of the following. Prepare them well in advance and add at the last minute.

CELERY CURLS: cut sticks of prepared celery into even lengths – about 2 inches. Make a number of cuts in one end of each nearly to the bottom. Leave in iced water for 1–2 hours until curly.

RADISH ROSES: prepare the radishes, then make 4–6 cuts crossing at the centre of each. Leave in iced water for 1–2 hours to open out.

TOMATO WATERLILIES: wipe the tomatoes, choosing small ones if possible. Using a pointed knife make V-shaped cuts all round – pull the two halves apart.

GREEN SALAD

Lettuce, 1
Cucumber, ¼
Watercress, 1 bunch
French dressing (page 90)

Prepare the salad ingredients. Just before serving place in a bowl and toss with a little French dressing.

Any combination of green salad vegetables can be used, though it is usual to include one 'leafy' variety, like lettuce or watercress, and one 'crunchy', like cucumber or green peppers. A little finely chopped onion can also be added. A sliced hardboiled egg makes a good garnish.

Apple Pie

MIXED SALAD

Lettuce, 1
Tomatoes, 4
Cucumber, ¼
Mustard and cress, 1 box
Beetroot, 2 small
French dressing or mayonnaise
  (page 91)

1 Prepare the lettuce and mustard and cress. Peel and slice the tomatoes and slice the cucumber. Dice the beetroot.

2 Arrange the lettuce on a shallow dish and place the tomatoes, cucumber, mustard and cress and beetroot in separate lines on the lettuce. Serve with French dressing or mayonnaise.

This can be made into a main course salad by the addition of some form of protein like hardboiled eggs, sliced cold meat, grated cheese or flaked canned salmon. Arrange the eggs or meat attractively on the lettuce-lined dish and place the salad ingredients round.

Arrange ingredients in separate lines on the lettuce

Baked Apples

POTATO SALAD

New potatoes or waxy old potatoes,
  1½ lb/600 gm
Salt and pepper
Mayonnaise (page 91) or salad cream
Chopped parsley or chives, to garnish

1 Scrub the potatoes and cook in boiling salted water until tender. Drain and cool. Peel. Cut into ½-inch dice and place in a bowl.
2 Add the mayonnaise or salad cream a little at a time, stirring carefully until the potatoes are evenly coated. Season with salt and pepper. Chill.
3 Just before serving turn into a bowl and garnish with chopped parsley or chives.
Note: This salad can also be made with canned or left-over boiled potatoes.

VARIATIONS
1 Add chopped chives or finely chopped onion to the mayonnaise.
2 Fry 3–4 rashers of streaky bacon until crisp, then crumble over the salad as a garnish in place of the chopped parsley.

TOMATO SALAD

Tomatoes, 4
Salt and pepper
French dressing (page 90)
Chopped chives or mint

Layer the tomato slices in a dish

1 Peel the tomatoes and slice thinly. Layer the slices in a dish, seasoning well with salt and pepper.
2 Pour over enough French dressing to moisten and leave for 1–2 hours. Serve garnished with chopped chives or mint.

VARIATIONS
1 Add a pinch of mixed dried herbs or ½ teaspoon chopped fresh herbs to the French dressing.
2 Layer the tomatoes with chopped spring onions.

CUCUMBER SALAD

Cucumber, ½
Salt and pepper
French dressing (page 90)

1 Wipe the cucumber and peel if desired. Slice thinly. Place in a bowl, season with salt and pepper and leave for 1 hour.
2 Pour off any excess moisture and arrange in a serving dish. Pour over a little French dressing.

VARIATIONS
1 A little dried dill is a delicious addition to the salad.
2 For a special occasion replace the French dressing with a carton of soured cream. Sprinkle with chopped parsley before serving.

7 Eggs and cheese

Eggs Eggs are an essential ingredient of a variety of made-up dishes, sauces, cakes and puddings and are the basis of many dishes which we eat every day.

In Britain and the E.E.C. eggs are graded according to a uniform system. They are classified by gram weight, size 1 (over 70 gm) being the largest and size 7 (under 45 gm) being the smallest.

As a rule sizes 3 and 4 are satisfactory for all made-up dishes, although you may prefer the larger eggs for boiling and poaching.

BOILED EGGS

Bring a pan of water to the boil, lower the eggs into the pan and bring quickly back to the boil. Simmer gently for 3 minutes for a lightly boiled egg, or 4½ minutes for a firmer set. Drain and serve immediately.

Very fresh eggs or eggs taken straight from the refrigerator need slightly longer cooking – 4–5 minutes.

For a *hardboiled egg*, simmer for about 10 minutes. Drain and cool under running cold water. This enables the shell to be peeled off easily and prevents the dark rim round the yolk which occurs if the eggs are left to cool slowly.

FRIED EGGS

Heat a little lard in a frying pan. Break the eggs one at a time into a cup and slowly slide into the fat. Cook gently until the white is set. The eggs can be turned or the yolks can be basted with the fat, using a spoon. Lift carefully from the pan using a slice, drain and serve immediately.

SCRAMBLED EGGS

Butter, 2 oz/50 gm
Milk, 4 tablespoons
Salt and pepper
Eggs, 8
Buttered toast

1 Heat the butter and milk until the butter is melted. Season well with salt and pepper.
2 Break the eggs into a bowl and whisk lightly. Pour into the pan and cook over a gentle heat, stirring until the mixture begins to thicken. Remove from the heat and stir until thick but not overcooked. Serve on buttered toast.

Never overcook scrambled eggs as they separate and become very unappetising. The mixture continues to cook while it is in the pan even if it is not on the heat, so it is important to have the toast ready and the plates hot before you start to cook the eggs.

Trifle *and opposite,* **Cherry Loaf, Plain Oven Scones, Drop Scones**

POACHED EGGS

Eggs in a poaching pan

Special poaching pans are available, though a frying pan is a convenient substitute. Bring a little water to the boil in the base of the poacher. Butter the cups and place in the poacher until butter is melted. Break the eggs into a cup and slowly slide into the heated cups. Replace the lid and simmer gently until the whites are set. Loosen the edges with a knife and turn out on to buttered toast. Serve immediately.

If you have no poacher, half fill a frying pan with water adding 1 teaspoon vinegar. (This helps to keep the eggs a good shape.) Bring to the boil. Break the eggs into a cup and gently slide into the water. Simmer until the whites are set. Remove from the pan with a slice; make sure they are well drained, and place on buttered toast. Serve immediately.

Omelettes There are two varieties of omelette – plain and soufflé. Both can be served plain or with a filling – generally savoury for a plain omelette and sweet for the more unusual soufflé omelette.

PLAIN OMELETTE

Illustrated on page 57

Eggs, 2
Water, 1 tablespoon
Salt and pepper
Butter for frying
Filling – see below

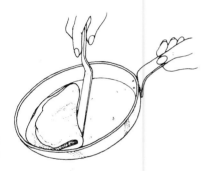

Use a palette knife to fold the sides over

1 Beat the eggs with the water, salt and pepper until well mixed.
2 Heat a small frying pan or special omelette pan gently and melt a knob of butter in it. Tip the pan so that the fat coats the base and sides evenly and pour out the surplus.
3 Pour the beaten eggs into the pan, and cook quickly. Stir the mixture with a fork so that the cooked egg is drawn from the sides to the centre and the liquid egg cooks. When the egg is lightly set, stop stirring and let the base become golden.
4 Add the chosen filling along the centre and fold the sides over, using a palette knife. Slide on to a heated plate and serve immediately.
Serves 1.

VARIATIONS
1 Plain – do not add any filling but season the basic mixture well.
2 Mixed herbs – add ½ level teaspoon mixed dried herbs or 1 level teaspoon chopped mixed fresh herbs to the basic mixture.
3 Cheese – add 1 oz/25 gm grated cheese.
4 Mushroom – fry 1 oz/25 gm mushrooms, sliced, in a little butter until tender. Drain and keep warm while the omelette is being made.
5 Ham – add 1–2 oz/25–50 gm cooked ham, chopped.

SOUFFLÉ OMELETTE

Eggs, 2
Sugar, 1 level teaspoon
Water, 2 tablespoons
Butter for frying

1 Separate the eggs and place the yolks in a bowl with the sugar and water. Beat lightly until evenly mixed.
2 Whisk the egg whites until stiff and fold in the beaten yolk mixture with a metal spoon.
3 Prepare the pan as described for Plain Omelette. Pour in the egg mixture and cook, without stirring, until the base is golden.
4 Meanwhile, heat the grill and when the base is browned place the pan under the grill until the top puffs up and is lightly browned.
5 Place the chosen filling along the centre, fold in half using a palette knife and slide on to a heated plate.
Serve immediately.

VARIATIONS
1 Plain – as above.
2 Jam – add 2–3 tablespoons warmed jam and serve sprinkled with caster sugar.
3 Fruit – 2–3 tablespoons fruit purée or canned pie filling.

Whisk egg whites until stiff

SCOTCH EGGS

Illustrated on page 56

Eggs, 5
Flour
Sausagemeat, 8 oz/200 gm
Browned breadcrumbs
Lard or oil for deep frying

1 Hardboil 4 of the eggs (see page 71). Cool and shell. Dust with flour.
2 Divide the sausagemeat into 4 portions and shape one portion round each egg, using a little flour if it is very sticky. Try to make the sausagemeat into an even layer and make sure there are no gaps. Chill the covered eggs for a short time.
3 Beat the remaining egg and place the breadcrumbs on a piece of kitchen paper. Coat the covered eggs with the beaten egg and roll in the breadcrumbs until evenly coated.
4 Heat the lard or oil in a deep-fat pan. Place the eggs in the basket and lower gently into the fat. Fry, turning once, for about 8–10 minutes in all. The breadcrumbs should be golden brown.
5 Drain on kitchen paper. Serve hot with a tomato or brown sauce, mashed potato and vegetables, or leave to cool and serve halved, cold, with salads. Scotch eggs are good picnic food.
Note : This quantity of sausagemeat gives only a thin coating. It can be increased to 12 oz/300 gm. Scotch eggs can also be shallow fried. Use about 1 inch of lard or oil in a large frying pan. Heat, then add the eggs and cook for 8–10 minutes in all, turning several times. Make sure the coating is evenly browned.

Simple Fruit Cake
and below, **Gingerbread**

Cheese Cheese is an essential part of our diet. It is an easy way to end a meal, a useful basis for every type of snack and is an important ingredient of many more substantial dishes.

There are hundreds of types of cheese made in, and imported into, this country. Most are eaten either with biscuits, or bread and butter, but a lot of the harder cheeses and some of the cream types are also used in cooked dishes. Be adventurous when you are buying cheese and try the more unusual ones when you see them.

The cheese quantities given in recipes may have to be varied according to the strength of the cheese.

Here are some notes on the most common types:

CHEDDAR: a hard yellow cheese, made in many countries. Canadian Cheddar tends to be strongly flavoured, New Zealand much milder, but both these types and English Cheddar are very useful for cooking and eating on their own.

CHESHIRE: another popular English cheese available in red or yellow varieties. It is more mellow in flavour than Cheddar and has a crumbly texture. Good cooked or uncooked.

STILTON: a blue cheese with a distinctive flavour which is eaten uncooked.

DANISH BLUE: a blue, crumbly cheese which is generally eaten uncooked but is sometimes used in made-up dishes like cheese dips and flans.

EDAM: a Dutch cheese made in the shape of a sphere, with a bright red rind. It has a smooth texture and is eaten uncooked.

GRUYÈRE: a hard Swiss cheese eaten uncooked or cooked in classic dishes like Cheese Fondue and Quiche Lorraine.

PARMESAN: a very hard Italian cheese that is always grated. It has a strong flavour and is used in made-up dishes and served, sprinkled, over pasta dishes.

CREAM CHEESE: there are a variety of cream cheeses, sold loose or packeted. Mostly they are eaten as they are but they can be used in made-up dishes like cheesecake and dips.

PROCESSED CHEESES: these are basically one of the common cheeses like Cheddar which have been broken down and further treated. They are generally sold packeted and sometimes sliced. They are useful for sandwiches and snacks and can be used in made-up dishes like flans and sauces. Some of the creamy types are further flavoured with herbs, shrimps, ham, etc., and are useful for quick sandwich fillings.

Cheese as a separate course

Cheese is often served as a separate course after or instead of a pudding. Serve a selection of cheeses, if possible, including a hard cheese like Cheddar, a blue cheese and a creamy variety. Buy new cheeses in small quantities and try them.

Serve plenty of bread (white, brown and crusty), biscuits and butter with, perhaps, a glass of celery sticks or a bowl of trimmed radishes for extra texture.

A selection of cheeses

Cheese snacks

Cheese is very useful as the basis of many snacks. Here is one quick idea :

FLUFFY CHEESE OPEN SANDWICHES

Bread, 4 slices
Butter
Ham, 4 slices
Processed cheese, 4 slices
Eggs, 4
Salt and pepper

1 Toast the bread on both sides until golden brown. Butter and arrange on the grill grid.
2 Top each piece of toast with a slice of ham and a slice of cheese. Grill until the cheese is hot and beginning to melt.
3 Meanwhile separate the eggs and place the whites in a clean bowl. Keep the egg yolks separate in 4 cups.
4 Whisk the egg whites with the salt and pepper until very fluffy. Divide between the toasted sandwiches, piling it up into a pyramid on the top of the cheese.
5 Make a small hollow in the top of each and carefully slide in the egg yolks, being careful not to break them.
6 Replace under the grill and cook under a medium heat until the whites are lightly browned. Serve immediately.

4 separate layers topped with egg yolk and grilled

8 Vegetables

Vegetables are used as an accompaniment to all main dishes, as starters and as the basis of many excellent snacks and supper dishes. Nutritionally, they are rich in vitamins and are an essential ingredient in a satisfactory diet.

Choose fresh vegetables carefully, buying ones which are clean and unblemished with few, if any, discoloured portions.

Root vegetables can be kept for 2–3 weeks in a cool, airy place but other vegetables should be used within 48 hours of buying. Store in a cool place or in a polythene bag or the special salad compartment of your refrigerator.

Allow 6–8 oz/150–200 gm of root vegetables per portion and about 4 oz/100 gm of other vegetables. Spinach shrinks on cooking – allow 8 oz/200 gm per portion.

Cooking and serving

Most vegetables are cooked by boiling in salted water until tender. Do not overcook as this spoils the flavour; they should still have a little 'bite'. Drain carefully after cooking and serve quickly, either tossed in butter with a garnish of parsley or with a white or flavoured sauce poured over them.

Other methods of cooking

BRAISING: celery, leeks, chicory and onions can be braised in the oven. Prepare according to type, place in an ovenproof dish with 6 tablespoons (to 4 portions) of brown sauce or gravy. Cover and cook in the centre of a moderate oven (350°F, 177°C, Mark 4) for 45–60 minutes or until tender.

GRILLING: tomatoes and mushrooms can be grilled. Prepare, halving tomatoes. Place on the grill grid, brush with oil or melted butter and grill under a medium heat until tender – about 5–7 minutes. Turn mushrooms halfway through cooking.

FRYING: tomatoes, mushrooms and onions can be fried. Halve tomatoes and slice onions. Leave mushrooms whole unless large. Fry in oil, butter or lard, turning until tender. Onions should be browned – about 7–10 minutes. Tomatoes and mushrooms take 5–7 minutes only.

BAKING: tomatoes and mushrooms can be baked. Prepare and place in an ovenproof dish. Season with salt and pepper and dot with butter. Cover and bake in the centre of a moderate oven (350°F, 177°C, Mark 4) for 15–20 minutes. Onions and parsnips can be baked in the fat round the joint like roast potatoes (page 84). Cook in exactly the same way, leaving onions whole and halving parsnips if very large. Allow 45 minutes for onions, 1–1¼ hours for parsnips.

Vegetables – Quick Reference Summary

VEGETABLE (in season)	PREPARATION	COOKING	SERVING
Artichoke – Jerusalem (autumn–winter)	Peel thickly	Boil for 20–30 minutes	Tossed in butter Serve with white sauce
Broad beans (summer)	Shell	Boil for 15–20 minutes	Tossed in butter Serve with parsley sauce
French and runner beans (summer)	Top, tail and string; leave small ones whole, slice larger	Boil for 10–15 minutes	Tossed in butter
Beetroot (all the year)	Trim leaves (do not damage skin before cooking as colour bleeds)	Boil for 1–2 hours; peel after cooking	Tossed in butter Serve with white sauce
Broccoli (winter)	Trim thick stalks, remove discoloured leaves	Boil for 10–25 minutes	Tossed in butter Serve with white sauce
Brussels sprouts (winter)	Trim base and remove outer leaves	Boil for 7–12 minutes	Tossed in butter
Cabbage (all the year)	Trim stalk and remove outer leaves; shred	Boil for 10–15 minutes	Tossed in butter Serve with white sauce
Carrots (all the year)	Scrape new carrots, leave whole; peel and slice or dice old carrots	Boil new for 10–15 minutes, old for 20–30 minutes	Tossed in butter and parsley
Cauliflower (summer and autumn)	Trim stalk and outer leaves	Boil for 15–30 minutes	Tossed in butter Serve with white or cheese sauce

VEGETABLE	PREPARATION	COOKING	SERVING
(in season)			
Celery (winter)	Trim leaves and root; scrub sticks well	Boil for 30–45 minutes (also braised)	Tossed in butter or served with white sauce
Leeks (winter)	Trim roots and most of green leaves; wash well	Boil for 15–20 minutes (also braised)	Tossed in butter or served with white sauce
Marrow (autumn)	Peel, halve and remove seeds; dice or slice	Boil for 10–15 minutes (also baked)	Tossed in butter or served with white or cheese sauce
Mushrooms (all the year)	Wash; leave whole or slice	Fry, grill or bake	
Onions (all the year)	Trim roots and remove outer coloured skin	Boil for 30–45 minutes (also baked, fried)	With white or brown sauce
Parsnips (winter)	Peel thickly; halve or slice	Boil for 25–35 minutes (also baked)	Tossed in butter
Peas (summer)	Shell	Boil for 10–25 minutes (add sprig of mint)	Tossed in butter
Spinach (all the year)	Tear leaves, removing stems; wash well	Boil for 7–10 minutes in a little water	Tossed in butter
Swedes (all the year)	Peel thickly; dice	Boil for 40–60 minutes	Mashed with butter
Turnips (all the year)	Peel thickly	Boil for 35–45 minutes	Tossed in butter or served with white sauce

Frozen vegetables

Frozen vegetables should be stored and cooked as directed on the packet for best results. They are cooked during processing so the cooking times are much shorter than for the same fresh vegetable. Do not store for longer than recommended and put them in the frozen food compartment of your refrigerator while still frozen.

As well as serving as accompaniments, frozen vegetables are useful to add to stews and casseroles, and as the basis of snacks on their own. Here are some ideas to add colour and interest:

PEAS: add to a Brown Stew about 10 minutes before the end of cooking.

SLICED BEANS: add 2 peeled, chopped tomatoes to a packet of beans which are already cooked.

BROAD BEANS: add a packet of cooked broad beans to ½ pint/ 250 ml parsley sauce – place on fried bread and top with crisp bacon rashers for an unusual snack.

SPINACH: cook a packet of spinach and drain. Top with poached eggs for a snack.

MIXED VEGETABLES: add a packet, cooked, to plain boiled rice for a quick savoury rice to serve with grilled chops, chicken joints, etc.

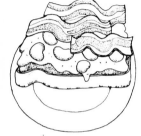

Broad beans in parsley sauce on fried bread, topped with bacon rashers

Canned and dehydrated vegetables

These, though lacking the texture of fresh or frozen vegetables, are useful store-cupboard items because of their ease of storage. Heat canned types in their own liquid and drain well. Use as accompaniments or in the same way as the ideas suggested above. Cook dehydrated vegetables as directed on the packet.

Potatoes

Available all the year, but new potatoes come into season in the spring.

Preparation

New potatoes need only to be scrubbed well or scraped, but old potatoes must be peeled before cooking in most ways. It is best not to prepare potatoes until you are ready to cook them, though they can be stored for a short time without discoloration in a bowl of salted water.

BOILED POTATOES

Old or new potatoes,
 1½–2 lb/600–800 gm
Salt
Butter, a knob
Chopped parsley

1 Prepare the potatoes and cook in boiling salted water until tender – about 12–15 minutes for new potatoes and 20 minutes for old.
2 Drain and return to the pan with the butter and chopped parsley. Toss until evenly coated, then serve immediately.

CREAMED OR MASHED POTATOES

Old potatoes, 1½–2 lb/600–800 gm
Salt and pepper
Butter, 1 oz/25 gm
Milk, 2–3 tablespoons

1 Prepare and cook the potatoes as for boiled potatoes.
2 Drain and return to the pan with the butter, milk, salt and pepper.
3 Beat until smooth over a gentle heat using a fork, potato masher, wooden spoon or electric mixer. Serve immediately.

CHIPPED POTATOES

Illustrated on page 61

Old potatoes, 1½–2 lb/600–800 gm
Oil or lard for deep frying
Salt

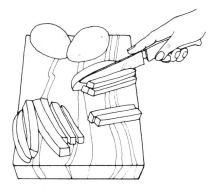

*Cut sliced potatoes into
even strips*

1 Peel the potatoes and cut into ½-inch thick slices. Cut the slices into strips the same width. Keep in salted water to prevent discolouration.
2 Heat the oil or lard in a deep-fat pan to about 370°F, 191°C. Drain the potatoes and pat dry in a cloth. Place half the amount in the chip basket and lower slowly into the hot oil. Cook for about 6 minutes or until the chips are tender but not coloured. Remove the basket from the pan and tip out the chips.
3 Re-heat the oil and fry the remaining chips in the same way. Remove the basket.
4 Re-heat the oil to 390°F, 200°C; return half of the chips to the basket. Fry for 2–3 minutes or until they are browned. Drain on kitchen paper, sprinkle with salt and keep warm in a low oven.
5 Re-heat the oil and repeat this second frying with the remaining chips. Drain, salt and serve immediately.

ROAST POTATOES

Old potatoes, 1½–2 lb/600–800 gm
Lard or dripping

Oven temperature : hot (400°F, 204°C,
Mark 6)

1 Peel the potatoes and cut into even-sized pieces. Dry thoroughly.
2 Place the lard or dripping in a roasting tin and heat in the oven until melted. Put the potatoes in the tin, turn in the fat so that they are evenly coated and place at the top of the oven for about 1 hour. Turn after 30 minutes.
3 Drain carefully and serve with roast joints and poultry.
Note : Roast potatoes can be cooked at any temperature between 375°F, 191°C, Mark 5 and 425°F, 218°C, Mark 7, according to what temperature is necessary for the joint. Adjust the cooking time of the potatoes accordingly, allowing 1¼–1½ hours at the lower temperature and only about 45 minutes at the higher.

BAKED POTATOES

Potatoes, 4 large
Butter to serve

Oven temperature : hot (400°F, 204°C,
Mark 6)

1 Choose even-sized potatoes. Scrub carefully and prick all over with a fork.
2 Cook at the top of the oven for 1–1½ hours depending on size – they should be soft when tested with the fingers.
3 Cut slits in the top and serve immediately with a knob of butter in the potato.

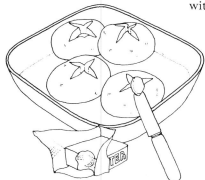

*Put a knob of butter in the slits
on top of a baked potato*

VARIATION
For a special occasion, the butter may be replaced by a sour cream dressing made by mixing a carton of sour cream with 1 tablespoon chopped chives or 1 small chopped onion.

FROZEN chipped potatoes should be cooked according to the directions on the packet.

CANNED new potatoes are a useful standby for the store-cupboard. Heat through with a sprig or two of mint in the water. Use cold for potato salad.

DEHYDRATED mashed potato is also excellent for emergencies or when time is short. For extra flavour stir in grated cheese.

CAULIFLOWER CHEESE

Cauliflower, 1 medium-sized
Butter, 1 oz/25 gm
Flour, 1 oz/25 gm
Milk, ½ pint/250 ml
Strong cheese, 3–4 oz/75–100 gm
Salt, pepper and dry mustard
Browned breadcrumbs, 1 tablespoon

1 Trim the cauliflower and cook in boiling salted water until tender – about 20–25 minutes.
2 Meanwhile melt the butter and stir in the flour. Cook for 2–3 minutes then remove from the heat and slowly stir in most of the milk.
3 Return to the heat and stir until thickened. Bring to the boil, add most of the cheese and season with salt, pepper and a pinch of dry mustard. Add a little more milk if necessary to give sauce a coating consistency. Simmer for 3–5 minutes, then keep warm.
4 When the cauliflower is cooked, drain and place in an ovenproof dish. Pour over the hot sauce and sprinkle with the breadcrumbs and remaining cheese. Place under a medium grill and cook until the cheese is melted and the top is browned and crispy. Serve immediately.

VARIATIONS
1 The breadcrumb topping can be replaced with crushed crisps.
2 The sauce can be flavoured with cheese and bacon (add 4 cooked rashers of bacon, chopped) or ham (2–3 oz/50–75 gm cooked ham, diced) or shrimps (2 oz/50 gm fresh, frozen or canned).

Pour hot cheese sauce over the cooked cauliflower

9 Sauces, stuffings and salad dressings

In this chapter we give the recipes for all the well-known sauces, together with salad dressings and stuffing recipes. Although you will probably find that your local shop has packet mixes of most of these recipes, they are rather expensive to use continually. However, it is useful to keep one or two packets in stock in case you do not have some of the ingredients for the home-made alternatives.

Packet sauces When you are using packet sauces, make them up as directed on the packet. You may find that some of them are rather bland in flavour so extra salt, pepper or lemon juice may be necessary.

Packet bread sauce is very useful but is often improved with a pinch of ground cloves.

Cans of sieved apples are available; they are a good alternative to home-made apple sauce. For two people, the cans of sieved apples made by the baby food manufacturers are useful as there will be no waste.

WHITE SAUCE

Butter, 1 oz/25 gm
Flour, 1 oz/25 gm
Milk, ½ pint/250 ml
Salt and pepper

1 Melt the butter and stir in the flour. Cook for 2–3 minutes then remove from the heat and slowly add most of the milk, stirring continuously.

2 Return to the heat and stir until thickened. Bring to the boil, season well and cook for 3–5 minutes. Add more milk if necessary to bring to the required consistency.

Note: These quantities give a sauce of coating consistency; for a pouring sauce use ¾ oz/18 gm flour to the same quantity of milk.

White sauce is served with various foods, including boiled cauliflower, marrow, eggs, fish and chicken. It forms the basis of many flavoured sauces and is an essential ingredient in made-up dishes such as Fish Pie (page 24).

VARIATIONS
This sauce can be varied in many ways by adding the following ingredients after the sauce has thickened. Re-heat, stirring, and adjust the seasoning if necessary.

Quantities are for a sauce made using the above recipe.

PARSLEY: add 1 tablespoon chopped parsley – serve with fish, boiled ham, boiled chicken, broad beans.

CHEESE: add 2 oz/50 gm grated cheese and a pinch of dry mustard – serve with vegetables, eggs, pasta.

SHRIMP: add 2 oz/50 gm fresh, frozen or canned chopped shrimps and a squeeze of lemon juice – serve with fish or eggs.

CAPER: add 2–3 tablespoons capers and the juice of ¼ lemon – serve with boiled mutton.

EGG: add 2 hardboiled eggs, chopped – serve with fish.

ONION: fry 2 onions, peeled and chopped, in 1 oz/25 gm butter until cooked. Drain and add to the sauce – serve with Roast Lamb.

MUSHROOM: cook 2 oz/50 gm sliced button mushrooms in 1 oz/25 gm butter until tender. Drain and add to the sauce – serve with fish, grilled chops, fried chicken.

MUSTARD: add 1 level teaspoon dry mustard to the sauce with the flour. Serve with Grilled Mackerel.

Gravy Gravy is an essential accompaniment to any roast joint and is generally made in the roasting tin after the joint has been placed on the serving dish, though it is possible to make it in a saucepan using dripping from the joint as a base.

If the gravy is very pale, add a little gravy browning. Some varieties are very concentrated so add a drop at a time, stirring well, until the gravy is a good colour.

THICKENED GRAVY

Pour off most of the fat from the roasting tin, leaving about 2 tablespoons and the sediment. Place the tin on the heat, add 1 tablespoon flour and stir in well. Gradually stir in ½ pint/250 ml vegetable water, stock or water. Bring to the boil, stirring, until thickened. Season with salt and pepper and strain into a sauce-boat.

THIN GRAVY

Make as above, pouring off all the fat but leaving the sediment behind and omitting the flour.

MINT SAUCE

Fresh mint leaves, 2 tablespoons,
 chopped
Sugar, 1 level teaspoon
Boiling water, 1 tablespoon
Vinegar, 2 tablespoons

1 Place the sugar and boiling water in a sauce-boat and stir until dissolved. Add the mint and vinegar.
2 Leave for about 1 hour before serving with Roast Lamb.
3 Left-over sauce may be stored in a screw-top jar in a cool place.

APPLE SAUCE

Cooking apples, 1 lb/400 gm
Water, a little
Butter, a knob
Sugar

1 Peel, core and slice the apples. Cook with a little water until soft.
2 Beat until smooth, adding the butter and enough sugar to give a sharp but not sour taste. Serve with Roast Pork.

BREAD SAUCE

Onion, 1
Cloves, 4
Milk, 1 pint/500 ml
Salt and pepper
Fresh white breadcrumbs, 2–3 oz/
 50–75 gm

1 Peel the onion and stud with the cloves. Place in a saucepan with the milk, salt and pepper. Bring to the boil and simmer for 10 minutes. Leave to stand for up to 1 hour.
2 About 15 minutes before serving, remove the onion and add most of the breadcrumbs. Stir, bring to the boil and simmer until thickened, adding more breadcrumbs if necessary to give a thick but 'pourable' sauce.
Serve with Roast Chicken, Roast Turkey and sausages.

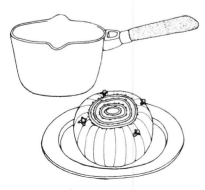

For Bread Sauce, stud the onion with cloves before placing in saucepan

TOMATO SAUCE

Tomatoes, 12 oz/300 gm
Onion, 1 small
Streaky bacon, 2 rashers
Butter, ½ oz/12 gm
Flour, ½ oz/12 gm
Chicken stock or water, ½ pint/250 ml
Salt and pepper
Mixed herbs, ½ level teaspoon
Bay leaf, ½

1 Chop the tomatoes roughly. Peel and chop the onion. Rind and dice the bacon.
2 Heat the butter in a saucepan and fry the onion and bacon until cooked but not coloured. Stir in the flour and cook for 2–3 minutes. Remove from the heat and slowly add the stock. Return to the heat and cook, stirring, until thickened.
3 Add the tomatoes, salt, pepper, herbs and bay leaf and bring to the boil. Simmer, uncovered, for 30 minutes.
4 Sieve to remove the tomato skins, re-season if necessary and re-heat.
Serve with pasta, grilled meats and made-up dishes.
The fresh tomatoes may be replaced by a 15 oz/375 gm can of whole tomatoes. Use the juice in place of some of the stock.

JAM SAUCE

Jam, 6 tablespoons
Water, 2 tablespoons
Lemon juice, a squeeze

Heat the jam and water together gently in a small saucepan until nearly boiling. Stir well and sharpen with the lemon juice.

Stuffings A stuffing adds extra flavour and bulk to many roast joints and poultry, and fills up the body cavity or the space of a bone. Stuff loosely as it tends to swell on cooking. Stuffing may also be formed into small balls and cooked in the fat round the joint until browned and crisp – they take about 20 minutes.
Note : Stuffing should not be made until just before it is needed.

SAGE AND ONION STUFFING

Onions, 2 large
Sage leaves, 6 fresh
  or dried sage, 3 level teaspoons
Butter, 1 oz/25 gm
Fresh white breadcrumbs, 4 oz/100 gm
Salt and pepper

1 Peel and chop the onions. Place in a saucepan, cover with water and bring to the boil. Cook until tender – about 5–7 minutes. Drain.
2 Wash and chop the sage. Melt the butter. Remove from the heat and stir in the onions, sage, breadcrumbs, salt and pepper. Mix well and use as required.
This stuffing is generally used for stronger flavoured meats such as pork, though many people also like it with chicken.

HERB STUFFING

Streaky bacon, 2 rashers
Butter or lard, 1 oz/25 gm
Fresh white breadcrumbs, 3 oz/75 gm
Shredded suet, 1 oz/25 gm
Chopped parsley, 1 tablespoon
Mixed herbs, 1 level teaspoon
Salt and pepper
Egg, 1

1 Rind and dice the bacon and fry until browned in the butter. Drain and mix with the breadcrumbs, suet, parsley, mixed herbs, salt, pepper and enough beaten egg to bind.
2 Use as required. This stuffing is suitable for chicken, turkey (use double quantities for one end of a 12 lb/4½ kg bird), veal and lamb.

Packet stuffings Packet stuffings are a useful store-cupboard item – several different flavours are now available.

Follow the directions on the packet for making up quantities, and cooking. For a change try the following:

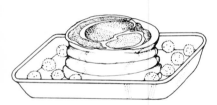

Cook small stuffing balls
in the fat around a joint

1 Add 2 rashers ot streaky bacon, de-rinded, diced and fried.
2 Add the fried, chopped chicken or turkey liver to the packet of made-up stuffing for a bird.
3 Add a little extra seasoning, fresh herbs or lemon juice.
4 Add the grated rind of a lemon.
5 Make up a packet of stuffing into balls as directed on the packet, fry until golden and add to a casserole for extra flavour.
6 Use dry packet stuffing instead of fresh breadcrumbs to coat chicken joints for frying or baking.

Salad dressings

FRENCH DRESSING

Salt, ¼ level teaspoon
Pepper, dry mustard and sugar, a pinch of each
Vinegar, 1 tablespoon
Oil, 3 tablespoons

Place the salt, pepper, mustard and sugar in a screw-top jar or bowl with the vinegar. Shake or mix with a fork until blended. Add the oil and shake or beat again until evenly mixed. The oil will separate out on standing, so shake or mix again before use.

VARIATIONS
The vinegar can be replaced by lemon juice if preferred, and the dressing can be flavoured with garlic, chopped onion or herbs.

MAYONNAISE

Egg yolk, 1
Salt, ½ level teaspoon
Pepper, dry mustard and sugar, a
  pinch of each
Oil, 6–8 tablespoons
Vinegar or lemon juice, 1–2 teaspoons

1 Place the egg yolk and seasonings in a small bowl. Mix with a wooden spoon. Slowly add the oil, drop by drop, beating thoroughly between each addition. When the mixture starts to thicken, the oil can be added ¼ teaspoon at a time. If it gets too thick, add a little of the vinegar or lemon juice.

2 When all the oil has been added, stir in enough vinegar or lemon juice to thin slightly and flavour; do not add it all without tasting.

3 Use immediately or store in an airtight container in a cool place – not in the refrigerator.

If the mayonnaise curdles, place another egg yolk and seasonings in a clean bowl and gradually add the curdled mixture, beating well between each addition.

Add the oil, drop by drop, beating well between each addition

Though there is a wide variety of bought salad dressings they tend to have a sharp unnatural flavour and most people find it well worthwhile to make their own. Both these recipes can be made and kept for a short time without deterioration.

10 Pastas and rice

Pasta

Pasta, made from wheat, often mixed with egg, is a delicious accompaniment to many main courses and a basic ingredient of various made-up dishes. All shapes are easily obtainable, from tiny soup shapes, cooked in clear soups, to the larger spaghetti, lasagne and noodles. Most of the more unusual types have cooking times on the packet, but these are some general cooking hints.

Cook pasta in plenty of boiled salted water until just tender – test a little piece by biting. The pasta should be firm, not over-cooked and mushy.

VERMICELLI (very thin): total cooking time 5 minutes

SPAGHETTI (thicker): total cooking time 12–15 minutes

MACARONI (tubular): total cooking time 15–20 minutes

NOODLES (ribbon): total cooking time 10–12 minutes

SOUP PASTAS: total cooking time 8–10 minutes

CANNERONI (thick tubular): total cooking time 12–15 minutes.

When serving pasta *as an accompaniment*, drain well and return to the pan with a knob of butter or a little olive oil. Toss until evenly coated, turn on to a heated serving dish and supply grated cheese to sprinkle over. Parmesan cheese is the traditional one to use, but finely grated strong Cheddar can be substituted.

Cooked pasta can also be served as a substantial snack with grated cheese and tomato sauce (page 89).

In this country, the large tubular pasta used in the recipe given below (Canneroni with Tomato Sauce) is often wrongly described as *cannelloni*. These are really large squares of pasta which are usually stuffed and rolled up before baking.

Pasta should be cooked until tender but firm, never over-cooked and mushy

CANNERONI WITH TOMATO SAUCE

Canneroni, 8 pieces
Lard, 1 oz/25 gm
Onion, 1
Mushrooms, 2 oz/50 gm
Raw minced beef, 12 oz/300 gm
Salt and pepper
Chopped parsley, 1 tablespoon
Tomato soup, 10 oz/250 gm can
Parmesan cheese

Use a greased ovenproof dish
Oven temperature: fairly hot (375°F, 191°C, Mark 5)

1 Peel and chop onion, wipe and chop mushrooms. Fry in melted lard until soft.
2 Add the meat and fry for a further 5 minutes, stirring.
3 Season with salt and pepper. Add the parsley.
4 Cook the canneroni in boiling salted water for about 15 minutes; drain well.
5 Fill the canneroni with meat mixture. Arrange in the dish and pour the soup over.
6 Bake for 20 minutes; serve sprinkled with grated Parmesan chese.

SPAGHETTI WITH MEAT SAUCE

For the sauce:
Raw minced beef, 8 oz/200 gm
Chicken livers, 4 oz/100 gm
Streaky bacon, 4 oz/100 gm
Olive oil, 1 tablespoon
Onions, 2
Carrot, 1
Garlic, 1 clove
Mushrooms, 2 oz/50 gm
Celery, 1 stick
Tomato purée, 2 tablespoons
Tomatoes, 6 oz/150 gm can
Dry red wine, chicken stock or water,
  4 tablespoons
Salt, 1 level teaspoon
Pepper
Dried oregano, 1 level teaspoon
Basil, ½ level teaspoon
Bay leaf, 1

Spaghetti, 8–12 oz/200–300 gm
Butter
Finely grated cheese

The sauce can be made in advance and re-heated when required.

1 Mix mince with chopped livers. Rind and dice the bacon and fry in the oil until lightly browned.

2 Peel and chop onion, peel and grate carrot, crush garlic. Wipe and chop mushrooms and celery.

3 Add to bacon and fry for 5 minutes, stirring. Add meats and fry for a further 10 minutes, stirring, until browned.

4 Add remaining sauce ingredients, stir well and bring to the boil. Cover and simmer for 1–1¼ hours, stirring from time to time. Add a little extra stock or water if the sauce gets too thick. Put on one side if not being used at once.

About 20 minutes before serving time, bring a large saucepan of salted water to the boil. Holding the spaghetti upright, slowly lower it into the pan, curling it round. Return to the boil and cook until tender – about 15 minutes. Drain and place in a serving dish, topped with a knob of butter. Serve the meat sauce poured over the spaghetti or in a separate dish. Grated cheese is sprinkled over each serving individually.

VARIATIONS
1 Omit chicken livers and increase the amount of minced beef to 12 oz/300 gm.
2 Vary the herbs or replace by 1 level teaspoon of mixed dried herbs.
This is a very good choice for an informal party as the sauce can be made up in advance and re-heated while the spaghetti is cooking. Increase the quantities as necessary.

*Hold the spaghetti upright and slowly
lower it into the boiling salted water*

Rice

This is another accompaniment which is also used in a wide variety of made-up dishes, both savoury and sweet.
There are four main types of polished (white) rice available:

LONG GRAIN (PATNA TYPE): when cooked, this rice has fluffy, separate grains. It is the type used when rice is served as an accompaniment to savoury dishes like curries and also for savoury made-up dishes.

SHORT GRAIN (CAROLINA OR 'PUDDING' TYPE): this is a smaller, rounder grain rice which gives a moist, sticky result when cooked. It is used for puddings and for savoury recipes and stuffings which need moisture.

PAR-BOILED: this is a long grain rice which has been steam treated. It is very easy to cook and gives a perfect result every time, so many people are prepared to pay a little extra for it. Use for the same dishes as long grain rice and cook as instructed on the packet.

PRE-COOKED: an instant rice which has been completely cooked, so only needs re-heating. Follow the directions exactly. It is useful for really quick snacks.

Top: long grain rice
Bottom: short grain rice

Quantities

Allow 1½–2 oz/37–50 gm per head.

Cooking method

The easiest way to cook long grain rice which is to be served as an accompaniment is the *1–2–1 method*:

Rice, 1 cup
Cold water, 2 cups
Salt, 1 teaspoon

1 Place these in a saucepan, bring to the boil, stir, cover tightly and leave to simmer for about 15 minutes. After this time the water will have been absorbed and the rice grains will be dry and separate.
2 Fluff with a fork, season with salt and pepper and turn on to a serving dish with a knob of butter. This quantity is enough for 3–4 people. Increase the quantities as needed, always using double the volume of water to rice.

SAVOURY RICE

A good accompaniment to main courses such as sausages, grilled lamb or pork chops. Cook rice as above and stir in fried onion rings, fried mushrooms, a few peas, etc., varying the additions as you like.

11 Hot and cold puddings

This chapter gives recipes for a variety of hot and cold puddings. Some are 'family puddings' like crumbles and pies, while others are more exotic and suitable for special occasions. Also described are ways of using some of the many packaged and canned puddings, such as jellies and pie fillings, which you will find in your supermarkets.

Using cream   In many of these recipes you will notice that either cream is included in the ingredients or it is suggested that you may serve the pudding with cream.

Cream is available in various different forms, the most common being *single* and *double*.

Single cream is a pouring cream and is suitable for serving with a pudding or in coffee. It cannot be whipped.

Double cream has a higher butterfat content and can be whipped until stiff. It can be served with puddings but is generally only used when cream is used in the pudding; see Trifle, (on page 101).

A mixture of single and double cream in equal proportions will also whip, and can be used in place of the double cream mentioned in these recipes.

Whipping cream, which can be whipped, is halfway in butterfat content between single and double cream, and is available in some parts of the country. It is cheaper than double cream and can be used in any of these recipes.

To whip cream, turn into a basin and whisk with a rotary or spiral whisk or an electric beater until thickened. This may happen very quickly so watch the mixture and do not overbeat.

RICE PUDDING

Short grain rice, 1½ oz/40 gm
Caster sugar, 2 oz/50 gm
Milk, 1 pint/500 ml
Butter
Grated nutmeg

Use a buttered ovenproof dish
Oven temperature: cool (300°F, 149°C, Mark 1–2)

1 Wash the rice and place in the dish with the sugar. Pour in the milk. Cut a knob of butter into very small pieces and dot over the milk. Sprinkle with grated nutmeg.
2 Place the dish on a baking tray and bake at the bottom of the oven for about 2 hours until creamy and golden brown on top. Stir the pudding after about 45 minutes.
Serve Rice Pudding hot or cold.

BAKED CUSTARD

Eggs, 3
Milk, 1 pint/500 ml
Caster sugar, 1½ oz/40 gm
Grated nutmeg (optional)

Use a buttered ovenproof dish
Oven temperature: warm (325°F,
163°C, Mark 3)

1 Beat the eggs in a basin.
2 Warm the milk with the sugar until hot but not boiling. Pour on to the eggs, beating well.
3 Strain into the dish and sprinkle the top with grated nutmeg if desired.
4 Place the dish in a baking tin containing about 2 inches cold water and bake in the centre of the oven until the custard is set and the top browned – about 40–50 minutes.
Serve hot or cold – alone or with a fruit sweet.

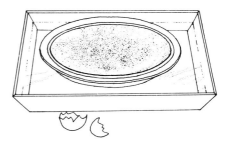

*Stand the dish of custard in a baking tin
containing a little cold water*

CUSTARD

Custard powder, 1½ level tablespoons
Milk, ½ pint/250 ml
Sugar, 1 level tablespoon

*Bowl of custard covered
with wetted greaseproof paper:
this prevents a skin forming*

1 Blend the custard powder in a small bowl with about 2 tablespoons milk until smooth. Heat the remainder of the milk with the sugar until nearly boiling.
2 Pour the hot milk on to the blended custard, stir well and return the mixture to the saucepan.
3 Heat, stirring, until boiling and thickened.
Serve hot or cold with pies, tarts or a fruit sweet. If you are serving the custard cold, pour it into a bowl and cover the surface closely with a piece of wetted greaseproof paper to prevent a skin forming. Before serving, remove the paper, stir and turn into a serving dish.

BAKED JAM SPONGE

Illustrated on page 64

Jam, 4 tablespoons
Butter, 3 oz/75 gm
Caster sugar, 3 oz/75 gm
Egg, 1
Self raising flour, 5 oz/125 gm

Use an ovenproof dish
Oven temperature : moderate (350°F,
  177°C, Mark 4)

The sponge mixture covers a layer of jam

1 Butter the dish and cover the base with the jam.
2 Cream the butter and sugar together until light and fluffy. Beat the egg and gradually add to the creamed mixture, beating well between each addition. Sift the flour and fold into the creamed mixture, adding a little milk if the mixture is very stiff.
3 Cover the jam with the sponge mixture, level the top and bake in the centre of the oven for about 25–40 minutes, until risen and golden.
This pudding can be made in an ovenproof basin. When using this, cook for about 40 minutes, covering the top of the basin with greaseproof paper if the sponge becomes brown too quickly. Turn out before serving.
Serve with single cream, custard or a jam sauce.

VARIATIONS
1 Replace the jam in the base of the dish with marmalade.
2 *Eve's Pudding:* Peel, core and slice 3 medium-sized cooking apples and place in the base of a buttered ovenproof dish with 3–4 tablespoons Demerara sugar. Spread the sponge mixture over the apples and bake as above.
3 A quick-mix sandwich mixture can be used in place of the creamed cake mixture given above. Use the recipe given on page 116 to top the prepared jam. Cook and serve as directed above.

Preparation of fruit   Fruit can be prepared for crumbles, pies, etc., as follows :

1 APPLES : peel, core and slice or leave in quarters.

2 RHUBARB : wipe, trim the leaves and root ends and cut into even lengths. Remove any coarse threads.

3 PEARS : peel, quarter and core.

4 PLUMS : wipe, halve and remove the stones.

5 GOOSEBERRIES : wash, top and tail.

APPLE PIE

Illustrated on page 68

Apples, 1½ lb/600 gm
Sugar, 4 oz/100 gm
Cloves, a few
  or ground cloves, ½ level teaspoon
Water, 2 tablespoons
Shortcrust pastry (page 107), 4 oz/
  100 gm

Use an ovenproof dish
Oven temperature: hot (425°F, 218°C,
  Mark 7)

1 Peel and quarter the apples. Slice into an oven-proof dish, sprinkling each layer with some of the sugar and cloves. Add the water.
2 Make up and roll out the pastry to a shape about 1 inch larger all round than the pie dish.
3 Cut a 1-inch strip from the edge. Damp the rim of the dish and press this strip into position. Damp the strip and cover the pie with the pastry.
4 Press well all round to seal the edges, trim and decorate. Cut slits in the top to allow the steam to escape.
5 Place the dish on a baking tray and bake the pie in the centre of the oven for about 30–40 minutes, until the pastry is browned. If it gets overbrown, lower the temperature to fairly hot (375°F, 191°C, Mark 5).
6 When the pie is cooked, dredge the top with sugar and serve with cream or custard. Any other fruit, prepared as on page 97, can be used in place of the apples in this recipe.
For a crunchy topping, brush the pastry with milk and sprinkle with sugar before baking.

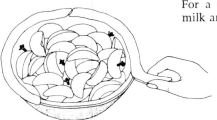

*Press a 1-inch strip of pastry
onto the rim of the dish*

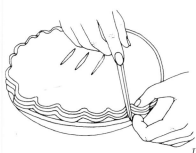

Decorate the edge of the pastry

BLACKBERRY AND APPLE CRUMBLE

Cooking apples, 3 medium
Blackberries, ½ lb/200 gm
Caster sugar, 3 oz/75 gm
Water, 2 tablespoons

For the crumble topping:
Plain flour, 6 oz/150 gm
Butter, 3 oz/75 gm
Caster sugar, 3 oz/75 gm

Use an ovenproof dish
Oven temperature: fairly hot (400°F,
   204°C, Mark 6)

1 Peel, core and slice the apples. Butter the dish and arrange the apples and blackberries in it, sweetening well with sugar. Add the water.
2 Sift the flour into a basin, add the butter and rub in using your fingertips until the mixture resembles fine breadcrumbs. Stir in the sugar. Sprinkle this topping over the fruit in an even layer.
3 Place the dish on a baking tray and bake at the top of the oven until cooked and browned. Serve with cream or custard.

VARIATIONS
1 Use any fresh fruit, prepared as on page 97.
2 Use canned, well-drained peach slices.

Arrange fruit in the dish

BAKED APPLES

Illustrated on page 69

Cooking apples, 4 medium
Demerara sugar
Butter
Water

Use a shallow ovenproof dish
Oven temperature: fairly hot (400°F,
   204°C, Mark 6)

1 Wash the apples and remove the core using an apple corer or vegetable knife. Cut a slit round the centre of each apple and place in the dish.
2 Fill the centre hole in each apple with sugar and top with a knob of butter. Pour 3–4 tablespoons water into the dish and bake in the centre of the oven for 35–45 minutes or until the apples are soft but not broken.
The upper half of the skin can be removed before cooking.
Serve with single cream or custard.

VARIATIONS
Replace the sugar by:
4 tablespoons mincemeat, *or*
4 tablespoons marmalade, *or*
4 tablespoons mixed dried fruit (including mixed cut peel if possible, or sprinkle with grated lemon rind) and 2 tablespoons Demerara sugar, *or*
4 tablespoons chopped dates mixed with a few chopped nuts.

Apples ready to be baked

APRICOT AMBER

Shortcrust pastry (page 107), 4 oz/
   100 gm
Apricots, 15 oz/375 gm can
Eggs, 2
Butter, 1 oz/25 gm
Caster sugar, 3 oz/75 gm

Use a 7-inch flan ring or pie plate
Oven temperature: hot (425°F, 218°C,
   Mark 7)

1 Make up the pastry and roll out. Use to line the flan ring placed on a baking tray or a pie plate. Bake blind (see page 106) at the top of the oven for about 15 minutes.
2 Open the can of apricots and drain off the juice. Sieve the fruit. Separate the eggs and melt the butter. Stir the egg yolks and butter into the fruit and turn into the flan case. Level the top.
3 Reduce the oven heat to moderate (350°F, 177°C, Mark 4) and bake the flan for 12–15 minutes or until the filling is just beginning to set.
4 Meanwhile whisk the egg whites until stiff. Add half the sugar and whisk again until really stiff. Fold in the remaining sugar. Remove the flan from the oven and pile the meringue on to the filling, making sure that it completely covers the apricot mixture. Return the completed flan to the oven and cook until the meringue is lightly browned – about 10 minutes.
Serve hot with cream.

FRUIT SALAD

Grapefruit, 2
Oranges, 2
Red-skinned eating apples, 2
Banana, 1

For the sugar syrup:
Sugar, 4 oz/100 gm
Water, ½ pint/250 ml
Lemon juice

Preparing the fruit

1 *Syrup:* Place the sugar and water in a pan, bring to the boil, simmer for 5 minutes, then pour into a bowl and leave to cool. When cold, sharpen with lemon juice.
2 About 2–3 hours before serving, peel the grapefruit and oranges and carefully remove the flesh, discarding pips, white pith and any skin. This can either be done by removing each segment in turn or alternatively the peeled fruit can be sliced across into 6–8 slices and the slices then quartered. Pips and any central white pith should be removed. Save any juice and add to the syrup with the fruit. Leave to stand.
3 Just before serving, wipe, quarter and core the apples and slice very thinly. Peel and slice the banana and add to the bowl with the apples.
Serve with single cream.
Any combination of fruits, fresh or canned, may be used in Fruit Salad. If using canned fruit the fruit syrup may be used in place of the stock sugar syrup used above. Sharpen with lemon juice if necessary.
For a special occasion, add 1–2 tablespoons brandy or fruit liqueur to the syrup.

TRIFLE

Illustrated on page 72

Sponge cakes, 6 small
  or sandwich cake, 1 7-inch round
Jam
Fruit, e.g. peaches, fruit cocktail,
  15 oz/375 gm can
Custard, ¾ pint/375 ml
Double cream, ¼ pint/125 ml
Glacé cherries and angelica to decorate

*Decorate with cherries,
angelica or almonds*

1 Split the cakes and spread with jam. If using sandwich cake, cut into 6 portions, split and spread with jam. Place in a shallow glass bowl.
2 Drain the fruit, and spoon 4–6 tablespoons of the syrup over the cake. Arrange the drained fruit over the sponge cakes. Make up the custard, cool quickly and pour over the fruit. Leave to set.
3 Just before serving, whip the cream and use to decorate the trifle. Either spoon on to the custard or place in a piping bag fitted with a star pipe, and pipe it on to the custard. Decorate with pieces of glacé cherry and angelica.

VARIATIONS
This very basic recipe can be varied in many ways.
1 The fruit can be replaced with ½ pint/250 ml jelly.
2 The cakes can be moistened with sherry or a mixture of sherry and fruit juice.
3 The amount of cream may be increased to ½ pint/250 ml.
4 Toasted, blanched almonds can be used with or in place of the cherries, and angelica used to decorate the trifle.

Quick puddings

*Blancmange layered
in a tall glass*

On every supermarket shelf there are lots of canned and packeted puddings and it is always a good idea to have a selection in your store-cupboard. Among the puddings you will find are:

1 BLANCMANGE: available in lots of flavours. It can be made up with instant milk granules or evaporated milk. Try layering two varieties of blancmange, made up as directed, in tall glasses with pieces of fresh fruit or crushed macaroons, boudoir biscuits or warmed jam.

2 LEMON OR ORANGE PIE FILLINGS: use to make a quick lemon or orange meringue pie as directed on the packet (use a pastry flan case – see recipe for Apricot Amber on opposite page). Or make up a packet as directed, cool slightly and fold in a whipped egg white. Place some grated chocolate or chocolate chips in the base of two glasses, top with the lemon mixture and decorate with more chocolate.

Fruit Condé

3 CANNED FRUIT FILLINGS: although these are really meant for pies and flans, quick puddings can be made by layering the pie filling with blancmange, whisked jelly (see below) or crushed digestive biscuits. They are super, too, served warm over ice cream.

4 CANNED MILK PUDDINGS: use these cold as a basis for Fruit Condé. Divide a can of rice pudding between 4 sundae dishes and top with half a canned or fresh pear. Warm some red currant jelly or sieved raspberry jam and carefully spoon enough over the pear to cover it. Or serve the puddings mixed with canned or fresh chopped fruit or pieces of chopped fudge.

Jelly ideas Make up packet jellies according to the directions.

To turn out a jelly from a mould, loosen the jelly round the sides using your fingers or the back of a teaspoon. Invert the serving dish over the jelly, hold the mould and dish together and turn the whole lot upside down, so that the dish is underneath. Give it a little shake and the jelly should slip out. If it is obstinate, dip the mould in hot water for a moment and try again.

There are various ways of making a packet jelly more interesting:

1 MILK JELLY: dissolve the jelly cubes in ½ pint/250 ml boiling water and leave to cool. When cold make up to 1 pint/ 500 ml with cold milk or diluted evaporated milk. Stir and leave to set.

2 WHISKED JELLY: make up jelly in the usual way and leave until nearly set – the consistency of unbeaten egg white. Whisk until frothy, turn into the serving bowl and leave to set. This can be varied by using ¾ of the water and adding a small tin of evaporated milk while whipping.

3 JELLY WITH FRUIT: drain a can of fruit and make up the jelly with the fruit juice and boiling water. Fold the fruit into the jelly and leave to set. Fresh fruit can be folded into a jelly made in the usual way.

4 Make up jelly as usual and pour into two separate bowls. When nearly set, whip one bowl of jelly until frothy, then leave both to set. Before serving turn out the plain jelly on to a piece of wetted greaseproof paper and chop with a wet knife. Spoon portions of the two jellies alternately into tall glasses and chill.

5 Decorate jellies with whipped cream and pieces of fresh, crystallized or glacé fruit.

Ice cream   Although we tend to think of ice cream as something we buy to eat immediately, it can also be served as a sweet. Ice creams can be served with meringues (see page 117), whipped cream, fruit (fresh or canned) or a home-made sauce (see below).

CHOCOLATE SAUCE

Plain chocolate, 4 oz/100 gm
Golden syrup, 2 tablespoons
Butter, 1 oz/25 gm
Water, 2 tablespoons

1 Place all the ingredients in a basin over a pan of hot water and heat gently until the butter and chocolate are melted and the sauce is hot.
2 Stir well and use while hot.

BUTTERSCOTCH SAUCE

Butter, 2 oz/50 gm
Demerara sugar, 2 oz/50 gm
Golden syrup, 2 tablespoons

1 Place all the ingredients in a small pan and heat, stirring, until boiling.
2 Boil for 1 minute then use immediately. A little lemon juice may be stirred in, if desired, and 1–2 oz/25–50 gm chopped walnuts may be added.

BAKED ALASKA

Illustrated on page 65

Strawberries, 8 oz/200 gm, fresh or frozen
Sandwich cake, 7-inch round
Vanilla or flavoured ice cream, 1 family-size block
Egg whites, 3
Caster sugar, 6 oz/150 gm

Use an ovenproof plate
Oven temperature: very hot (450°F, 232°C, Mark 8)

1 Wash the fruit and drain. Thaw frozen fruit. Slice or mash, sweetening if necessary.
2 Place the cake on the plate and cover with the fruit. Chill thoroughly.
3 Just before serving, place the ice cream on top of the fruit, cutting into slices if necessary.
4 Whisk the egg whites until stiff, add half the sugar and continue to whisk until really stiff. Fold in the remaining sugar. Cover the fruit, ice cream and cake with the meringue mixture.
5 Place at the top of the oven for 3–5 minutes until the meringue is browned.
Serve immediately.
Any drained canned fruit, or fresh or frozen raspberries may be used in place of the strawberries. The cake may be moistened with fruit juice or sherry.
Although this appears a spectacular sweet, it is not too difficult to make for a dinner party. Assemble the cake and its topping of fruit in advance. Separate the eggs, weigh out the sugar and turn the oven on before the meal. While the main course dishes are being cleared away, make the meringue and finish the sweet, then bake and serve at once.

Flans Flans are a popular cold sweet and are easy to serve as they can be made well in advance. They are very decorative and are ideal for parties as well as everyday.

Flan cases are made from pastry, sponge and biscuit crust. The fillings can be any combination of fresh or canned fruit, jelly, whips, etc. They are either decorated with, or served with cream.

To make a pastry flan, make as directed for Apricot Amber (see page 100). Cook for about 15 minutes. Cool and fill as desired.

BISCUIT CRUST FLAN

Digestive biscuits, 7 oz/175 gm
Butter, soft, 3–4 oz/75–100 gm
Demerara sugar, 1 oz/25 gm

1 Crush the biscuits with a rolling pin and place in a bowl. Melt the butter. Stir the sugar into the biscuit crumbs and add enough butter to bind together.

2 Place the mixture in an ovenproof pie plate, glass dish about 8 inches in diameter, or 7–8 inch flan ring placed on a plate. Using the back of a teaspoon, press the mixture against the sides and the base, forming an even layer and an edge about 1½ inches high. Chill until firm. Remove flan ring carefully.

Use the back of a teaspoon to press the crumb mixture into position

Flan fillings 1 FRESH FRUIT: prepare in the usual way, removing any discoloured portions and washing if necessary. Slice or chop. Arrange in the flan case. Glaze with 3–4 tablespoons of red currant jelly, warmed. Or pour ½ packet of jelly over, made up as directed on the packet. Do not use the jelly until nearly set, otherwise it will tend to sink into the flan.

Try: Fresh strawberries or raspberries
     Sliced banana (dipped in lemon juice to prevent browning)
     Sliced oranges and halved black grapes

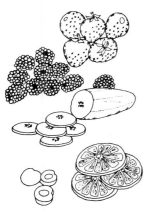

2 CANNED FRUIT: any canned fruit (drained) may be used as a filling. To make a glaze, blend a little of the fruit juice with 3 level teaspoons cornflour or arrowroot. Boil about 6 tablespoons of the fruit juice, pour on to the blended mixture, stir and return to the pan. Heat, stirring, until clear and thick, add a little sugar and lemon juice if necessary for sharpness and flavour. Cool slightly then pour over the fruit.

Try: Mandarin oranges
Pineapple chunks mixed with a little preserved ginger.
Sliced peaches
Pear halves

3 CANNED FRUIT FILLINGS: these are very useful as they come in many different flavours and need no glazing. Just pour the filling into the flan, level and chill.

Use a variety of fruits for distinctive flan fillings

All these fillings can also be used with bought sponge flans.

PARTY CHEESECAKE A special party recipe:

Biscuit crust flan, an 8-inch flan
Cream cheese, 12 oz/300 gm
Caster sugar, 4 oz/100 gm
Plain flour, 1 oz/25 gm
Sherry or fruit juice, 1 tablespoon
Orange rind, ½ level teaspoon, grated
Lemon rind, ½ level teaspoon, grated
Eggs, 2
Soured cream or plain yoghurt, a
  5 oz/125 gm carton

Use an 8-inch flan ring on a baking
  tray or ovenproof pie plate
Oven temperature: moderate (350°F,
  177°C, Mark 4)

1 Make the biscuit crust flan case as directed on page 104, pressing the mixture over the base and sides of the ring or pie plate. Chill until firm.
2 Beat the cream cheese until softened, then cream in the sugar. Add the flour, sherry, orange and lemon rind. Separate the eggs, and beat the yolks into the mixture. Fold in the soured cream.
3 Whisk the egg whites until stiff and fold into the cheese mixture. Pour into the prepared flan case.
4 Bake in the centre of the oven for about 45 minutes. After this time, turn off the oven heat, open the door and leave the cheesecake to cool in the oven. Remove the flan ring.
Serve warm or cold, decorated with a twist of fresh lemon. Serves 6–8.
This is delicious served as a dessert or as a gâteau at a special tea or morning coffee party.

Decorate a Party Cheesecake with a twist of fresh lemon

12 Pastry

The ingredients for pastry should be cool and the pastry should be made quickly with as little handling as possible. Fingers rather than the whole hand should be used for rubbing in.

If pastry is difficult to handle when it has been made, wrap it in foil and chill for about 30 minutes, or until firm.

Use butter, margarine, lard or blended or whipped up vegetable fats. Each gives a slightly different result and as a rule a mixture of butter or margarine with a white fat is recommended for the best flavour and texture. Made pastry can be stored in the refrigerator for up to a week, providing it is well wrapped in foil to prevent drying out.

Note: when a recipe calls for 4 oz/100 gm pastry, this means pastry made with 4 oz/100 gm flour; calculate other weights similarly.

Baking blind

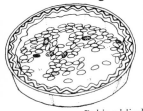

Baking blind

Tarts and flan cases are often baked 'blind', that is, unfilled. Roll out the pastry and line the flan ring placed on a baking tray or pie dish. Trim the edges. Cut a circle of greaseproof paper a little larger than the flan ring, place it in the flan and cover the base with dried beans, crusts or rice to keep the pastry flat. Bake at the top of a hot oven (425°F, 218°C, Mark 7) for about 20 minutes, removing beans and paper after 15 minutes. Cool on a wire rack.

Empty pastry cases can be stored in an airtight tin for some time before using.

Pastry using special whipped up white fats or special margarines

Any of the traditional recipes may be made using these modern fats but a much better result, with far less effort, will be obtained if the special recipes recommended by the manufacturers are used. These are generally printed on the carton and are often in the manufacturers' literature or advertisements. It is important to follow the recipe exactly for the best results. The pastry can be used in the same ways as the traditionally-made pastry and cooked at the same temperatures. The texture may be softer and the flavour will probably be blander than pastry made with lard and ordinary margarine. Here is a recipe for a quick-mix shortcrust suitable for use with a whipped up white fat.

QUICK-MIX SHORTCRUST PASTRY

Self raising flour, 4 oz/100 gm
Salt, a pinch
Whipped up white fat (e.g. Trex), 2 oz/50 gm
Cold water, 1 tablespoon

1 Sift the flour and salt into a bowl. Add the fat and water.

2 With a fork, work the fat into the flour until a smooth ball of dough is formed.

3 Turn the dough on to a well–floured board and roll out and use as desired.

This amount of pastry is enough for the items listed on opposite page under Shortcrust Pastry.

SHORTCRUST PASTRY

Plain flour, 4 oz/100 gm
Salt, a pinch
Fat, 2 oz/50 gm
Cold water

This amount of pastry is enough for:
A 7- or 8-inch flan case
Topping a pie using a 7–8-inch round
 dish
12–15 small tarts using 2½–3-inch
 patty tins
A dozen 2-inch sausage rolls
For a double crust pie in a 7–8-inch
dish, use double this recipe.

1 Sift the flour into a bowl with the salt. Add the fat and rub in lightly with the fingertips until the mixture resembles breadcrumbs.
2 Add water, a teaspoonful at a time, mixing with a knife until the dough starts to stick together. Only about 4 teaspoonsful of water should be needed and it is very important not to make the pastry wet and sticky or it will bake very hard.
3 Turn the pastry on to a floured board and knead gently until smooth. Roll out with a floured rolling pin.

FLAKY PASTRY

Plain flour, 8 oz/200 gm
Salt, a pinch
Fat, 6 oz/150 gm
Cold water
Lemon juice, 1 teaspoon

This amount of pastry is enough for:
24 × 2-inch sausage rolls
Two tops for pies made in a 1 pint/
 500 ml pie dish

1 Sift the flour into a bowl with the salt. Soften the fats on a plate, using a knife. Mix them together if you are using two kinds of fat. Divide into four portions and rub one into the flour.
2 Mix about 8 tablespoons water with the lemon juice and slowly add to the flour, mixing with a knife, until a soft dough is obtained.
3 Turn out on to a floured board. *Roll out into an oblong, using a floured rolling pin. Dot a portion of the fat over the top two-thirds of the dough. Fold the bottom third up and the top third down. Seal the ends, wrap in foil and chill in the refrigerator for 30 minutes until firm.*
4 Unwrap and replace on the floured board with the sealed edges top and bottom. Repeat from * to * twice more, turning the pastry through a right angle each time.
5 After the final chilling, roll out before using.

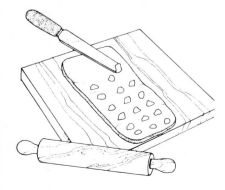

Dot some of the fat over the top
two-thirds of the dough

CHEESE PASTRY

Plain flour, 4 oz/100 gm
Salt, pepper and dry mustard, a pinch
Fat, 2 oz/50 gm
Grated cheese, 2 oz/50 gm
Beaten egg yolk, 1
Water

This amount of pastry is enough for:
A 7–8-inch flan case
12–15 small tarts using 2½–3-inch
  patty tins
About 10 savouries
About 40 cheese straws

1 Sift the flour into a bowl with the salt, pepper and mustard.
2 Add the fat and rub in lightly with the finger-tips until the mixture resembles fine bread-crumbs. Add the cheese.
3 Beat the egg yolk with a little water and add gradually to the pastry, mixing with a knife until the dough sticks together.
4 Turn on to a floured board and knead gently until smooth. Roll out with a floured rolling pin.

SUET PASTRY

Self raising flour, 6 oz/150 gm
Salt, a pinch
Shredded suet, 3 oz/75 gm
Cold water

This amount of pastry is enough for:
A fruit-filled suet pudding using 1¼ lb/
  500 gm fruit and a 1½ pint/750 ml
  basin
A roly-poly using 4–6 tablespoons jam
A meat pudding using ¾–1 lb/300–400
  gm meat and a 1½ pint/750 ml basin

1 Sift the flour into a bowl with the salt. Add the suet and mix.
2 Gradually add the water (about 6 tablespoons should be needed), mixing with a knife until the soft dough is formed.
3 Turn on to a floured board and knead lightly.

Packet pastry mixes and ready-made pastry

Excellent packet pastry mixes are available which give good results. Ready-made pastry is also available either frozen or chilled.

For the best results, prepare and use the pastry mixes, and thaw and cook the ready-made pastry, as directed on the packets. They can be used in place of home-made pastry in any of the recipes in this book.

Remember that some ready-made shortcrust pastry is sweet-ened, so is obviously only suitable for puddings.

If you find ready-made pastry shrinks on cooking, try rolling out and then leaving for about 15 minutes before shaping and cooking. When cutting out pastries, be careful not to stretch the pastry as it will tend to give a misshapen finished product.

Ready-made pastry products like sausage rolls and vol-au-vent cases are also available frozen. Thaw and cook as directed.

13 Cakes and biscuits

This chapter contains recipes for traditional cakes and biscuits, together with icing recipes and ways of finishing sandwich cakes. A recipe for a quick-mix cake and some unusual American biscuits are also included.

Remember that before you start to make any of these recipes you must preheat the oven and prepare the cake tins or baking trays as directed in the recipes and diagrams. Use melted lard or oil to grease the tins, and greaseproof paper to line them. Aluminium foil can be used successfully if you have no greaseproof paper, and can be used over and over again if care is taken when removing the cakes from the tin.

To test whether or not a cake is cooked, open the oven door and look at the cake. If it is cooked, it will have risen and will have begun to shrink from the sides of the tin. Small cakes will be firm to the touch. Larger cakes should be pressed lightly with a finger. The impression should disappear quickly when you remove your finger.

Cool cakes in the tins and biscuits on the trays for a few minutes, then invert on to a cooling rack and remove the tin and any paper. Leave, right side up, on the cooling rack until quite cold. Store in an airtight container.

Packet mix cakes Cake, small cake and cookie-type packet mixes can be bought everywhere. These work out more expensive than home-made recipes but are useful to have in the store-cupboard. Most require only the addition of liquid and an egg, but for best results be careful to follow the directions exactly, with regard to making up, cooking container used and baking times and temperatures.

Sandwich cakes made with packet mixes can be finished in any of the ways given on pages 118—119

CHERRY LOAF

Illustrated on page 73

Glacé cherries, 6 oz/150 gm
Self raising flour, 8 oz/200 gm
Salt, a pinch
Butter, 4 oz/100 gm
Caster sugar, 4 oz/100 gm
Egg, 1
Milk, about 8 tablespoons

Use an 8 × 4½-inch loaf tin, greased and lined (see page 111)
Oven temperature: moderate (350°F, 177°C, Mark 4)

1 Quarter the cherries, place in a sieve and sprinkle with a little of the flour until lightly coated.
2 Sift remaining flour with the salt and rub in the butter. Add the sugar and cherries.
3 Beat the egg and stir into the mixture with enough milk to give a dropping consistency.
4 Put the mixture into the tin and level the top.
5 Bake in the centre of the oven for about 1–1¼ hours or until risen and golden brown.

SIMPLE FRUIT CAKE

Illustrated on page 76

Self raising flour, 8 oz/200 gm
Mixed spice, ½ level teaspoon
Salt, a pinch
Butter, 4 oz/100 gm
Caster sugar, 4 oz/100 gm
Mixed dried fruit and peel, 4 oz/
  100 gm
Eggs, 2
Milk

Use a 7-inch round tin, greased and
  lined (see opposite page)
Oven temperature: moderate (350°F,
  177°C, Mark 4)

1 Sift the flour with the spice and salt and rub in the butter. Add the sugar and fruit.
2 Beat the eggs and stir into the mixture with enough milk to give a dropping consistency.
3 Put the mixture into the tin and level the top.
4 Bake in the centre of the oven for about 1 hour or until risen and browned.

ROCK CAKES

Self raising flour, 8 oz/200 gm
Mixed spice, ½ level teaspoon
Salt, a pinch
Butter, 4 oz/100 gm
Caster sugar, 4 oz/100 gm
Mixed dried fruit and peel, 4 oz/
  100 gm
Egg, 1
Milk

Use a greased baking tray
Oven temperature: fairly hot (400°F,
  204°C, Mark 6)

1 Sift the flour with the spice and salt and rub in the butter. Add the sugar and fruit.
2 Beat the egg and stir into the mixture with enough milk to give a stiff consistency. Drop spoonfuls of this mixture on the prepared tray, forming about 12–14 buns.
3 Bake at the top of the oven for about 15 minutes or until risen and browned.
Makes 12–14 cakes.

Spooning Rock Cake mixture on to the tray

GINGERBREAD

Illustrated on page 76

Dark brown sugar, 8 oz/200 gm
Butter, 6 oz/150 gm
Treacle or golden syrup, or a mixture
  of both, 12 oz/300 gm
Milk, ½ pint/250 ml
Egg, 1
Plain flour, 1 lb/400 gm
Ground ginger, 1 level tablespoon
Bicarbonate of soda, 1 level
  teaspoon
Baking powder, 1 level tablespoon

Use an 8-inch square tin, greased
and lined (see opposite page)
Oven temperature: warm (325°F,
  163°C, Mark 3)

1 Place the sugar, butter and treacle in a sauce-pan and heat slowly until the butter is melted. Do not boil. Beat the milk with the eggs.
2 Sift the flour with the ginger, baking powder and bicarbonate of soda. Stir in the melted mixture and beaten egg and milk. Mix thoroughly then beat until smooth. Pour into the prepared tin.
3 Bake in the centre of the oven for about 1½ hours, until risen and beginning to shrink from the sides.

VARIATIONS
1 Add up to 6 oz/150 gm mixed dried fruit and peel to the mixture if desired.
2 Decorate the finished gingerbread with preserved ginger, or sprinkle with caraway seeds.

To line a round or square cake tin

Grease the tin and measure its depth and circumference. Cut a piece of greaseproof paper the length of the circumference + 2 inches and twice the depth + 2 inches. Fold in half lengthwise.

Fold folded edge up 1 inch, crease and flatten. Make slanting cuts at 1-inch intervals from fold to crease. Place inside tin with cut edge on the base, fitting paper to the sides of tin. Grease the paper.

Cut two layers of greaseproof paper the size of the base and place inside tin. Grease the paper.

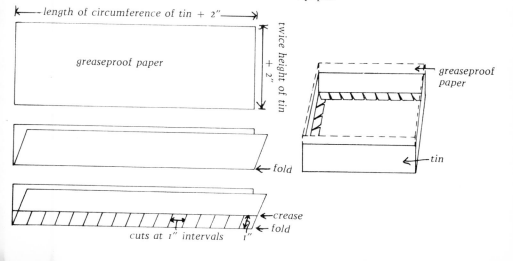

length of circumference of tin + 2"

greaseproof paper

twice height of tin + 2"

greaseproof paper

tin

fold

cuts at 1" intervals

crease

fold

1"

Scones Scones can be made and baked in about 30 minutes so they are ideal if you have unexpected guests or not much time to spare.

Freshly-made scones are best served with butter and jam, or cream. Scones more than a day old can be toasted and served with butter.

PLAIN OVEN SCONES

Illustrated on page 73

Self raising flour, 8 oz/200 gm
Salt, a pinch
Butter, 1½ oz/38 gm
Milk to mix

Use two greased baking trays
Oven temperature: very hot (450°F, 232°C, Mark 8)

1 Sift the flour into a bowl with the salt. Rub in the butter, stir in enough milk, about 8 tablespoons in all, to give a soft dough. Turn on to a floured board and knead lightly. Divide into two portions and form each into a round.

2 Put the rounds of scone dough on the trays and press with the hand or a rolling pin into circles about 8 inches across. Mark with a knife into wedges and bake at the top of the oven for 20–25 minutes or until risen and browned.

3 Break into wedges and serve plain or cut in half and buttered. Alternatively, serve cut in half and filled with whipped cream and strawberry jam. Makes 8–12 wedges.

If you prefer round scones, roll out the dough to ½ inch thick and cut into rounds using a 2-inch cutter. Place on a greased baking tray and bake at the same temperature for 7–10 minutes only. Makes about 12 scones.

VARIATIONS

Sweet: Add 1–2 oz/25–50 gm caster sugar to the flour before rubbing in the butter.

Fruit: Add 1–2 oz/25–50 gm mixed dried fruit after rubbing in the butter.

Cheese: Add 3 oz/75 gm grated cheese after rubbing in the butter. A pinch of dry mustard added with the salt is an improvement. Cheese scones can be served plain, buttered for a quick snack or picnic, or halved and buttered with a slice of tomato placed in the scones before serving.

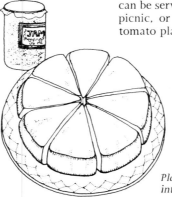

Plain oven scone dough can be formed into wedges or cut into rounds

DROP SCONES

Illustrated on page 73

These scones are very quick to make. A proper girdle is difficult to find but a heavy frying pan makes an effective substitute.

Self raising flour, 4 oz/100 gm
Salt, a pinch
Caster sugar, ½ oz/12 gm
Egg, 1
Milk, about ¼ pint/125 ml
Pork fat, oil or lard, to grease

1 Sift the flour with the salt and add the sugar. Beat the egg and add it to the flour with some milk, stirring well. Beat until a smooth batter is obtained, adding more milk if necessary to give a pouring consistency.

2 Heat the girdle over a low heat. Grease lightly with a piece of pork fat or a brush dipped in oil or melted lard.

3 Drop spoonfuls of the batter on to the girdle and cook until bubbles rise to the surface, turn and cook until the underside is browned – about 5 minutes in all. Cool between the folds of a tea towel on a cooling rack. This keeps the scones moist.
Serve plain, or with butter, or whipped cream and jam.
Makes about 20 drop scones.

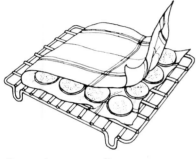

Dropped scones cooling

Sandwich cakes

There are two types of sandwich cake – a Victoria Sandwich which contains fat and is made by the creaming method, and the true Sponge which contains no fat and is made by the whisking method. Both are served filled with cream and jam, or jam alone, or butter cream. However, a Victoria Sandwich keeps better and has a firmer texture, so it is a good choice if you plan to ice the cake with glacé icing or butter cream. The light texture of a Sponge combines well with fruit and so is often used as the base for a gâteau to be served as a sweet.

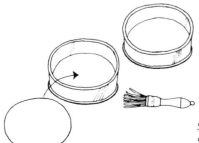

Sandwich tins, greased and lined with a disc of greaseproof paper, for Victoria Sandwich

VICTORIA SANDWICH

Butter, 4 oz/100 gm
Caster sugar, 4 oz/100 gm
Eggs, 2
Self raising flour, 4 oz/100 gm
Jam and icing sugar to finish

Use two 7-inch sandwich tins, greased
  and with the bases lined with discs of
  greaseproof paper
Oven temperature: fairly hot (375°F,
  191°C, Mark 5)

1 Cream the butter with the sugar until light and fluffy. Beat the eggs and slowly add to the creamed mixture, beating well between each addition. Sift the flour and fold into the creamed mixture with a metal spoon. Do not beat.

2 Divide the cake mixture evenly and place half in each tin. Level the top and bake at the top of the oven for 20–25 minutes or until risen, golden brown and just beginning to shrink from the sides of the tin.

To serve, place one cake upside down on a plate, and spread with jam. Top with the other cake and sprinkle with sifted icing sugar.

For other ideas on finishing the cake, see page 119.

This basic mixture can be flavoured in any of the following ways:

1 ORANGE OR LEMON: add the grated rind of 1 orange or 1 lemon to the creamed fat and sugar. Use orange or lemon butter cream (see page 117) to sandwich together.

2 COFFEE: dissolve 3 teaspoons of instant coffee in a little hot water and add to the creamed mixture with the egg. Sandwich together with coffee butter cream (see page 117).

3 CHOCOLATE: add 2 level tablespoons of cocoa in place of the same amount of flour in the recipe. Sift together twice before folding in. Sandwich together with plain or chocolate butter cream (see page 117).

*Victoria Sandwich mixture
can be cooked in
individual paper cases*

A Victoria Sandwich mixture can also be cooked in waxed paper cases. Divide the mixture between 15 paper cases, placed on a baking tray. Bake at the top of a fairly hot oven (375°F, 191°C, Mark 5) for 15–18 minutes until risen and lightly browned.

This mixture can be flavoured in the same way as suggested for Victoria Sandwich or may have the following items folded in with the flour:

2 oz/50 gm sultanas – makes Queen Cakes
2 oz/50 gm glacé cherries, chopped – makes Cherry Cakes
2 oz/50 gm chocolate chips – makes Chocolate Buns

Plain Buns may also be iced with glacé icing or butter cream.

SPONGE CAKE

Caster sugar, 3 oz/75 gm
Eggs, 3
Plain flour, 3 oz/75 gm
Hot water, 1 tablespoon
Jam and icing sugar to finish

Use two 7-inch sandwich tins,
  greased and dusted with flour
Oven temperature: fairly hot (375°F,
  191°C, Mark 5)

1 Place the sugar and eggs in a bowl over a saucepan of hot water and whisk until thick and creamy. Remove the bowl from the heat and whisk until cooled.

2 Sift the flour and fold into the whisked mixture with the hot water. Use a cutting action; do not beat.

3 When the flour is evenly incorporated, pour the mixture into the tins. Level and bake at the top of the oven for 20–25 minutes or until risen and browned.

Serve sandwiched together with jam and topped with sifted icing sugar.

FRUIT GÂTEAU

Round sandwich cakes, two 7-inch
Fresh strawberries or sliced peaches,
  12 oz/300 gm or 15 oz/375 gm can
Double cream, ½ pint/250 ml
Icing sugar
Angelica to decorate if using peaches

1 Make the sandwich cakes using either a Victoria Sandwich or a Sponge Cake mixture.

2 Wash and drain the strawberries and slice most of them, reserving about 8 medium-sized ones for decoration. Drain the peaches if used and chop half.

3 Whip the cream until just thickened. Sweeten with sifted icing sugar if using strawberries.

4 Place the bottom sandwich cake on a serving plate and spread with some of the cream. Cover with some of the sliced fruit and top with the other cake.

Top each whirl of cream with a strawberry

5 Use most of the remaining cream to spread on the top, and arrange the remaining fruit attractively in the centre. Put the rest of the cream in a piping bag fitted with a star vegetable pipe, and pipe 8 whirls round the outside. Top each with one of the reserved strawberries or a piece of angelica. Chill for 1–2 hours before serving. Serves 6–8.

Note: This type of gâteau makes a good sweet for the end of a dinner party. The fruits can of course be varied according to what is in season or in the store-cupboard. The cakes can also be moistened with 2–3 tablespoons fruit juice or fruit liqueur, such as Kirsch, before the cream and fruit are put in place.

Quick-mix cakes Sandwich and fruit cakes, as well as gingerbreads and biscuits, can all be made using whipped-up white fats, special margarines or oil. However, special recipes are necessary for acceptable results. These are published by all the manufacturers, but here is an easy recipe for a sandwich cake, which can be varied in any of the ways given for traditional recipe sandwich cakes, and finished in any of the ways given on page 119.

QUICK-MIX SANDWICH CAKE

Self raising flour, 4 oz/100 gm
Baking powder, 1 level teaspoon
Special margarine, e.g. Blue Band,
 4 oz/100 gm
Caster sugar, 4 oz/100 gm
Eggs, 2
Jam and icing sugar to finish

Use two 7-inch sandwich tins, greased
 and with the bases lined with discs of
 greaseproof paper
Oven temperature: warm (325°F,
 163°C, Mark 3)

1 Sift the flour and baking powder into a bowl. Add the margarine, sugar and eggs.
2 Mix well, then beat with a spoon for 2 minutes. Do not beat for longer.
3 Divide the mixture between the tins and bake at the top of the oven for 25–30 minutes or until risen, golden brown and just beginning to shrink from the sides of the tin. Finish in the same way as the Victoria Sandwich, page 114.

MERINGUES

Egg whites, 2
Caster sugar, 4 oz/100 gm
Double cream, ¼ pint/125 ml

Use a baking tray
Oven temperature: cool (275°F,
135°C, Mark ½)

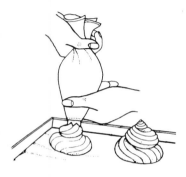

*Piping the meringue mixture
onto the prepared tray*

1 Line the tray with a piece of non-stick (silicone treated) paper or, if this is not available, greaseproof paper. Oil lightly if using greaseproof paper.
2 Place the egg whites in a clean bowl and whisk until very stiff. Add half of the sugar and whisk again until very stiff and smooth. Fold in the remaining sugar with a metal spoon.
3 Place this mixture in a large piping bag fitted with a star vegetable pipe, and pipe whirls of the mixture on to the prepared tray. If no piping bag is available use two teaspoons to spoon the mixture into even-sized piles on the baking tray.
4 Place at the bottom of the oven and dry off for about 2 hours or until crisp but still white. If the meringues start to brown, leave the oven door ajar.
5 To serve, whip the cream until thick and sandwich the meringues together in pairs.
Makes about 6–8 complete meringues.
Meringues can be served at tea but also make an excellent sweet when served with ice cream or fruit.

Icing recipes

BUTTER CREAM

Icing sugar, 8 oz/200 gm
Butter, 4 oz/100 gm
Flavouring – see below
Milk if necessary

1 Sift the icing sugar.
2 Cream the butter until softened, add the sugar and beat until light and creamy.
3 Add the flavouring if used and milk if necessary, to give a spreading consistency.

These are generous quantities, enough to top and fill a 7-inch round sandwich cake-or to coat the sides. Reduce to 6 oz/150gm sugar and 3 oz / 75 gm butter if you do not like too much icing.

FLAVOURINGS

VANILLA: add 1 teaspoon vanilla essence.

ORANGE or LEMON: add the grated rind of 1 orange or 1 lemon and enough juice to give a spreading consistency.

CHOCOLATE: add 2 oz/50 gm melted chocolate.

COFFEE: add 3 level teaspoons instant coffee.

GLACÉ ICING

Icing sugar, 4 oz/100 gm
Water to mix
Flavouring and colouring

Sift the sugar into a bowl and add the water, a little at a time, stirring until a smooth icing is obtained. Flavour and colour as desired. Use at once. If the consistency is too runny, add a little more icing sugar – the icing should coat the back of a spoon.

This quantity of glacé icing is enough to coat the top of a 7-inch round sandwich cake. To coat the top and sides use 8 oz/200 gm icing sugar.

FLAVOURINGS

ORANGE or LEMON: add the strained juice of an orange or lemon in place of the water. Colour with edible food colourings.
CHOCOLATE: mix 3 level teaspoons cocoa with 1 tablespoon hot water and use in place of the water in the recipe.
COFFEE: mix 2 level teaspoons instant coffee with 1 tablespoon hot water and use in place of the water in the recipe.

COLOURINGS: any edible food colourings can be used to tint the icing; use carefully as a little goes a long way.

Decorating a Victoria or Sponge Sandwich cake

All the quantities mentioned here are based on cakes made using 7-inch round sandwich cake tins.
When decorating a sandwich cake
1 Place the cooled cake on a wire rack.
2 Prepare the filling.
3 Prepare the butter cream, jam, etc., for the sides if you plan to ice them.
4 Prepare the butter cream for the top. If you plan to use glacé icing, do not make it yet but sift the icing sugar into a bowl.
5 Prepare the decorations – for easy ideas, see below.
When the icing has set, carefully transfer the complete cake to a serving plate with two palette knives or slices.

FILLINGS

1 The simplest filling is jam, which can be melted slightly to make it easy to spread.
2 Whipped double cream (allow about ¼ pint/125 ml) can be used alone or with jam, but remember that the cake will have to be eaten within 24 hours of decorating or the cream may go sour. If possible, it should be stored in a refrigerator.
3 Butter cream (using 4 oz/100 gm icing sugar) can be used. Spread it evenly using a palette knife.

FOR THE SIDES

The sides of a sandwich cake can be left plain but for a special occasion they can be coated with jam, butter cream and nuts. Prepare the coating (chopped nuts, sieved cake crumbs, desiccated coconut or chocolate vermicelli) and place on a plate. Fill and sandwich the cake together, then brush the sides with melted apricot or raspberry jam, or spread evenly with butter cream (using 6–8 oz/150–200 gm icing sugar) and press the chosen coating on to the sides with a knife. Alternatively, roll the cake in the coating. Brush off surplus crumbs.

Rolling the coating onto the sides of the cake

FOR THE TOPPING

Top sandwich cakes with butter cream or glacé icing after filling the cake and coating the sides.

BUTTER CREAM: spread the top evenly with the butter cream (using 4 oz/100 gm icing sugar) and then mark a pattern using the prongs of a fork or a skewer. Press any decorations used into place, or decorate with some of the butter cream in a piping bag fitted with a small star pipe, after spreading the rest in an even layer. Add decorations.

GLACÉ ICING: make up and pour on to the top of the cake. Spread evenly over the top and ease to the edges using a knife – do not allow to run down the edges. Add decorations and leave to set.

DECORATIONS

The simplest decorations include nuts (whole or halved walnuts and almonds), crystallised or glacé fruit (cherries, angelica cut into small pieces), chocolate chips or buttons, grated chocolate, small sweets like jellies, chocolate beans and dolly mixtures.

Ideas for simple gâteaux

1 A jam-filled sandwich topped with white glacé icing, decorated with glacé cherries and angelica.
2 A chocolate sandwich filled and topped with orange butter cream, decorated with halved, crystallised orange slices and chocolate chips.
3 A coffee sandwich filled and coated round the sides with coffee butter cream, with the top iced with coffee glacé icing and decorated with halved walnuts.

A simple decoration

FLAPJACKS

Demerara sugar, 2 oz/50 gm
Golden syrup, 1 tablespoon
Butter, 3 oz/75 gm
Rolled oats, 4–5 oz/100–125 gm

Use a greased 7-inch square tin
Oven temperature : cool (300°F,
    149°C, Mark 1–2)

1 Place the sugar, syrup and butter in a sauce-pan and heat gently until the fat melts. Place 4 oz/100 gm of the oats in a bowl, pour on the melted mixture and mix well, adding more oats if the mixture is very soft.
2 Press the mixture into the tin. Bake in the centre of the oven for about 45 minutes or until lightly browned.
Mark into squares or fingers while warm.
Cool in the tin.

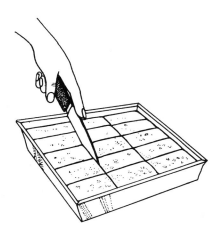

BOSTON BROWNIES

Self raising flour, 2½ oz/62 gm
Salt, a pinch
Butter, 2½ oz/62 gm
Chocolate chips, 2 oz/50 gm
Caster sugar, 6 oz/150 gm
Eggs, 2
Walnuts 2 oz/50 gm

Use a greased oblong tin about
    11 × 7 × 1½ inches deep
Oven temperature : moderate (350°F,
    177°C, Mark 4)

1 Sift the flour with the salt. Place the butter and chocolate in a basin over a pan of hot water until melted.
2 Place the sugar and eggs in a large bowl and beat until mixed. Stir in the chocolate alternately with the sifted flour. Chop the walnuts and add, mixing well. Turn into the prepared tin and bake in the centre of the oven for 30–40 minutes, until risen.
3 Cool in the tin. When quite cold cut into fingers. Do not store in a tin with crisp biscuits as it will make them go soft.
Makes about 15–18 pieces.

CHOCOLATE CHIP OATMEAL COOKIES

Butter, 8 oz/200 gm
Light brown sugar, 6 oz/150 gm
Caster sugar, 2 oz/50 gm
Vanilla essence, 1 teaspoon
Plain flour, 6 oz/150 gm
Salt, ½ level teaspoon
Bicarbonate of soda, 1 level
  teaspoon
Water, 3 tablespoons
Oats, 8 oz/200 gm
Chocolate chips, 4 oz/100 gm

Use 2 lightly greased baking trays
Oven temperature: moderate (350°F,
  177°C, Mark 4)

1 Soften fat and cream with the sugars. Add the vanilla essence, flour and salt, and mix in well. Dissolve the soda in the water and add with the oats and chocolate chips. Mix together well.
2 Drop spoonfuls of the mixture on to the trays, leaving space for spreading. Flatten the mounds slightly and bake in the centre of a moderate oven for about 15 minutes.
Makes about 40 cookies.

SHORTBREAD

Plain flour, 5 oz/125 gm
Rice flour or ground semolina,
  1 oz/25 gm
Caster sugar, 2 oz/50 gm
Butter, 4 oz/100 gm
Caster sugar to dredge

Use a lightly greased baking tray
Oven temperature: cool (300°F,
  149°C, Mark 1–2)

1 Sift the flours and add the sugar.
2 Using your fingers, knead the butter into the dry ingredients, keeping the butter in one piece if possible. Work the mixture until it is a smooth dough. If it becomes very sticky, wrap in waxed paper or foil and chill in the refrigerator for about 30 minutes.
3 Flour a 7-inch sandwich tin, and press the mixture into it in an even layer. Invert on to the baking tray. Decorate the edges, prick with a fork and bake in the centre of the oven until firm and lightly coloured – about 1–1¼ hours.
4 When cool, dredge with sugar and cut into wedges. Store in an airtight tin for not more than 1 week.
Makes about 8 wedges.

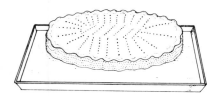

Crimp the edges and prick the top before baking Shortbread

VARIATION
Instead of making the Shortbread in a round, it can be rolled out and cut into fingers. Transfer to a lightly greased baking tray, prick well and bake in the centre of a moderate oven (350°F, 177°C, Mark 4) for 15–20 minutes or until lightly coloured. Cool on the tray for 1–2 minutes then transfer to a cooling rack.

Index

Note: figures in square brackets denote colour illustrations

The River Cottage

Mushroom Handbook

The River Cottage
Mushroom Handbook

by John Wright

introduced by

Hugh Fearnley-Whittingstall

www.rivercottage.net

BLOOMSBURY

First published in Great Britain 2007

Text © 2007 by John Wright
Mushroom photography © 2007 by John Wright
Recipe photography © 2007 by Colin Campbell
Additional photography © 2007 by Alan Outen, Gordon Dickson,
Alan Hills, Bryan Edwards and Marie Derome

The moral right of the author has been asserted.

Bloomsbury Publishing Plc, 36 Soho Square, London W1D 3QY

A CIP catalogue record for this book is available from the British Library.

ISBN 9780747589327
10 9 8 7 6 5 4 3 2 1

Designed by willwebb.co.uk
Printed by Arti Grafiche Amilcare Pizzi s.p.a, Italy

All papers used by Bloomsbury Publishing are natural, recyclable products made from wood
grown in well-managed forests. The manufacturing processes conform to the environmental
regulations of the country of origin.

www.bloomsbury.com/rivercottage

Contents

Mushroom hunting can be a perilous pursuit for the unwary and
I have walked a narrow path in this book between gently encouraging
you, dear reader, and frightening you to death.

I would like to say that this is the only book on mushrooms you will ever
need, but I would be lying. I regularly consult over 50 books and, while
you may not need to go to such anorak-y extremes, I do recommend
that you buy at least one more identification guide.

And before you go any further, it is essential that you read the
advice on p.45.

It's a thrill to introduce the first of the River Cottage Handbooks, in which we intend to explore some of the more specialised areas of our approach to food (and indeed to life), to share our passion for them, and generally show you the ropes. In mushrooms, I believe we could not have chosen a better subject to start the series. And in John Wright, I am certain that we could not have found a better man to write it.

The first time I went out foraging with John we had our sights set on one of the greatest fungal prizes of them all: the Summer Truffle. I had never found one – and didn't seriously expect to. But John was full of confidence. He knew there were Truffles to be rustled at his secret location – and he insisted on blindfolding me on the way there. (Luckily he was driving.)

At John's suggestion, we had recruited a third party to the hunt. She was known to have an instinctive nose for a Truffle, and I had done my best to hone her skills beforehand. John had given me a phial of a chemical called dimethyl sulphide – the synthesised version of the natural Truffle smell – and I had successfully trained her to find and dig up potatoes steeped in this pungent elixir. The only problem was that she would insist on eating them. 'She' was my resident breeding saddleback sow, Delia.

When we arrived, Delia was released into the undergrowth. She clearly found the whole experience thrilling. Right from the start she was snuffling up little treats from the forest floor. For all I could tell, she might have eaten ten truffles in the first half hour. John made a couple of valiant attempts to get between her snout and whatever morsel seemed to be exciting it; on one occasion he rescued an acorn, on another a small stone.

Finally, after a good couple of hours, John intervened in a particularly focused bout of Delia's nose-digging, and scrabbled a slightly muddy lump from the ground. As he brushed the earth from its stippled black surface he said, in a cautious, almost disbelieving voice: 'It's a Truffle. It really is … a Truffle.' We ate it right there and then in the woods – grated onto eggs scrambled over a camping stove. And Delia also managed to get her nose in the pan.

It was the beginning of a journey, and a friendship based around foraging, that has led meanderingly to this book. Of course mycologically speaking we are leagues apart – John is one of Britain's foremost mushroom experts, whereas I'm just a happy-go-lucky enthusiast, keen to find and eat as many species as possible, ideally without poisoning myself. But that is rather the point. This is the mushroom book I have been waiting for – the one that has been missing from my life.

Some years back I mentioned to John that, much as I enjoyed some of the existing literature on mushrooms (Roger Phillips for his taxonomic details, Jane Grigson for her gastronomic inspiration), there wasn't really a book that I felt hit the right note for those starting out on the mushroom adventure – or indeed for those who, like me, already loved mushroom hunting but wanted to consolidate their somewhat random knowledge and patchy experience. What I wanted to know (without becoming a fully fledged fungus academic) was how to be a better mushroom hunter, and how to enjoy my mushrooms more. Did he know of a book that could help me? 'Probably not,' he said. Then he added, with a twinkle, 'Perhaps I'll just have to write one.'

In the meantime, I realised, the best way for me to achieve my goal was simply to spend more time looking for mushrooms with John. He is a great person to forage with, generous with his vast knowledge (but never excessively so). He has a gift for capturing the charms or quirks of a species, and its place in the great scheme of things (I've always loved John's 'fact' that a Morel is as far from a Cep in the chain of life as a Christmas tree is from a cabbage). In explaining mushrooms, he never dissipates their mystery, but instead celebrates their sheer fabulousness – in the true sense of the word.

A couple of years back I asked John if he would like to host some mushroom foraging days for us at River Cottage HQ. And I have discovered that it isn't just me who finds his take on mushrooms so engaging. After their day with John, our guests leave us feeling charged with the confidence to go forth and forage on their own.

When the opportunity to make a River Cottage mushroom book came along, of course I wanted John to write it. I wondered, though, if it was too much to hope that the same wit and sparkle that he shows when leading a forage would find its way onto the page. I needn't have worried. One shouldn't expect to laugh out loud when reading about mushrooms – but I promise you will. John may take the fear out of fungus, but never the fun.

Hugh Fearnley-Whittingstall, Dorset, June 2007

Starting Out

What are mushrooms and toadstools?

'Venomous and muthering', 'evil ferment', 'poysonous damp weeds'. Few people of the past had a good word to say about fungi and, until the early eighteenth century, no one had the faintest idea what these 'earthie excrescences' actually were, though this did not stop people making something up. Fitting uncomfortably into the more familiar world of plants and animals, these mysterious agents of putrescence, decay and sometimes death have always been treated with great suspicion. But, practical people as they had to be, the ancients sensibly classified the fungi into two important groups: the 'esculenti' and the 'perniciosi'. This attitude, shared by this present book, was neatly expressed in the sixteenth-century *Grete Herball*, where we find the best known of all fungal quotations:

> *'Fungi ben mussheroms; there be two manners of them, one maner is deedley and slayeth them that eateth them and be called tode stoles, and the other doeth not.'*

These pretty words go most of the way to answering the question I am asked most often after 'Can I eat it?' – 'What is the difference between a mushroom and a toadstool?' I think that the simplest differentiation is this:

> *'A toadstool has a cap and a stem and you can't eat it, a mushroom has a cap and a stem and you can.'* Slayeth and doeth not.

Much has been written about the derivation and meaning of the words 'mushroom' and 'toadstool' and little agreed upon. 'Mushroom' is from the Old French 'mousseron', itself derived from 'mousse', which means 'moss' and is probably a reference to the soft texture of most fungi. The word 'toadstool' is very likely no more than it seems; the 'toad' part reflecting a perception of that animal's poisonous nature and the 'stool' a simple reference to shape. 'Toadstool' has sometimes, as above, been rendered as 'tode stole' with 'tode' being the German word for death. Whichever derivation one accepts, it is clear that 'toadstool' is a pejorative term, while 'mushroom' is not. There is a narrower definition that is very useful, though it can contradict the first one:

> *'A mushroom is a member of the genus* Agaricus.'

The genus *Agaricus* includes *A. bisporus*, *A. campestris*, *A. arvensis* and *A. silvicola*, the Cultivated, Field, Horse and Wood Mushroom respectively, so you can see the sense of it. Indeed, the term 'the true mushrooms' is often used for *Agaricus* species.

The contradiction exists because there is also *A. xanthodermus*, the Yellow Stainer, which is poisonous. A pity, really. One last word on etymology: the word 'fungus' is derived from 'spoggos', which is Greek for sponge. By this time, most of my enquirers have regretted their question.

While there will always be more to learn, the essential nature of fungi has now been firmly established. Their inexplicable ability to appear suddenly in the same spot year after year, without apparent roots and sometimes in those mysterious rings, is now all explained. Mushrooms and toadstools – and most of the many other fungal forms one sees in the woods and fields – are not organisms. They are organs. The bulk of the organism is underground (or within some other sub-stratum, such as wood) and takes the form of microscopically thin (about a tenth of the diameter of a human hair) fibres called hyphae. These form a largely invisible, but nevertheless huge, cotton wool-like mass called a mycelium. Our mushrooms and toadstools are, quite simply, the reproductive organs, the fruit bodies, of this larger organism; their sole purpose is to produce and disperse spores. Billions of them.

So now we understand that mushrooms and toadstools grow quickly because all of their raw materials are ready and waiting in the mycelium, and they grow in the same place year after year because that is where the actual organism is situated. Mushrooms and toadstools do have the equivalent of roots, but they are usually too thin to see and they sometimes form rings because the mycelium from which they spring grows outwards from a central point and dies off in the middle. No lightning, no dragons, no pixies.

Early writers were correct in their assessment that fungi fitted poorly into the world of plants and animals. Fungi are neither. They inhabit their own great kingdom – Kingdom Fungi – which now sits alongside the other great kingdoms – Plantae, Animalia, and two or three more.

Organisms belong to their particular kingdom simply because their parents did, and not because they have certain characteristics (in the same way that dolphins still wouldn't be fish even if they looked twice as fishy as they do). Nevertheless, fungi do have certain properties which, taken together, distinguish them from members of the other kingdoms. Their cells are, in fact, the hyphae mentioned above and, unlike most plant and animal cells, need many nuclei scattered along their length to control the various cell functions. The cell walls are made not from cellulose as in plants, or proteins as in animals, but of chitin, a material more familiar as the crunchy bit of cockroaches. Their most important property viewed from an ecological viewpoint is an inability, shared with all animals and a very few plants, to make their own food. They either externally digest organic matter and absorb the resulting simple, soluble soup through their cell walls, or are provided for by plants with which they have formed a symbiotic relationship.

As with plants and animals, fungi are divided up into family groups. Of the major divisions of the fungi there are two that interest the mushroom hunter – the *Ascomycota* and the *Basidiomycota*. The former contains species as diverse as Truffles and Morels; the latter contains most of the rest of the species in this book. They are sometimes more approachably called the 'spore shooters' and the 'spore droppers'. These names are references to the hugely complex microscopic mechanisms by which the spores are formed and released.

Brian Spooner and Peter Roberts in their highly readable book *Fungi* point out that there is a lot more going on behind the scenes than the average mushroom hunter can imagine. I do hope that some of the excitement and wonder of mycology rubs off on you as you search for your supper.

How to collect fungi

There is a pure and all-consuming joy that comes from foraging for one's own food, a joy where other worries are forgotten in the single-minded pursuit of a quarry. Foraging is a deep instinct that has been shared by all our ancestors right back to that famous protozoan we can all call Grandmother and we are the poorer when we ignore it. Nevertheless, as with most joys, there are a few practical issues that need to be considered. Most of the rest of the book deals with that most practical issue of how not to poison yourself; this chapter considers all the others.

Mushroom hunting and the law

The laws governing the activities of us simple foragers are surprisingly complicated and not entirely settled.

The 1981 Wildlife and Countryside Act, which is often quoted when the legality of picking mushrooms is discussed, is steadfastly irresolute and vague on the whole matter and of almost no help at all. There is, however, a general acceptance in common law, enshrined in the 1968 Theft Act, that a person may collect the 'four Fs' – Fruit, Flowers, Foliage and Fungi – as long as these are growing wild and are collected for personal use. This right applies everywhere, even on private land, but there are exceptions and caveats:

i. In some places there are bylaws that prohibit or restrict picking. If this is the case, there should be a notice to that effect.
ii. It appears to be illegal to collect plants or any part of a plant (which would include blackberries!) from 'Right to Roam' land, but whether this includes fungi is unclear.
iii. A question of legality hangs over collecting from 'sites of special scientific interest' (SSSIs), though it is unlikely that picking a few common mushrooms from such sites will land you in trouble.

If you are collecting commercially, even on a very small scale, you must ask permission from the landowner. If you don't, then you will be stealing.

While you might be allowed to pick fungi at a particular location, you might not be allowed to be there to do it; you could be trespassing. The law of trespass (England and Wales only; there is no Scottish law of trespass) says that if you go onto land that does not belong to you without the permission of the owner and if your action is not covered under legislation such as 'Right to Roam' or 'Rights of Way', then you are trespassing. (Incidentally, despite all those

'Trespassers will be Prosecuted' signs, you cannot be prosecuted – though you could, in principle, be sued.) If the landowner asks you to leave, you must do so immediately by the quickest route. It is an interesting fact that the landowner is not entitled to claim any mushrooms you might have picked from his land, though having established yourself so firmly on the moral lowground it would be an inopportune moment to argue the matter!

Many of the places you are likely to go to pick mushrooms, such as Forestry Commission or local authority land, are places where public access may be permitted, but it is just that – permission, not a right. Some organisations and authorities impose a limit on the amount you can collect per visit as part of a 'code of conduct'. This is usually one and a half kilograms and seems generous enough to me.

Britain has so far avoided most of the closed seasons, licences and quotas that have been introduced in mainland Europe, but as the popularity of mushroom hunting increases, it is unlikely that we will escape them for much longer.

To sum up: Don't trespass to pick fungi and, if in doubt, ask permission.

Mushroom hunting and conservation

While a casual consideration of the matter would suggest that pulling a mushroom out of the ground is as destructive as pulling a plant out of the ground, in fact, it is not. When you pull up a plant that is the end of it, but when you pull up a mushroom all you are doing is removing a reproductive organ. Eye-watering, yes; fatal, no. The main part of the organism, the cotton wool-like mycelium, is underground or within the log on which the mushroom is growing, and picking a mushroom is more like picking an apple off a tree – pick all the crab apples you want and the tree remains. Of course, you may affect the long-term reproductive success of the organism concerned, but consider how much crab apple jelly you would have to make before crab apple trees went into decline! What you cannot do by picking a mushroom is damage the fungus itself.

Does this mean that we can pick as many mushrooms as we like without damaging their viability? Well, maybe it does. It is probably only in mushrooming hotspots, where every single mushroom is picked shortly after it takes the unwise decision to pop its head out of the ground, that there is a real threat to the long-term survival of popular species, and then only locally. Furthermore, by the time mushrooms are found, they have usually produced billions of spores and, despite the best efforts of mushroom hunters, many more mushrooms go undiscovered than find their way into the kitchen.

Research in this area is extremely difficult and while many conservation bodies, zealous in the defence of their patch, point to over-picking as a cause of any perceived decline in mushroom populations, actual hard evidence is completely lacking. Few people would deny that there has been a decline, but some of this may have been caused by pollution and most, perhaps nearly all, has been caused by habitat loss. The loss of meadow and pasture, of ancient woodland and heath, has put great pressure on many species and impoverished us all. The conservation and creation of wildlife habitats will do far more for fungi than any amount of self-denial by foragers looking for their dinner.

Having argued forcefully that picking mushrooms does no damage, I am now going to beat a small retreat. Fungi expend enormous resources in producing their fruit bodies (mushrooms) and do so for a reason. On this basis I take the entirely unscientific view that, despite any lack of evidence that extensive picking is damaging, one should err on the side of caution and exercise some restraint. For each of the edible species described in this book I give some indication as to how common they are and sometimes indicate how much of this restraint should be employed.

There are four fungi that are considered to be so endangered that they are specifically protected under the 1981 Wildlife and Countryside Act and it is illegal to pick them. They are the beautiful yellow and purple Royal Bolete (*Boletus regius*), a frankly rather dull bracket fungus called *Buglossoporus pulvinus*, and a 'Puffball on a stick' known as the Sandy Stiltball (*Battarraea phalloides*). It is an extraordinary if inconsequential fact that the fourth member of the select quartet, the Lion's Mane Fungus (*Hericium erinaceus*), while still rare in the wild is now cultivated and can be bought in delicatessens. It is rather like setting up a panda farm and selling panda-burgers.

If you need further persuasion, here are a few other reasons for leaving at least some of the edible mushrooms you find where they are:

Picking only 'middle aged' mushrooms has some advantages – the youngsters have not usually acquired their full flavour (or size) and have not had chance to produce any spores at all, and the oldies, while past their culinary best, are producing spores by the billion.

Maggots do nothing to endear themselves to the mushroom hunter, but then the reverse is also true. Fungi play an extremely important role in supporting a huge variety of insect larvae and other organisms, many of them specially adapted to take advantage of these ephemeral habitats. The wholesale removal of fruit bodies can seriously affect these invertebrate populations.

Forests that have been scoured clean by bands of mushroom hunters have a distinctively barren look to them, so do leave some for others to enjoy.

The mushroom hunter's toolkit

This is a small and simple affair, consisting, at its most basic, of a basket, a knife and a determined expression. For those who want to take more, this is what I recommend:

A basket: it does not matter which sort. The notion that using one with an open weave allows spores to be scattered through the forest as you walk is fanciful in the extreme.

Plastic containers: to protect the more delicate species and in which to quarantine those as yet unnamed specimens which must always be kept away from your known edible finds. Plastic bags are completely useless, by the way, as the mushrooms sweat and become squashed. If your intellectual curiosity is roused by any of the species of tiny fungi that abound alongside their larger, edible cousins, then one of those compartmented boxes beloved of fishermen is ideal for transporting them back home in good condition.

A knife: for cutting mushrooms from trees (a perilous occupation, as I know to my cost) and for digging mushrooms out of the ground. If you want to look really professional, you can buy special knives that have a little cleaning brush on the end.

A hand lens: one of the folding 'loupe' variety is invaluable for looking at some of the finer identifying characteristics on your mushroom finds. It also instantly gives you an authoritative air when you hang it on a cord around your neck.

A notebook or a digital camera: to record the habitat in which the mushroom was found. Habitat is often an important clue in identification – some mushrooms are only found in pine woods, some only in beech woods, and so on.

A good field guide: the one you are holding should serve you well though you can never have too many. I have over 50 books that I use to identify my finds and they are getting very heavy to carry around. There are another 40 or so on my Christmas list. The main reason for actually taking a book with you is to prevent the heart-rending dilemma that comes when you find a huge patch of very promising-looking fungi and don't know whether to pick them or not.

A hat: as well as keeping the rain off, a hat will help protect your head from brambles and low branches, shield your eyes so that you can spot mushrooms lurking on a dark forest floor and, *in extremis*, act as an emergency mushroom basket.

When to look

While flowering plants produce their fruit and flowers to a timetable that seldom varies by more than a couple of weeks, fungi have a more independent spirit and take delight in appearing almost at random during the year and sometimes not at all. However, despite the vagaries of many species, there is undoubtedly a mushroom season and that, of course, is in the autumn.

The start of the season is ultimately a matter of rainfall; if August and September are dry, the season will be delayed. The end of the season occurs with the first hard frost, though a mild spell after this may revive mushroom hunting fortunes for a while. Of course, the climate is not the same everywhere and there will be considerable variation between one part of the country and another.

Sometimes we have a lovely wet, cool summer (I will sulk all the way through a hot August) and then the mushrooms come up from June to November. In a mild winter, mushrooms can be found until January. Occasionally, we have both, though there is a limit to how many fruit bodies a fungal mycelium can produce in one year.

In addition to the autumn, there is a distinct spring season when two notable mushrooms can be found: St George's Mushrooms and Morels. There are also several species that like the summer months: many of the Boletes, some *Agaricus* species, and Giant Puffballs. Even during autumn itself, some succession is discernible with species such as Blewits, Waxcaps and Velvet Shanks coming late in the year, giving us welcome continuation and variety.

Where to look

The rudest question you can ask a mushroom hunter is, 'Where did you find those?', but I am in a generous mood and prepared to pass on a few tips.

Very broadly there are two types of places worth looking – grassland and woodland. Apart from those rare lucky days when your basket fills with woodland Ceps and Chanterelles, it is in grassland that the big feasts are found. A good Field Mushroom field or Parasol patch can yield mushrooms by the tens of kilograms. I once found about 35kg of Giant Puffballs in a single field, and I remember on one glorious day standing on a hillside where the Parasols were beyond counting.

Grassland tends to come in varying grades according to, among other things such as acidity, how long it has been left undisturbed. Field Mushrooms can appear in quite young grassland while the wonderful Waxcaps, which take much longer to become established, are familiar in very old grassland. Grassland species are nearly always saprotrophs (they live on dead organic matter). As they grow outwards, they often enrich or impoverish the grass, producing distinctive rings. These give a clue to the presence of the mycelium even before the mushrooms appear in the familiar fairy ring pattern. Rings of dark grass can often be seen from across a valley and you can make a mental note of them for later exploration. Sometimes fairy rings are complete, with mushrooms all the way round; more often they are partial and mushrooms appear only on fragmentary arcs of the original ring.

Grass that has grazing animals on it is far richer in fungi than are hay meadows. The best demonstration of this is the Field Mushroom, which has a strong preference for fields where horses are kept. Mushrooms do not like to fight their way through tall grass, so intensively grazed land is nearly always the best. Grass that is a beautiful lush green has probably been 'improved' with nitrates and phosphates and is unlikely to be a happy home for many fungi.

While grassland provides us with delicious mushrooms in abundance, the real gourmet fungi – the ones you pay a lot for in restaurants – come from the woods. Ceps, Chanterelles, Horns of Plenty, Morels and Truffles are all woodland species. It is also true to say that there are more woodland fungi, edible or not, than grass-land fungi; two-thirds of the mushrooms in this book are found in woods.

Because many fungi can only grow near certain tree species with which they can form a symbiotic relationship, it is possible to approach a patch of forest with an educated optimism about what you might hope to find.

Beech and oak jointly lead the field in having the largest number of fungal species found near them. Over 2,000 fungal species have been found in association with, or at least in close proximity to, both these trees. Next come birch and pine with 1,600 species each. Many other types of tree are associated with fungi, but the fact that some are not explains why ash and sycamore woods prove to be such poor hunting grounds. The worst large tree for finding fungi of any description is the yew.

How, or indeed if, the wood is managed has a strong bearing on its ability to produce fungi. Fungal fruiting bodies do not like competition, and undergrowth is a major limiting factor; anything that reduces it, such as physical intervention, the encouragement of a heavy forest canopy or the introduction of grazing, will open out the forest and allow the fungi to establish a foothold. On the other hand, over-tidy foresters who habitually remove fallen trees deprive us of fungi such as Oyster Mushrooms that depend on this dead wood for their livelihood.

So, there you are, standing in the middle of a nice open piece of beech wood-land expecting to be surrounded by mushrooms. Except that the mushrooms are mysteriously absent. The depths of a seemingly perfect wood are often almost devoid of fungi. The problem is not that the fungal mycelium from which the mushrooms grow is unhappy here, but that it is *too* happy. Life is easy, so why bother to expend any energy on an ungrateful future generation? It is only when the mycelium runs out of food or is otherwise threatened that it gives any thought to the morrow and decides to reproduce. This is the 'car park' effect. Experienced mushroom hunters seldom set off straight away into the depths of a wood but hang around the edge of the tarmac. Fungal mycelia cannot eat car parks and they'll start to panic; it is then that they produce their fruiting bodies. Of course, it is not just car parks that have this effect; so do any other places where there is a change from one environment to another – wood margins, paths, soil change, different vegetation, earth banks. Life on the edge.

It is obvious that the countryside is where most wild mushrooms will be found, but the city dweller does not always have to travel so far. Many mushrooms are quite at home in odd corners of the urban environment: parks and gardens, road verges and, my particular favourite, cemeteries, can all be very productive. Certain species of Morel are the best-known of the metropolitan mushrooms, having acquired pieds-à-terre in the forest bark mulch that covers so many domestic and municipal flowerbeds. Shaggy Inkcaps are found much more frequently on road verges than in fields, and there is one species, a close relative of the cultivated mushroom, called the Pavement Mushroom (*Agaricus bitorquis*), which effortlessly punches its way through tarmac leaving neat round holes.

A certain amount of extra caution is required when picking mushrooms in town because of the increased risk of pollution, both airborne and from soil residues (and, we must never forget, dogborne). Mushrooms are well known for their ability to concentrate heavy metals, though the risk from this unfortunate talent has reduced considerably since the removal of lead from petrol. But you do need your wits about you. I once picked a nice collection of Fairy Ring Champignons from a park in Stockholm only to realise, just in time, that the barely perceptible fine white powder on their caps was a fungicide.

How to look

During a British Mycological Society foray some years ago, our party of mushroom hunters bumped into a party of bird watchers – we were all looking down and they were all looking up.

It is surprising how bad people are at spotting mushrooms when they first try – it takes a while to train your eyes to distinguish rocks or leaves from mushrooms. Incidentally, the best mushroom hunters are children as they are enthusiastic, generally have better eyesight than their adult companions and are much nearer the ground. Sometimes people confuse fungus foraging with hiking and march off as though the hounds of hell are after them, forgetting that they are already where they want to be! So, slow right down, scan the ground as you go and follow as erratic a path as the terrain will allow. Most people do well with a gentle wander around, but I usually resort to a certain amount of energetic thrashing about in the undergrowth for fear of missing something.

When you find some fungi, remember that you have found two things – fungi *and* a place where fungi like to grow. Stop and look carefully all around as there are likely to be other species very nearby.

I seldom cut mushrooms to pick them. I much prefer to gently ease the whole fruit body out of the ground with a knife and so preserve the entire specimen for identification. There are several important characteristics at the base of the stem of many mushrooms that are crucial in establishing their identity; a colour change on cutting, a small root, a volva (bag). If you cut above the ground, these are lost to you. Of course, if you are absolutely sure you know what you are picking, then cutting will do no harm and your supper won't get covered in dirt. There is no conservation reason for choosing one method over the other.

One last tip: don't walk backwards; you're bound to squash something.

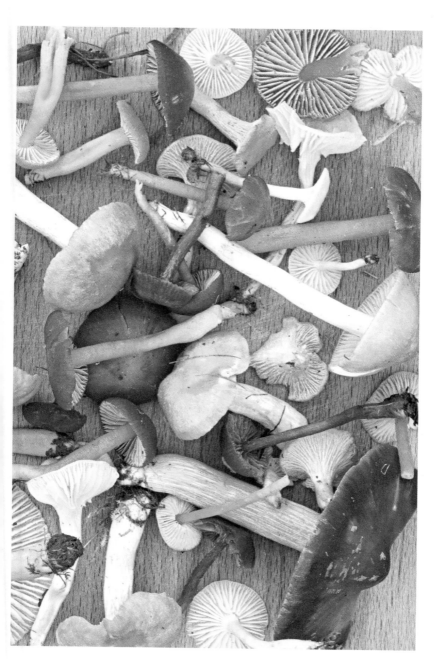

How to tell one fungus from another

It would be wonderful if all the edible fungi came with a little green sticker and all the poisonous fungi with a red one. Unfortunately, nature is not so accommodating and there are no such short cuts, not one. However, I do often hear of sure-fire tests that have worked for people over many years. Those for whom they haven't worked I don't hear from quite so often.

Just for the record, here are a few tests that I've come across that, if applied rigorously, will eventually lead you to an early grave:

'It is OK if you can peel the cap.'
I often show people how easily the skin of the Death Cap can be peeled.

'If other animals can eat it, then so can you.'
Slugs have a totally different metabolism to humans and can munch on a Death Cap with impunity, as, in fact, can rabbits!

'If it doesn't turn a silver spoon black, it is fine.'
This is complete nonsense.

'No mushroom that grows on wood is poisonous.'
… except for the Funeral Bell (*Galerina marginata*), Sulphur Tuft (*Hypholoma fasciculare*) and half a dozen others.

'It is fine if you only eat mushrooms with black gills …
or is it white gills?'

My favourite piece of useless advice comes from the second-century physician and poet, Nicander:

'The rank in smell, and those of livid show,
All that at roots of oak or olive grow,
Touch not! But those upon the fig-tree's rind
Securely pluck – a safe and savoury kind!'

So how do you know whether a mushroom is edible or not? You need to find out its name. I concentrate here on mushrooms and toadstools, that is, anything with a cap and a stem. Other fungi, such as the Jelly Ear, Puffball, Truffle and Beefsteak Fungus, are so distinctive that they should not prove too difficult to identify and are not easily confused with poisonous species.

Mushrooms and toadstools are notoriously difficult to identify with any great certainty. With the flowering plants there are many clear characteristics that help you to distinguish one species from another – number and colour of petals, shape of leaf, hairiness and so on – but when it comes to mushrooms and toadstools they all have a stem and a cap and everything else is a matter of detail. This similarity of form exists because, of course, mushrooms are *organs*, not *organisms*. In fact, they are reproductive organs and their form is simply a matter of function, which is why they all look much the same. Imagine you were given the task of identifying a selection of mammals just by studying their reproductive organs and you will see the problem. (Don't imagine it for too long.)

This difficulty is compounded because a young fungus may look quite unlike a mature one and different environments produce strikingly different examples of the same species. If you find it a frustrating task telling one fungus from another, then I must tell you that so do I. Often I will spend an hour or two with piles of books and a microscope studying a single toadstool only to be forced to admit defeat, whereupon I tear the offending specimen to shreds, then stamp on it, then throw it into the bin, then set fire to the bin. I did say it was frustrating. On the other hand, the joy and satisfaction of achieving an accurate identification is complete and I hope that you will embrace the little bit of hard work as simply part of the fun. Let us then put potential frustration to one side and consider the following positive thoughts:

There are fewer than 100 species, both edible and poisonous, described in this book and, if your interest is purely of a culinary nature, these are all the fungi you will ever want to learn.

Although there are thousands of mushrooms and toadstools, they do, mercifully, fall into natural groups or genera that usually share certain characteristics. So, among others, there are the Amanitas (white gills, ring on the stem, bag at the base of the stem) and the Russulas (stocky, gills brittle). This helps enormously as the human brain is very good at categorising things and if you can work out which genus a fungus belongs to, you are three-quarters of the way there.

Learning what a mushroom or toadstool looks like is similar to learning what a particular person looks like. Superficially, one person looks much like another, but subtle differences enable us to easily recognise a friend in a crowd. So it is with fungi – once you have become familiar with a species, you will be able to name it at 30 paces.

But where on earth do you start? Well, the time-honoured way is to pick up a mushroom book and flick through the pictures until you spot something that looks a bit like the fungus you have in your hand. Don't do it. In fact, I suggest that you put your books back on the shelf for a moment and turn your mind to the most important thing of all – looking at the mushroom.

There is no single process for identifying a fungus. It all depends on which fungus you are talking about and how much you know about it already. Here, however, is the basic process:

1 Take notes in the field or wood
2 Obtain a spore print
3 Study the fungus
4 Follow a 'key' to find a possible name for the fungus or at least which genus or group it belongs to
5 Check the answer with pictures and descriptions.

1 Take notes in the field

Your study should really begin at the moment you find your fungus. Take a note of where it was growing, under what sort of tree, whether it was growing singly, in a ring or in tufts or on wood, and so on. Check the smell and any colour change when the flesh is cut as these can be terribly important considerations that freshly picked specimens usually exhibit best.

2 Obtain a spore print

You may think that spore colour is rather an esoteric characteristic to consider, but do believe me when I say that it is one of the most important. For reasons that will become evident, if you know the spore colour, you will know where to start looking in your book. I must add that if you already have a reasonably good idea about the identity of the mushroom in front of you, a spore print may not be strictly necessary – spore prints are most useful when you haven't got the faintest idea where to start.

Spores come in several colours – white is the most common, but they move through many shades of cream to yellow and warm and cool browns through to dark browns, then black. You will also find, quite commonly, pink spores and there is one toadstool, the highly poisonous False Parasol (*Chlorophyllum molybdites*), which has green spores.

It is often possible to guess the colour of the spores by looking at the gills on which they grow. Unfortunately, this short cut does not *always* work, as sometimes either the gills themselves are highly coloured or they are pale and the coloured spores have yet to form. A much better way is to take a spore print. Cut off the cap and lay it on a piece of white paper. Alternatively, make a hole in a piece of white paper, push the stem of the mushroom through the hole and sit it on a glass or cup. If you can cover the top, it will prevent the mushroom from drying out.

Depending on the freshness of your specimen, a reasonably useful spore print can be ready in a couple of hours though overnight is certainly better. Although we are talking about 'prints', the shape is immaterial – we are only interested in the colour of the spore mass.

So what use is this hard-won piece of information? Knowing the spore colour does not, directly, tell you what your specimen is, but it can tell you a lot about what it is not. If the spores are white, you have eliminated half of all the fungi it could have been. If the spores are pink, you have eliminated over 90 per cent. Several of the popular books have the fungi arranged according to spore colour, usually with white at the front and black at the back. Most important is the use of spore colour in multi-choice and dichotomous keys.

Taking a spore print

3 Study the fungus

The more you know about a fungus, the more certain you can be of its identity, so it is well worth examining your find carefully and even, dare I say it, make notes! The good news is that the subtle details of which I spoke earlier are, on closer consideration, not so subtle after all. Here is a list of some of the main characteristics used in identification:

CAP:	Size, shape, colour, surface texture, peelability of the skin.
STEM:	Size, shape, colour, surface texture. Is there a ring? Is there a bag at the base?
RING:	If there is a ring, is it like a collar or a skirt? Is it coloured? Does it have markings on it?
GILLS OR TUBES:	Colour. How are they attached to the stem? How thick are they? How close together? Are they brittle or soft or waxy? Do they fork?
FLESH:	Texture – fibrous, rubbery or crumbly? Smell, taste (be careful!).
SPORES:	Colour.
HABITAT:	Where is it growing? Are they in groups, tufted, single?
SEASON:	Spring? Autumn?

Take, for example, the fungus pictured here. A cursory description would be 'a medium-sized toadstool with a scaly brown cap'. Let us see if we can do better with what can be seen just from the picture:

CAP:	Russet brown, paler at the edge, smooth but with movable pink/grey scales. Skin peelable, flesh white.
STEM:	Fairly robust, distinctly swollen at base, slightly rooting. Pinkish to white, roughened and showing distinctly pink where it has been damaged. Has a faint ring of scales at the top of the swollen base.
RING:	Large and fragile, white with little grooves running down it.
GILLS:	Close together, white but bruising pink.

I hope that you did not find that list too daunting – it only took a couple of minutes to make. It contains over 20 observations and if I were to read it, I would know straight away that it was describing *Amanita rubescens*, the Blusher.

4 Follow a 'key'

This is where that hard work begins. A key is a series of questions. The answer you give to one question will take you to the next question. When you run out of questions to answer, you will discover either the actual name you are looking for or the group within which your specimen may be found. Some keys will only give an answer if the mushroom in question is described within the book.

A key may, for example, ask if the cap skin peels easily. If it does you go to, say, question four, if not you go to question seven, and so on. I shall be frank with you: keys are difficult things. They always seem to ask ambiguous questions or demand seemingly impossible judgements. This is not a plot by key writers to drive you mad; keys are just very difficult to write. Still, in general, they do work and often work well, especially after you have had some practice.

Most keys will give you some sort of answer, be it a name or just a genus; the key I have included on the following pages is one that only gives you an answer if your specimen is in the book. Of course, this is an answer of a sort. If you cannot identify your fungus using the key, it is not in the book and you must not eat it!

To use the following key, first determine whether your specimen has spines, gills or tubes (see boxes i, ii and iii opposite). If it has gills, you will need to know the colour of the spores. Go to the beginning of the appropriate section and answer question 1.

So if, for example, you have a gilled, white-spored fungus, you would find yourself answering question 1 on the page opposite. If it has some sort of ring on the stem, you would then go to question 2 and, if not, you would turn the page to question 6. If you go to question 6, you are asked if it has a bag at the base. If it has, it is likely to be a Tawny Grisette; if not, you are led to question 7, and so on.

And you thought it was going to be complicated.

5 Check the answer with pictures and descriptions

If the key gives an actual name of a particular fungus, carefully check it with the description in your book and any photographs or drawings, making sure that all the characteristics tally with your specimen. Photographs generally capture one or two stages in the life of a fungus, so details that vary a great deal over time, like the shape of the cap, may not match your expectations. However, with a little practice you will be able to allow for such variations. It is worth taking a look at closely related species just to make sure you have the one you think you have.

If a key just gives you a genus or some other grouping, you either have to find a key to that genus or check all the possibilities that you have been given. The key in this book sometimes gives a list of three or four possibilities, but these are all very similar species dealt with in the same section. Don't expect to get an answer every time and don't make wild guesses. Do practise and don't get despondent.

Key to species with a stem and a cap

Unlike most mushroom keys, this is just a partial key referring only to the species described in this book. In other words, it won't always give you a result. If you don't get a result, you still don't know what it is and must not eat it! If you do get a result, check it with the descriptions and any photographs on the relevant page. I know it looks complicated, but just work through the key as carefully as you can. It is not as daunting as many others – I have one that is nearly 500 pages long! The drawings that are referred to appear on pp.36–7.

i	Cap with small, breakable spines underneath (drawing i), cream or foxy orange	*Hedgehog Mushrooms (p.114)*
ii	Cap with gills underneath	**Part 1**
iii	Cap with pores and tubes (drawing ii) underneath	**Part 2**

Part 1: Fungi with gills

SPORES WHITE OR CREAM TO PALE YELLOW

1	i. Ring (drawings vi, viii, xiv) or sheath-like or shaggy ring zone (drawing iii) on stem or just a fleecy stem (drawing iv).	2
	ii. No ring or fleece on stem.	6
2 cont. overleaf	i. Ring distinct, membranous (drawing xiv or vi) and not easily slid up and down stem.	3
	ii. Ring fragile or like a sheath or absent with just a shaggy ring zone or simply a fleecy stem. Caps usually less than 10cm diameter, with brown/orange scales (drawing vii).	*The Dapperlings (p.146)*

2 cont.	iii. Ring complex, usually double, will slide up and down stem without damage (drawing viii). Cap large, usually over 10cm, with immovable brown scales (drawing v).	*Parasol, Shaggy Parasol (p.75)*
	iv. Growing in tufts on wood. White, very slimy.	*Porcelain Fungus (p.58)*

3	i. Volva (bag) at base of stem (drawing x or xi).	4
	ii. No volva, stem base swollen and at least a little scaly (drawing xii or xiii).	5

4	i. White with green cap or white all over.	*Death Cap (p.140) Destroying Angel (p.143)*
	ii. Brown cap with pure white movable scales. No grooves on top of ring (drawing xiv).	*Panther Cap (p.150)*
	iii. Yellow cap, often with brown patches stuck to it. Smells of raw potatoes. Volva spherical (drawing xi).	*False Death Cap (p.143)*

5	i. Cap bright red or, rarely, orange, with white scales. Base fleecy (drawing xii).	*Fly Agaric (p.149)*
	ii. All parts slowly bruising pinkish, especially where nibbled by slugs. Grey movable scales, striation on top of ring (drawing vi).	*The Blusher (p.64)*

6	i. Volva (bag) at base of stem (drawing x). Orange brown cap, distinct grooves at edge (drawing xxvii).	*Tawny Grisette (p.68)*
	ii. No volva.	7

7	i. Growing on wood.	8
	ii. Not growing on wood.	9

8	i. Cap bright orange and sticky or slimy. Stem soon dark to black, velvety.	*Velvet Shank (p.81)*
	ii. Stem lateral or missing. Cap shell-shaped (drawing xv). Spores sometimes have a very pale lilac tint!	*Oyster Mushroom (p.56)*

9

i. Irregular funnel shape, gills decurrent (drawing xviii) and in the form of wrinkles (drawing xvi), or just faint veins. Bright yellow all over, or yellow stem and brown cap, or dark brown to grey to black.

Chanterelle (p.46)
Trumpet Chanterelle (p.78)
Horn of Plenty (p.83)

ii. Regular funnel shape, bright orange. Cap edge rolled under, flesh tough.

False Chanterelle (p.47)

iii. Not as above.

10

10

i. Stem thin, tough and fibrous (drawing xvii). Cap not white.

11

ii. Stem not tough and fibrous.

12

11

i. Cap pale orange, buff when dry, rounded with a central boss in older specimens. Gills cream. In grass, often in rings.

Fairy Ring Champignon (p.54)

ii. Orange-brown or lilac, scurfy. Gills broadly spaced. Woods.

The Deceiver, Amethyst Deceiver (p.66)

12

i. General waxy appearance, bright red or dull orange. Gills thick and widely spaced.

13

ii. White or whitish.

14

iii. Not as above.

15

13

i. Bright scarlet cap and stem, usually less than 5cm diameter.

Scarlet Waxcap (p.72)

ii. Crimson cap, yellowish tones elsewhere, cap over 5cm.

Crimson Waxcap (p.72)

iii. Orange cap, gills and stem buff. Gills decurrent (drawing xviii).

Meadow Waxcap (p.70)

14

i. Large, white to off-white all over, growing in spring. Strong mealy smell. — *St George's Mushroom* (p.62)

ii. Small, white-frosted cap, mottled with brown/pink patches. Gills cream. — *Fool's Funnel* (p.144)

iii. Small, white all over, rather waxy in appearance, no frosting on cap. Gills very decurrent (drawing xviii). — *Snowy Waxcap* (p.70)

15

i. Gills produce a milky latex when broken, decurrent (drawing xviii). Funnel-shaped (drawing xxvi). — 16

ii. Not producing a latex. Fairly squat in stature. White gills and stems, caps coloured with yellows or greens or with bright red. Gills usually brittle except the Charcoal Burner). — 17

16

i. Milk bright orange, maybe pockmarks on stem (drawing ix). — *Saffron Milkcap* (p.145) *False Saffron Milkcap* (p.61)

ii. Milk not orange. With birch or pine on acid soil. Smells of stock cubes when dried. — *Fenugreek Milkcap* (p.145)

iii. Milk not orange. Ring of pockmarks on cap. With oak. — *Oak Milkcap* (p.82)

17

i. Cap bright red. — *The Sickeners* (p.152)

ii. Cap yellow. — *Common Yellow Brittlegill, Yellow Swamp Brittlegill* (p.51)

iii. Cap with greens or blues. — *Powdery Brittlegill, Greencracked Brittlegill* (p.48)

iv. Cap with lilacs, greens and yellows, firm and slightly greasy. Gills not brittle. — *Charcoal Burner* (p.48)

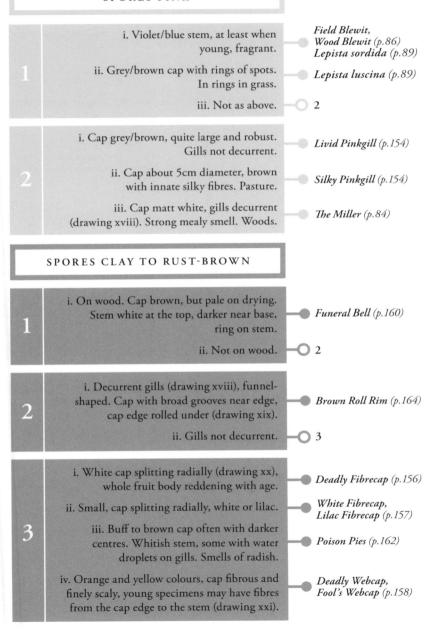

SPORES PINK

1
i. Violet/blue stem, at least when young, fragrant. — *Field Blewit, Wood Blewit (p.86) Lepista sordida (p.89)*

ii. Grey/brown cap with rings of spots. In rings in grass. — *Lepista luscina (p.89)*

iii. Not as above. — 2

2
i. Cap grey/brown, quite large and robust. Gills not decurrent. — *Livid Pinkgill (p.154)*

ii. Cap about 5cm diameter, brown with innate silky fibres. Pasture. — *Silky Pinkgill (p.154)*

iii. Cap matt white, gills decurrent (drawing xviii). Strong mealy smell. Woods. — *The Miller (p.84)*

SPORES CLAY TO RUST-BROWN

1
i. On wood. Cap brown, but pale on drying. Stem white at the top, darker near base, ring on stem. — *Funeral Bell (p.160)*

ii. Not on wood. — 2

2
i. Decurrent gills (drawing xviii), funnel-shaped. Cap with broad grooves near edge, cap edge rolled under (drawing xix). — *Brown Roll Rim (p.164)*

ii. Gills not decurrent. — 3

3
i. White cap splitting radially (drawing xx), whole fruit body reddening with age. — *Deadly Fibrecap (p.156)*

ii. Small, cap splitting radially, white or lilac. — *White Fibrecap, Lilac Fibrecap (p.157)*

iii. Buff to brown cap often with darker centres. Whitish stem, some with water droplets on gills. Smells of radish. — *Poison Pies (p.162)*

iv. Orange and yellow colours, cap fibrous and finely scaly, young specimens may have fibres from the cap edge to the stem (drawing xxi). — *Deadly Webcap, Fool's Webcap (p.158)*

1
i. Tiny, tall and slender, cap yellow when dry, nipple-like projection on cap (drawing xxii). — *Magic Mushroom (p.167)*

ii. Larger. — 2

2
i. On wood, sulphur-yellow. — *Sulphur Tuft (p.168)*

ii. Not on wood. — 3

3
i. Cap tall and elongated when young (drawing xxiii). — *Shaggy Inkcap, Common Inkcap (p.97)*

ii. Cap broader, permanent ring on the stem. — 4

4
i. Cap edge, ring on stem and the outside and especially the inside of the base of the stem turn *intensely* chromium yellow on bruising. Slightly unpleasant smell. — *Yellow Stainer, The Inky Mushroom (p.172)*

ii. Not yellowing at all or not so intensely. — 5

5
i. Cap covered in scaly brown fibres (drawing xxiv). — 6

ii. Cap white or whitish. — 7

6
i. Flesh reddening when cut, quite small (5–10cm). Woodland. — *Blushing Wood Mushroom (p.99)*

ii. Not reddening, large. — *The Prince (p.98)*

7
i. Cap bruising slightly yellow, pendulous ring on stem with 'cogwheel' markings (drawing xxv). Woodland. — *Wood Mushroom (p.99)*

ii. Large (10–30cm), in fields, often with 'cogwheel' marks on ring (drawing xxv). — *Horse Mushroom, Macro Mushroom (p.90)*

iii. White, smaller, gills bright pink when young. In fields. — *Field Mushroom (p.93)*

iv. Flat, compact, double ring. Growing in compacted soil, often in gardens and roadsides. — *Pavement Mushroom (p.95)*

Part 2: Fungi with tubes

1
- i. With bright red on stem. — ○ 2
- ii. Without red. — ○ 3

2
- i. Brown cap, yellow flesh that goes instantly and intensely blue. Stem covered in tiny red dots. — ● *Scarletina Bolete (p.110)*
- ii. Stem not swollen even when young, small. — ● *Red Cracked Bolete (p.106)*
- iii. Cap dingy white, flesh turns slowly pale blue. Stem covered in a red net. (Don't worry too much about this one; it is very rare.) — ● *Devil's Bolete (p.177)*

3
- i. Stem long and rough with raised orange or black dots. — ● *Orange Oak Bolete, Orange Birch Bolete (p.108), Brown Birch Bolete (p.109)*
- ii. Cap sticky or slimy. — ● *Slippery Jack, Weeping Bolete (p.112)*
- iii. Not as above. — ○ 4

4
- i. Stem relatively thin, brown, tubes pale yellow. Slightly bluing when bruised. — ● *Bay Bolete (p.106)*
- ii. Stem very swollen, at least when young. — ○ 5

5
- i. Tubes and pores pink (except in very young specimens), brown net on stem. — ● *Bitter Bolete (p.175)*
- ii. Pores and tubes white, cream or yellow. — ● *Cep, Dark Cep (p.102) Oak Bolete (p.104)*

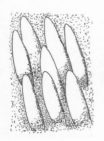

i
Hedgehog
Mushroom spines

ii
Tubes and pores of
Boletus species

iii
Shaggy, zoned stem of
some Dapperlings

iv
Shaggy stem of some
Dapperlings

v
Immovable scales
on many Parasols

vi
Grooves on upper surface of ring

vii
Scaly cap of the Dapperlings

viii
Double ring of
the Parasols

ix
Pockmarked stem of the
Saffron Milkcap

x
Volva at the base of
many Amanitas

xi
Volva at the base of
the False Death Cap

xii
Swollen, fleecy stem
base of the Fly Agaric

xiii
Swollen stem base

xiv
Pendulous ring

xv
Oyster Mushroom

xvi
Forked gills

xvii
Fibrous stem

xviii
Decurrent gills

xix
Inrolled margin

xx
Cap radially split as in
the Fibrecaps

xxi
The web-like fibres of
young Webcaps

xxii
Magic Mushroom

xxiii
Cylindrical cap of
the young Inkcaps

xxiv
Brown fibrous scales

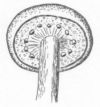

xxv
Horse Mushroom ring
with the 'cogwheel' visible

xxvi
Funnel shape typical of the Milkcaps

xxvii
The grooved margin of
the Grisettes

xxviii
Gills touching
the stem

xxix
Gills not touching
the stem

xxx
the Parasol's
'snakeskin' stem

Glossary

I have tried to avoid too much jargon in this book, but the following dozen or so words crept in because it was so difficult to do without them.

Ascomycete: A fungus that produces its spores, normally eight at a time, in little sausage-shaped cells then, usually, shoots them out of one end into the air, e.g. Morels, Truffles and yeast.

Basidiomycete: A fungus that produces its spores on little stalks, normally four at a time, at the end of cells called basidia, e.g. most mushrooms and toadstools.

Bracket fungus: A fungus with a fruit body that projects from a living or dead tree or branch and has the general appearance of a shelf.

Decurrent: Gills that run down the stem, e.g. Chanterelles (drawing xviii).

Genus: A closely related group of organisms, e.g. the genus *Russula* is all the so-called Brittlegills.

Hyphae: Long and very thin cells that make the bulk of a fungus.

Latex: A white, yellow or orange milky fluid that exudes from the broken gills and flesh of the Milkcaps.

Mycelium: A mass of hyphae.

Mycology: The study of fungi.

Mycophagy: The eating of fungi.

Mycophile: Someone who enjoys fungi.

Mycorrhizal: The relationship in which a fungus supplies water and minerals to a plant in exchange for sugars.

Saprotroph: An organism that lives off dead organic matter.

Species: A single type of organism. Usually defined as a group that can breed together.

Specific epithet: The last part of a scientific name, e.g. the *'cibarius'* part of *'Cantharellus cibarius'* (the Chanterelle).

Symbiotic: A relationship that is of mutual benefit between two organisms.

Taxonomy: The ordering of organisms into family hierarchies.

Umbo: A raised bump on the top of the cap.

Volva: The bag that is at the base of many mushrooms and toadstools (drawing x).

River Cottage
Magic Seven Mushroom Challenge

With any subject it is always difficult to know quite where to start. If you have ever collected a dozen assorted species of fungi and tried to match them to any of the 2,000 pictures in a book, you will know just what I mean. They all look the same and your confidence just drains away. An easier way – certainly a safer way – is to concentrate on and actively look for just a small number of species that are relatively easy to recognise.

Below is a list of wild mushrooms that should not be too difficult to find and which will give you increasing confidence as you tick them off. I have arranged them in order of the amount of challenge they present and anyone who gets through this list can consider him or herself a proper mushroom hunter. Maybe we ought to have a badge.

Shaggy Inkcap (*Coprinus comatus*), p.97
Probably more familiar to most people than the Field Mushroom, this striking fungus frequently makes an appearance on grassy verges.

Jelly Ear (*Auricularia auricula-judae*), p.126
Very common on elder trees and can be found at most times of the year.

Fairy Ring Champignon (*Marasmius oreades*), p.54
Not only very common (urban even) but delicious.

Hedgehog Mushroom (*Hydnum repandum*), p.114
Quite unmistakeable, fairly common, excellent eating and unusual.

Cep (*Boletus edulis*), p.102
Common (though you might need to get out a bit!), extremely good to eat and not one that any self-respecting mushroom hunter could admit to not having found.

Morel (*Morchella elata*), p.133
This is likely to prove the most difficult to find – keep a look out in forest bark garden mulches in spring. Nevertheless, it is easy to identify and a gourmet treat.

The Blusher (*Amanita rubescens*), p.64
Extremely common in woods and very good to eat, this slightly more difficult to identify mushroom will provide a final (not too final, I trust) challenge.

Edible Species

Edible Species *contents*

Of the approximately 4,000 species of larger fungi found in Britain, about a quarter are to some extent edible. The rest are too tough, too unpleasant or simply poisonous. Most of these edible species are either too small or tasteless to consider, too rare or too difficult to identify, and we are left with only 100 or so species that are commonly collected for food. Of these, I have chosen about 65 for this book. I have excluded a few of the popular species that are tricky to identify with any great confidence, so there are no *Tricholoma* species here and no red Russulas.

For many people, mushroom hunting is a matter of collecting Ceps, Chanterelles and one or two other 'high table' fungi. It is a pity that many other delicious fungi are disdainfully overlooked in the pursuit of their celebrated cousins, so I have made an effort to champion these underappreciated species. They are not always so straightforward to identify but their flavours can be just as good, and many of them are very common. Also it may be that a greater acceptance of these poor relations will take some of the pressure off the celebrities.

There is much more to mushroom hunting than the mere finding of a sustaining meal. Foraging for food is an instinctive activity and, as such, inherently pleasurable. One of the great joys of taking people on fungus forays is seeing the intense and primal delight in their eyes when they spot their quarry.

Nevertheless, wild fungi do have a nutritional value considerably greater than is often realised. Roughly speaking, fungi have a food value somewhere between that of meat and that of vegetables. Being low in fats and carbohydrates and high in proteins and vitamins, they are really very healthy foods indeed, though frying them in bacon fat can rather ruin their virtuous qualities. Most fungi contain good quality proteins, but do so rather unevenly with some like the Chanterelle containing almost none at all while certain of the *Agaricus* species contain over 40 per cent protein by dry weight. Most individual species lack certain of the essential amino acids and cannot be relied upon to provide all that is needed in a balanced diet, but since even the most enthusiastic mycophile is unlikely to rely entirely on mushrooms for sustenance, this is unlikely to be a problem. As their high levels of dietary fibre can be either a boon or a bane, depending on individual sensitivity, it is important to try a small portion the first time you eat any fungus.

I doubt if considerations of nutritional value or lack thereof are likely to be of major concern to the average mushroom hunter. He or she is concerned above all with taste, and in this wild fungi excel. The wealth of flavours that they provide remain unsuspected by those whose only experience of fungi comes from the ordinary cultivated mushroom, and there is much to look forward to.

A few words are in order about the names of the fungi. Very nearly every fungus in this book is provided with two names – one English, one scientific. Up until recently, there were hardly any English names for fungi, with fewer than one in twenty possessing one; an extraordinary state of affairs when one considers that nearly every last inconspicuous member of the flowering plants in Britain, down to the three-veined sandwort and the Portland spurge, sports at least one English name and often many more. In recent years, an effort has been made to provide an English name for most, if not quite all, of the larger fungi.

I cannot say that I have greeted this project with any enthusiasm; I like the scientific names because they are universal and precise and enable me to know what people are talking about when they use them. When, however, someone says that they saw some Scarlet Pixie Hoods or use some other ridiculous name for a perfectly respectable fungus, I seldom have the faintest idea what they are talking about. If only everyone would buckle down and learn the proper scientific names all would be well. Nevertheless, I understand that this is unlikely and I use the recommended list of English names with reasonable consistency throughout this book.

Finally a warning. Although this book contains a certain amount of levity, the business of collecting wild fungi for food is a very serious matter. With good sense it is a perfectly safe way of enjoying the fruits of nature, but if, through carelessness, you get it wrong, you or your loved ones could die a horrible death. I have seldom set foot in a wood in the autumn without seeing at least one deadly fungus, so if you are at all careless, you will eventually succumb. It is encouraging, nevertheless, to consider that it is indeed carelessness that proves to be people's undoing. I doubt that anyone who has taken their collection home and studied it carefully has ever come to harm.

Here are some important things to remember:

- *Never* eat a fungus if you do not know its name.
- Before you eat anything make sure that it agrees with the Key (pp.29–35) *and* the description *and* the photograph.
- Individuals within a species can vary greatly in size, shape and colour.
- Always consult more than one book. (I use dozens of them.)
- Many fungi can be eaten raw but some are seriously poisonous if they are not cooked. As a general rule it is safest to always cook what you pick.
- Some people react badly to even the most innocuous of mushrooms, so always try just a little the first time you try a new species.

Chanterelle *Cantharellus cibarius*

CAP:	4–8cm but very variable in size. Irregular and wavy, funnel-shaped but often with a flattish top. The cap edge rolls down slightly. Bright yellow.
STEM:	3–8cm by 0.6–1.5cm. Tapers downwards, same colour as the cap, but may show white patches.
GILLS:	Not true gills but really 'wrinkles' on the underside of the cap. They ***divide into pairs*** (anastomosing) and run down the stem. Bright yellow.
FLESH:	Paler than the surface. Smell of apricots (very faint except where large numbers are kept together in a container).
SPORES:	White to yellowish.
HABITAT:	Woodland, chiefly oak, beech and pine. Often in moss.
FREQUENCY:	Very common.
SEASON:	Late summer to late autumn.

THERE ARE FOUR varieties of wild fungi that enjoy undisputed celebrity status – the Cep, the Truffle, the Morel and the Chanterelle. For me, the Chanterelle wins the Oscar outright for the delicate flavour that persists even after long cooking, its unsurpassed texture and, perhaps most of all, its beauty. No other mushroom is so versatile; no other mushroom retains its good looks so well in cooking.

Although the Chanterelle is content to grow with many different species of tree, a rule of thumb is to look for them under beech and oak in the south, and pine in the north. They are very at home on mossy banks or half hidden in leaf litter. Sometimes they grow in groups of a dozen or so, but occasionally an entire woodland glade can fill with hundreds of them. They fruit quite reliably and the same spot will produce Chanterelles year after year. They also grow quite slowly, so it may be worth waiting for small ones to turn into big ones and a single location will often remain productive for weeks or even months. Find your spot, remember it, don't tell anyone.

Beware of the poisonous (and slightly luminous!) Jack O'Lantern (*Omphalotus illudens*). It looks a little like the Chanterelle, but it is so very rare in Britain that I have not included it in this book. It is known only in a few locations in southern England, and mainly grows in tufts on oak stumps. Someone once mistook the Deadly Webcap (p.158) for a Chanterelle with disastrous consequences, but it is so unlike the Chanterelle that it is difficult to understand how such a mistake could have been made. There is one fungus,

however, that can fool just about anyone; it is called, unsurprisingly, the False Chanterelle (*Hygrophoropsis aurantiaca*). Fortunately, this mushroom isn't poisonous, but it does have flaccid, tasteless flesh far removed from that of its tasty twin. It is bright orange rather than yellow, is more symmetrical, has an in-rolled edge to the cap, is soft and fibrous in texture and has narrow, true gills rather than ridges. Sadly, in one of those little tricks that nature enjoys playing on us, it is even more common than the real Chanterelle.

Chanterelle

False Chanterelle

Charcoal Burner,
Powdery Brittlegill & Greencracked Brittlegill

Charcoal Burner *Russula cyanoxantha*

CAP:	7–12cm. Firm and rather rounded, colour very variable with violets, pinks, greens, yellows and white.
STEM:	5–8cm by 1.5–3cm. White and firm. (Get your chemistry set and rub the stem with iron sulphate; it won't go orange!)
GILLS:	*Flexible* and slightly greasy to the touch, white.
FLESH:	White.
SPORES:	White.
HABITAT:	Broadleaved woods, mostly beech and oak.
FREQUENCY:	Very common.
SEASON:	Summer to autumn.

Powdery Brittlegill *R. parazurea*

CAP:	5–10cm. Flat convex. Matt *grey/blue/green*.
STEM:	4–7cm by 1–1.5cm.
GILLS:	White to cream.
FLESH:	White.
SPORES:	Cream.
HABITAT:	Broadleaved woods, mostly beech and oak.
FREQUENCY:	Fairly common.
SEASON:	Summer to autumn.

Greencracked Brittlegill *R. virescens*

CAP:	7–12cm. Rounded then flattened out and wavy, dull ochre green with darker *scaly green patches* all over.
STEM:	5–9cm by 2–3cm. White, rusty spots later. (Goes orange with iron sulphate, so a lot of fun to be had here.)
GILLS:	Cream, fairly brittle.
FLESH:	White, firm.
SPORES:	White to pale cream.
HABITAT:	Broadleaved woods, chiefly beech.
FREQUENCY:	Occasional.
SEASON:	Summer to autumn.

Charcoal Burner

Powdery Brittlegill

Greencracked Brittlegill

THESE ARE a selection from a group of Brittlegills with mostly greenish or bluish caps. The most common of these is the Charcoal Burner. It is singular among the Brittlegills in not having brittle gills and thus is a fine example of biology refusing to have any regard for rules.

With any Brittlegill you are not sure of, a quick nibble of the cap edge will determine if it is acrid and inedible (spit it out!) or mild and edible. The very hot ones, such as the Sickener (*Russula emetica*), p.152, generally cause some sort of gastric upset and must be avoided.

All the mild Brittlegills have a nutty flavour and a pleasing texture that is suitable and safe for salads. As they are undervalued by the average mushroom hunter obsessed with 'A-list' mushrooms such as Ceps and Chanterelles, the Brittlegills are passed by as too difficult to identify and not tasty enough – which leaves all the more for us.

P.S. It is easy to tell a Brittlegill from anything else, but apart from 20 to 30 well-known species out of the 200 or so on the British list, it is all but impossible to tell one from another. Still, at least you can eat some of them. Far worse is the notoriously difficult genus *Cortinarius* – the Webcaps. Its 400 species are appallingly hard to identify and only one is edible. Most of them are extremely rare with a suspiciously large number having been recorded only once, so even the keenest *Cortinarius* twitcher is unlikely to spot more than a third of them in a lifetime. I often advise people new to mycology and overwhelmed by confusion to specialise in just one genus (an excellent piece of advice I have never taken myself). If you decide to take this path, don't choose *Cortinarius* – that way madness lies.

Common Yellow Brittlegill
& Yellow Swamp Brittlegill

Common Yellow Brittlegill
Russula ochroleuca

CAP:	6–10cm. Rounded when young, soon flattening out, yellow ochre.
STEM:	4–7cm by 1.5–2.5cm. White.
GILLS:	Brittle, white.
FLESH:	White. Tastes rather acrid.
SPORES:	White to cream.
HABITAT:	Woodland.
FREQUENCY:	Extremely common.
SEASON:	Summer to early winter.

Yellow Swamp Brittlegill
R. claroflava

CAP:	6–12cm. Rounded when young, often flattening out to form a completely flat disc, very bright shiny yellow.
STEM:	5–10cm by 1.5–3cm. White bruising grey to black.
GILLS:	Brittle, ivory at first, then ochre.
FLESH:	White.
SPORES:	*Ochre.*
HABITAT:	Damp birch woods.
FREQUENCY:	Common.
SEASON:	Late summer to autumn.

WALK INTO just about any wood in the autumn and you will immediately tread on a Common Yellow Brittlegill. The huge genus *Russula* contains over 200 species, but the Common Yellow Brittlegill is almost as common as all the rest put together. So it is rather a pity that, though perfectly edible, it earns a place in this book more for its super-abundance than its flavour. In fact, the flavour is not at all bad, just a bit peppery, which is fine if you like peppery, otherwise you can just add one or two to a mixed mushroom dish. The good news is that they are much less spicy when cooked than a nibble of a raw specimen will lead you to expect. Of course, as with all strong-tasting

Common Yellow Brittlegill

Young Yellow Swamp Brittlegill

Easily broken gills

mushrooms (and indeed all mushrooms), you should try a small amount first to make sure it agrees with you.

Perhaps better, though less common, is the under-appreciated and not at all peppery Yellow Swamp Brittlegill. I suspect that the 'Swamp' part of its name has protected it from the frying pan more than any inherent esculent failing. With its firm texture, nutty flavour and ability to retain its bright yellow coloration during cooking, it makes a tasty and decorative ingredient in most dishes. It is also one of the few that I am happy to recommend adding to a salad.

Beware of the Geranium Scented Brittlegill (*Russula felea*). With their mostly bright caps, stocky outline and brittle gills, the Brittlegills are easily distinguished from the other genera. The Geranium Scented Brittlegill is one yellow *Russula* that should particularly concern us due to its acrid taste. It has more of an orange tinge to its yellow colouring than the other two, and smells, you guessed it, of geraniums.

P.S. One would think that all mushrooms and toadstools, because they all look more or less the same, would be closely related to one another. They are not. The toadstool shape has been invented independently by no less than six different branches of the fungal family tree.

Brittlegills and the closely related Milkcaps are actually a long phylogenic way from other mushrooms and are closer to a lot of weird stuff that grows on twigs. In fact, strange as it must seem, Boletes, Puffballs and even the Beefsteak Fungus (p.128) are more closely related to, say, Field Mushrooms (p.93) than are the Brittlegills. This may appear extremely odd (it is rather like discovering that humans were more closely related to cows than chimps), until one remembers that mushrooms and toadstools are organs, not organisms. It should be no surprise that since they are designed for the same function they look the same. The technical term for this biological phenomenon is 'convergent evolution' and it can be seen throughout the natural world.

The Brittlegill's evolutionary distance from other mushrooms is hinted at in the character that gives them their name – brittle gills. In fact, the whole mushroom is brittle and this is because the Brittlegills are built from round cells quite unlike the long cells that make other mushrooms more fibrous and hence tougher.

Nature is endlessly and startlingly inventive and these evolutionary paths can lead on to some astonishing places. The Brittlegills and their friends the Milkcaps have Truffle-like descendents – the so-called Milk Truffles. Simply put, Milk Truffles are mushrooms that have made a massive change in shape and career and have taken themselves off to live underground. Some habits die hard though and at least one of them – *Zelleromyces stephensii* – will still produce a milky latex when you cut it.

Fairy Ring Champignon

Marasmius oreades

CAP:	2–5cm. Convex then flat with a *central boss* when mature, wavy margin. Tawny to ochre, paler when dry.
STEM:	4–7cm by 0.3–0.5cm. White to cream, *tough and fibrous*.
GILLS:	Distinctly *beige*, broad and *spaced widely*.
FLESH:	Very thin, cream.
SPORES:	White.
HABITAT:	Short grass, lawns, parks, pasture. Often in rings.
FREQUENCY:	Very common.
SEASON:	Spring to autumn.
WARNING:	Must be cooked!

IF THE GARDENER'S No. 1 Most Hated Toadstool is the Honey Fungus, then No. 2 must be the Fairy Ring Champignon. The damage this fungus has inflicted on many a once spotless lawn has brought tears to the eyes of many a once proud gardener. It is all but impossible to eradicate and only the drastic measure of removing and then replacing half a metre of topsoil is guaranteed to work.

But there is good and surprising news – it is one of the very best of the wild mushrooms, in my opinion up there with the Ceps and Chanterelles. Better still it is very common, very prolific and so easy to identify that it would take heroic carelessness to mix it up with anything nasty. And who wants one of those dreary monoculture lawns anyway?

Fairy Ring Champignons are known to contain hydrogen cyanide, though they are perfectly safe to eat after being cooked. No, really. The quantities are tiny but the tell-tale smell of bitter almonds can still occasionally be detected. They suffer sometimes from maggots but seldom half-heartedly so; they are either all maggot-free or all infested. The stems are far too tough to eat, so just nip them off with a thumbnail as you pick them. The caps look and taste wonderful when pickled and preserved in oil (p.245) and, since they are viewed by many as toadstools, you get the irresistible chance to offer Pickled Toadstools to guests at tea time.

Beware of the Fool's Funnel

(*Clitocybe rivulosa*), p.144, which grows in similar habitats and is quite seriously poisonous. Don't worry too much as, with its 'frosted cake' bloom on the top of the cap, it is a very distinctive toadstool – just remember it is sometimes easy to lose concentration when picking lots of small mushrooms.

Fairy Ring Champignon

P.S. Few things in the fungal world stimulate more interest and puzzlement than fairy rings. These sometimes vast and ancient formations have received the attentions of productive imaginations for millennia. The largest one I know is around 70 metres in diameter and may be 200 years old, but they can live for a thousand years and grow up to half a mile across. Remember that we are talking about a half mile diameter single individual here – an individual organism that can dwarf any other on the planet! Well the mystery, if not the wonder, is now in the past.

Rings come about when the underground cotton wool-like mycelium of a fungus grows outwards from a central point and dies off in the middle. The mushrooms then grow from this underground ring. The ring zone of dead grass is caused by dehydration and by fungal toxins (cyanide again!), while the outer zone of lush grass is caused by the release of nitrogen from the feeding mycelium. The inner zone of lush grass is the result of nitrogen released from the dying mycelium. No fairies. Sorry.

Oyster Mushroom *Pleurotus ostreatus*

CAP:	5–12cm. Kidney-shaped, beige to grey, sometimes bluish.
STEM:	Short, lateral.
GILLS:	Whitish. Not branching.
FLESH:	White, thick near stem.
SPORES:	White to very pale lilac.
HABITAT:	Usually on deciduous trees, most often beech. In tiers.
FREQUENCY:	Very common.
SEASON:	Spring to early winter.

OYSTER MUSHROOMS are almost unmistakable and their chief peril arises when less than agile mushroom hunters wielding sharp knives try to clamber over piles of slippery logs. They really are some of the best mushrooms, and can be found in enormous quantities. Before you fill your basket, just check to see if their maggot-to-mushroom ratio is too high for your personal taste – they are rather prone to this particular aggravation. Actually, all is not necessarily lost. A mycological friend of mine who (oddly) didn't much like eating mushrooms took a basket of them home, proudly informing me a couple of weeks later that he had succeeded in hatching 15 different species of mushroom fly from the maggots in his collection. Result!

Also look out for the Pale Oyster (*Pleurotus pulmonarius*). If your Oyster Mushrooms seem to lack any stem, this is what they are more likely to be. Don't worry, they taste just as good. There is also the Branching Oyster (*Pleurotus cornucopiea*), which has gills down its stem and tastes of coconut. It became quite a common species a few years ago following an abundance of its favourite home, dead elm trees.

P.S. I am about to tell you more than you really want to know. Oyster Mushrooms grow on logs. Everyone is happy with this – Oyster Mushrooms are the good guys breaking down organic matter for future generations. But I am afraid they lead a terrible double life. Logs are made of cellulose and lignin, both of which are very low in nitrogen. Oyster Mushrooms need nitrogen and need to get it somehow. Until it fruits, the main part of an Oyster Mushroom exists as a cotton wool-like mass of fibres inside the log in which it is growing. On some of these fibres, tiny droplets of a powerful toxin form and proceed to stun passing nematode worms into immobility. Other fibres then grow to search out these hapless victims, enter their mouths and suck out their precious, nitrogen-rich fluids. Nasty. But nothing to worry about, unless, of course, you happen to be a nematode worm.

Oyster Mushroom

Oyster Mushroom

Porcelain Fungus *Oudemansiella mucida*

CAP:	2–10cm. Hemispherical, later convex.
	Translucent white/grey with an ochre flush in the centre of mature specimens. Very *slimy* indeed in wet weather, at least sticky in dry weather.
STEM:	3–8cm by 0.3–0.8cm. White, tough.
RING:	Distinct. Like a neat white collar.
GILLS:	White, distant.
SPORES:	White. This fungus is very productive of spores and a spore print can be formed inside an hour.
HABITAT:	In large tufts on beech trees, sometimes high up.
FREQUENCY:	Common.
SEASON:	Autumn to early winter.

DESPITE HAVING eaten around 120 species of fungi, I could never bring myself to try anything quite so slimy as the Porcelain Fungus. Then, quite recently, I met a couple with a basketful each of them. They dismissed my reasonably polite derision and assured me that they tasted a lot better than they looked. Thinking that they could hardly taste worse than they looked, I collected a few of them for supper. After the slime (and there is a lot of it) had been washed off and the stems removed, they sautéed well and had a surprisingly rich flavour. I am now a convert to the Porcelain Fungus.

Certainly it is a species well worth adding to your repertoire as during the season a mature beech wood can readily produce them by the hundredweight. Also there is not the slightest risk of mixing them up with anything else. I like to trim the stems as I pick and it is pretty essential to keep them away from other mushrooms in the basket because of the slime.

Porcelain Fungus

P.S. As you can see from the picture a Porcelain Fungus can completely take over a dead tree. It fights off rival fungi with its very own powerful fungicide. A study of this talent in the 1980s led to the creation of a new, very safe and very effective group of agricultural fungicides, the strobilurins, which have massively improved yields of crops such as wheat and fruits.

Porcelain Fungus – time for a ladder

Saffron Milkcap *Lactarius deliciosus*

CAP:	8–15cm. Convex, then flattened, then funnel-shaped. Dappled orange with darker concentric rings. Sometimes green in parts. Slightly sticky.
STEM:	4–7cm by 1.5–2cm. Pale and usually with *orange pits*.
GILLS:	Slightly decurrent. Pale orange/cream, bruising green. Milk *bright orange*, then slowly green.
FLESH:	Pale. Exuding orange milk fading to dull green.
SPORES:	Cream.
HABITAT:	Pines.
FREQUENCY:	Fairly common.
SEASON:	Autumn.

ANYONE ASKED to venture an opinion on the edibility of a fungus that is orange and exudes a bright orange milk that turns a lurid shade of green would probably give it the thumbs down. But of course, appearances count for nothing where edibility is concerned and the Saffron Milkcap is a good edible species, even if the 'deliciosus' epithet is something of an over-statement. Nevertheless, it is well worth collecting, especially if you like carrots, which it resembles in colour, texture and taste. Nineteenth-century authorities

recommend baking halved Saffron Milkcaps with a little butter and salt in a covered dish for half an hour. And very good it is too.

The Saffron Milkcap is fairly common and restricted to pine woods. It does suffer from the attentions of insect larvae, so do check them before picking a basket full of maggots.

Also look out for the rather censoriously named False Saffron Milkcap (*Lactarius deterrimus*). There are quite a few edible, orange Milkcaps,

Pockmarks often visible

Orange latex

but the False Saffron Milkcap is the most common (more common than the Saffron Milkcap). It is found only under spruce and is distinguished by the fact that the orange milk goes blood red and then green and by its tendency for the mushroom to turn green with age. The Traffic Light Mushroom would have been a better name. It is supposed to be less tasty than its companion, but the difference is slight. Most Milkcaps with bright orange milk are edible; make sure it is orange though, as there are a few very hot species with yellow milk.

P.S. Many trees are poor at extracting minerals and water from the soil; their fat rootlets present too small a surface area to absorb all they need. The huge mat of microscopic fibres (hyphae) that constitute the bulk of a fungus has no such problems. These fibres are able to absorb water and nutrients with great efficiency and will transfer them to a tree through a woolly sock of hyphae wrapped around its rootlets. The tree pays for its supper with sugar, and it is this sugar that forms the raw material from which many of our mushrooms are made. This equitable partnership is called mycorrhizal, and is of fundamental importance to the life of many fungi and trees.

Like our pine-loving Saffron Milkcap, many fungi are fussy when choosing a host tree and knowledge of which trees are around you will help you determine which mushrooms are at your feet. Some fungi, more catholic in their tastes, will grow with many types of tree, and if you have ever wondered why sycamore and ash woods are so useless for mushrooming, it is because they don't form such mycorrhiza at all.

Saffron Milkcap

St George's Mushroom

Calocybe gambosa

CAP:	6–12cm. Domed convex with the margin inrolled. White to beige with a brownish centre, often cracked, dry.
STEM:	3–6cm by 1–2cm. White.
GILLS:	White to pale cream, crowded.
FLESH:	White throughout. Very firm texture. *Strong smell of fresh meal.*
SPORES:	White to cream.
HABITAT:	Short grass. Old pasture, lawns. Often in rings.
FREQUENCY:	Locally common.
SEASON:	*Spring.*

LIKE A LOT OF my mushroom hunting friends, I go into a decline in the winter and spring. I still wander the fields and woods and I do take a genuine interest in the flowering plants, especially the edible ones, but somehow it is not quite the same. And then, towards the end of April, my mood changes because I know that now is the time to look for that first big mycological treat of the year – the St George's Mushroom.

These appear with surprising reliability on and around 23 April – St George's Day, hence the name. They can be found a week or two before, but most finds take place in May with a few rare sightings in June. It must be said that my attempts to predict the date of their appearance based on what type of winter or spring we have had have been consistently useless; the St George's Mushroom, like all mushrooms, comes up just when it feels like it. It is, however, something of a joy to actually pick them for tea on St George's Day and it is seldom that I have had to forgo this pleasure. I once gave a basketful to a restaurateur friend of mine who put them on the menu as a St George's Day special. It is a sad reflection on the caution of the average diner that he did not sell a single order. Perhaps all his customers were Scottish that night.

The St George's Mushroom is typically a species of permanent grassland, so old pasture and downland give the best crops. But lawns, municipal parks and road verges are also permanent grassland as far as mushrooms are concerned, so you may well find them in an urban setting. It is not really a woodland species, but it will often make an appearance on grassy wood edges

St George's Mushroom

and paths. It does not seem to be at all fussy about whether the soil is acid or alkaline.

St George's Mushrooms often grow in rings although it is not always obvious as the grass is neither damaged nor stimulated by the mycelium. You can sometimes work your way around the circle picking the best ones. The older fruit bodies can look a little shabby, but don't let appearances deceive you; they are just as good to eat as their younger brothers. They grow very slowly so you will be able to revisit the same spot more than once in the season and their spring fruiting means that they are nearly always free of maggots.

The firm, dry flesh possesses a rather overpowering aroma of fresh meal, which has been known to deter faint-hearted foragers, but it is reduced to a pleasant level with cooking. I know it is a cliché, but butter, garlic and cream suit St George's Mushrooms perfectly.

Beware of the woodland species, the Deadly Fibrecap (p.156), which is really the only toadstool that might be mistaken for the St George's Mushroom. The similarity is superficial, so just the normal level of caution is required. The fact that the St George's Mushroom seldom, if ever, appears after the end of May and the Deadly Fibrecap is a toadstool of the summer months does help. But the real clincher is the unmistakably strong smell of the St George's Mushroom.

The Blusher *Amanita rubescens*

CAP:	8–15cm. Almost spherical when young, opening to a broad umbrella. Reddish brown with a covering of movable *grey/pink scales*. Damaged areas showing pink/red.
STEM:	8–15cm by 1.2–2.5cm. White, bruising pink/red with a swollen base covered in rings of scales.
RING:	Membranous and (this is important) has lots of *fine grooves* on its upper surface.
GILLS:	White, slowly bruising pink/red.
FLESH:	White, slowly turning pink/red.
SPORES:	White.
HABITAT:	Deciduous and coniferous woods. Most common with beech.
FREQUENCY:	Very common indeed.
SEASON:	Summer to late autumn.
WARNING:	Must be cooked!

I HESITATE to include the Blusher in this book. Not because it isn't delicious – it is – and not because it is an endangered species – it isn't – but because, like a Queen's Scout whose brothers are all in a young offenders' institute, it has some very unfortunate relatives. These relatives are, indeed, the very worst one could hope for, including as they do the Death Cap (p.140), Destroying Angel (p.143) and, most relevant in this case, the Panther Cap (p.150). Nevertheless, once you get a feel for its distinctive appearance you will be able to spot a Blusher at 30 paces. It is certainly one well worth learning as it is very tasty and very common, first appears in the summer when other mushrooms still have their heads down and, frankly, you aren't going to have a lot of competition from other mushroom hunters. Having just convinced you that maybe it is worth a try I am now going to ruin it by telling you that the Blusher actually contains a toxin. However this toxin, like the one in kidney beans, is destroyed by heat, so cook it and you will be fine. No salads.

It is an irritatingly variable species, differing in size and general shape enormously, but it has a most striking feature in that any damaged or bruised parts very slowly turn pinky red. This is usually most noticeable where slugs have had a nibble or at the base of the stem where it has been handled in picking.

Beware of the Panther Cap (*Amanita pantherina*), p.150, which has distinct separate white scales on the cap, has unchangingly white gills and stem and no grooves on the ring's upper surface. This is a seriously poisonous species, though seldom deadly.

The Blusher

Grooved ring and scaly base

Blushing where nibbled

P.S. Amanitas have quite a complex structure. The scales on the top and at the base of Blushers and the famous white spots on the Fly Agaric are the remains of the veil that once enclosed the young fruit body. In the Death Cap the veil remains intact as a sheath at the base of the stem. Amanitas also have a partial veil going from the middle of the stem to the edge of the cap, forming a ring on the stem that hangs down after detaching itself from the edge of the cap.

The Deceiver *Laccaria laccata*

CAP:	2–4cm but very variable, tawny, drying paler. A distinctly *scurfy* look to the surface and usually with a wavy, grooved margin.
STEM:	4–10cm by about 0.4cm. Similar colour to the cap, tough, fibrous and sometimes twisted.
GILLS:	*Flesh-coloured* and *very widely spaced.*
FLESH:	Thin, pale.
SPORES:	White.
HABITAT:	All types of woodlands.
FREQUENCY:	Very common.
SEASON:	Summer to early winter.

THE DECEIVER is so-called because it varies so confusingly in size and shape; so much so that after 30 years of familiarity with this species, I am still sometimes deceived. However, it does have some very straightforward characteristics that happily make identification certain.

With the tough stems discarded, this very common species, if not up there with the Chanterelles and Ceps, is a useful addition to a mixed mushroom dish. There – I said it. 'Useful in a mixed mushroom dish' is mushroom book code for 'tasteless, but you might not notice if you have anything decent to go with it'. Actually, it is not all that bad. Give it a try.

Beware of any of the anonymous 'Little Brown Toadstools' that often abound on the forest floor, which can look superficially like our Deceiver. The genus *Inocybe* (p.156) springs to mind, but these all have brown gills and spores. The Deceiver's scurfy cap, fibrous stem and widely spaced, flesh-coloured gills are distinctive characteristics.

Also look out for the Amethyst Deceiver (*Laccaria amethystina*), which is one of the most stunning mushrooms you will ever see. Its colour is quite amazing and the caps look splendid in a salad. (Remember to just try one or two the first time you eat them raw.) They fade with drying, so keep them covered in the fridge and perhaps soak them in water for a little while just prior to serving. The colour successfully survives cooking, however, and you can do no better aesthetically than serving them with saffron rice. It is, if anything, even more common than its cousin, and will often grow in large troops. The moderately poisonous Lilac Fibrecap (*Inocybe geophylla* var. *lilacina*), p.157, is similar in colour and size, but should not present a problem for the careful collector.

The Deceiver

Amethyst Deceiver

Tawny Grisette *Amanita fulva*

CAP:	5–8cm in diameter. Rounded then flattened. ***Bright orange/brown*** with a ***grooved margin***. Quite sticky, frequently with patches of the volva adhering.
STEM:	8–12cm by 1cm. Tapering from the bottom upwards. White to pale orange. Sheath-like volva at the base, which is white and spotted with rusty patches. There is ***no ring or any sign that it ever had one***.
GILLS:	White, free of the stem.
FLESH:	White.
SPORES:	White.
HABITAT:	Beech and oak, but also sweet chestnut, birch and occasionally pine.
FREQUENCY:	Very common in small groups.
SEASON:	Autumn.
WARNING:	Must be cooked!

SINCE THE AMANITAS include several of the deadliest toadstools on the planet, many writers eschew the consumption of members of this genus altogether. This seems to me like plain cowardice. There are, in fact, a few Amanitas that with due caution you can quite safely eat. The Tawny Grisette is notably easy to distinguish from its lethal brethren because of the deep grooves on the cap edge, its bright colour and its lack of a ring. It can often be found in little groups of three or four and will sometimes dominate a woodland. It is one of the prettiest of the fungi with its lovely, slightly sticky orange-brown top pushing its way through the enveloping sheath, looking just like a fresh date. The flavour is mild and pleasant but you must remember to cook them. They are very fragile mushrooms, so do keep them separated from your weightier finds or they will get hopelessly squashed.

Beware of the deadly Amanitas and know what they look like (see pp.140, 149 and 150). Never pick one in the anonymous 'egg' stage.

Distinctively grooved cap

Young Tawny Grisette

Mature Tawny Grisette

P.S. There is a mushroom, *Amanita vaginata*, that is simply called The Grisette. It is often collected for the table, but I have not recommended it here because its grey coloration makes it less easy to identify and because the Tawny Grisette is about ten times more common. You may also come across the beautiful but inedible Snakeskin Grisette (*Amanita ceciliae*). It was once gloriously known as *Amanita strangulata*, surely the best name for a toadstool ever.

If you are wondering how the Grisette got the last part of its Latin name, it just means a 'sheath', referring to the sheath-like volva at the base of the stem. There are several fungi with Latin names that would be unwelcome in polite company. Two that spring readily to mind are the Stinkhorn (*Phallus impudicus*) and the Earth Star (*Geastrum fornicatum*). As you will know if you have ever seen one, the Stinkhorn hardly needs to justify its scientific appellation but our otherwise retiring Earth Star does seem to have some explaining to do. This particular *Geastrum* raises itself from the ground in an arch. The Latin for 'arched' is '*fornicatus*' and it was underneath the arches that Roman ladies of the night could be found. I came slightly unstuck once at an adult education course I was running when I wrote the names of our finds on a table and forgot to wipe them off. During the week, an elderly art student found the foldaway table and complained bitterly about the 'filthy words' he had been exposed to.

Meadow Waxcap *Hygrocybe pratensis*

CAP:	4–8cm. Convex when young, eventually flattened except for a broad central bump. *Matt, pale orange.*
STEM:	3–6cm by 0.6–1.2cm. Cream.
GILLS:	*Thick*, broadly spaced, *waxy*, cream, *decurrent.*
FLESH:	Cream, thick at the centre.
SPORES:	White.
HABITAT:	Short grass on poor soils, nearly always with moss and often growing in rings.
FREQUENCY:	Locally abundant.
SEASON:	Late autumn, early winter.

I STILL REMEMBER my first sight of a field of Waxcaps. It looked as though some child had taken his box of toys and, in a shocking tantrum, had thrown them down the hillside. The incredibly bright colours of the Waxcaps are the most striking in the fungal world, ranging from white to yellow to orange to red to almost purple, with one beautiful pink species – the Pink Waxcap – and one extraordinary green one – the Parrot Waxcap. Several members of this dazzling genus are edible and the best of these is the Meadow Waxcap.

Its flavour is very pleasant but a little too mild to constitute a mushroom dish entirely unaided and I always try to mix it with stronger-tasting species such as the Horse Mushroom.

Also look out for the Snowy Waxcap (*H. virginea*). It is really quite tasty although its diminutive size (only about 3cm in diameter) means that it will take a while to pick enough for a meal. It is very like the Meadow Waxcap in its general appearance, except that it is white, smaller and comparatively slender.

Beware of the seriously poisonous Fool's Funnel (*Clitocybe rivulosa*), p.144, which could conceivably be confused with the Snowy Waxcap as it is white and also grows in grassland.

P.S. I have always taken a great delight in Latin names, but they do get me down sometimes. Many of the fungi, presumably in an effort to keep one step ahead of the police, are constantly changing them. I first knew the Meadow Waxcap as *Hygrophorous pratensis*, then it changed to *Camarophyllus pratensis*, then *Cuphophyllus pratensis*, and now *Hygrocybe pratensis* – and it may not stop there. It is hard enough learning them once without having to learn them four times. In the more cynical circles of mycology there is a general and not unfounded belief that if you wait long enough the name will always return to the one you learnt first.

Meadow Waxcap

Snowy Waxcap

Scarlet Waxcap
& Crimson Waxcap

Scarlet Waxcap *Hygrocybe coccinea*

CAP:	3–6cm. Convex. *Scarlet*, drying to yellowish in the centre. Scurfy and not slimy.
STEM:	3–5cm by 0.5–0.8cm. Dry. Yellow through orange to red. Paler at the base. Not blackening with age.
GILLS:	*Waxy*, creamy yellow, reddish when young.
FLESH:	Yellowish, thin.
SPORES:	White.
HABITAT:	Short mossy grass on poor soils. Often growing in rings.
FREQUENCY:	Common.
SEASON:	Late autumn, early winter.

Crimson Waxcap *H. punicea*

CAP:	8–12cm. *Broadly conical. Crimson to slightly purple.*
STEM:	5–12cm by 1–2cm. Yellow, sometimes flushed orange.
GILLS:	*Waxy*, **thick** and broadly spaced. Yellow.
FLESH:	Whitish.
SPORES:	White.
HABITAT:	Short mossy grass on poor soils. Usually in small groups.
FREQUENCY:	Uncommon.
SEASON:	Late autumn, early winter.

THE SCARLET and Crimson Waxcaps must be among the most beautiful of all the mushrooms. The Scarlet Waxcap is really very common and it is a pity that its mild flavour does not entirely match its remarkable good looks. The larger Crimson Waxcap is less common and almost too pretty to pick, so I collect it just occasionally. As with all the Waxcaps, they like old, mossy grassland and are equally at home on blasted moors and slightly neglected suburban lawns. There are many red Waxcaps, but they are generally smaller and often slimy. They are probably harmless, but it's best you avoid them.

The culinary strength of these bright Waxcaps lies chiefly in their striking colours. They look great in risottos or sliced thinly as an exotic garnish to an autumn salad. If the salad idea appeals, remember to try just a tiny amount the first couple of times you eat them to make sure that they agree with you.

Scarlet Waxcap

Crimson Waxcap is much larger

The magnificent Parasol

Parasol & Shaggy Parasol

Parasol *Macrolepiota procera*

CAP:	15–35cm. Always with a little bump on the top. Fleecy and cream-coloured, covered in concentric, fixed, light brown scales. The scales form a central brown patch.
STEM:	Up to 25cm by 2cm. Bulbous base. Pale, covered in the typical '*snakeskin*' markings. With care it can be pulled out of its socket in the cap without damage.
RING:	Large and double, can be moved up and down the stem.
GILLS:	Cream/white.
FLESH:	White, unchanging when bruised. Smells of boiled milk.
SPORES:	White.
HABITAT:	Meadows, roadsides, parks.
FREQUENCY:	Common.
SEASON:	Summer to autumn.

Shaggy Parasol *M. rhacodes*

CAP:	8–15cm. Cream-coloured, covered in *shaggy* grey/brown scales.
STEM:	12–18cm by 1–2cm. Very *bulbous* base, smooth, dirty cream bruising orange/red. Top bruises orange when pulled out of socket in cap.
RING:	Double, can be moved up and down the stem.
GILLS:	Cream/white, *bruising red.*
FLESH:	White, bruising orange/red immediately on cutting.
SPORES:	White.
HABITAT:	Woodland, copses, roadsides, parks.
FREQUENCY:	Common.
SEASON:	Summer to autumn.
WARNING:	Must be cooked, disagrees with a few people!

NOTE: Both species come in a number of varieties, but the snakeskin markings and red bruising are, respectively, definitive characteristics.

THERE IS NO MORE astounding sight in an autumn field than a stand of Parasols. These stately, delicious and often enormous mushrooms can sometimes be spotted a quarter of a mile away and it can be difficult to stop oneself from running to pick them. The trouble is that, when you get there, they can look too good to pick and you may find your aesthetic and culinary sensibilities at war. I content myself with just a few of the more closed caps and leave the open ones to both produce their spores and grace the landscape. Honestly.

Fully open, they do look just like little parasols, and as long as the gills are soft and fresh, they are very good to eat. The smell is strikingly like that of warm milk, and the texture, when cooked, is fibrous and soft like the thigh meat of roast chicken. It is a pity to waste the tough stems, so I always find a place for them in the stockpot.

Now, whoever it was who said that life was too short to stuff a mushroom had clearly never come across the 'drumstick' Parasol. If anything ever cried out to be stuffed, it is these – they were clearly designed for this very purpose by a beneficent god. I will not burden you with a recipe here but merely point out that something involving bacon is not likely to disappoint.

Beware of the very similar and closely related genus *Lepiota* – the seriously poisonous Dapperlings (p.146) – which contains many species that look rather like their big cousins the Parasols. All of the Dapperlings are smaller than our two Parasols, so if your collection has any strangely diminutive individuals there is a chance that you have picked a Dapperling by mistake. Parasols grow to the drumstick stage and then open out; they do not start life as small fully open Parasols and just get bigger. My rule is to never pick a Parasol which is, or is likely to be when open, less than 12cm in diameter.

Note, too, that the Shaggy Parasol disagrees with some people, so always cook it before consuming and try only a small portion the first couple of times you eat it to check that it likes you as much as you like it.

P.S. The Parasol's smell of warm milk is so distinctive I could identify it from this alone. Smell is such an important clue to the identity of many fungi that anyone deficient in olfactory sensitivity suffers a severe handicap. The aniseed odour of the Horse Mushroom is well known, but there are more exotic experiences waiting out there. There is the Coconut Milkcap, the Curry Milkcap and the carrot-smelling Oak Milkcap. We have coal gas in the Sulphur Knight, rotting meat in the Stinkhorn and the foul smell of the Dog Stinkhorn. The more subtle fungal odours have taxed the ingenuity of writers over the years and they have sometimes resorted to an excessive floridity of language. The most notorious example is for *Hebeloma sacchariolens*, once described as 'reminiscent of harlots', a characterisation that has always put me at a serious disadvantage in determining this species.

Shaggy Parasol

Shaggy Parasols bruise red

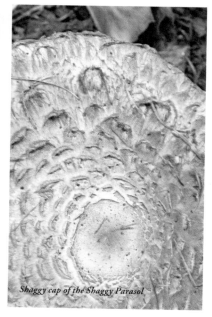

Shaggy cap of the Shaggy Parasol

Trumpet Chanterelle

Cantharellus tubaeformis

CAP:	2–7cm. Dimpled, funnel-shaped, *scurfy grey/brown*.
STEM:	2–10cm by 0.5–1cm. Often flattened with broad grooves. Tough and fibrous. *Bright yellow*.
GILLS:	*Wrinkles* instead of gills. Yellow/grey then greyish brown.
SPORES:	White.
HABITAT:	Woodland. Usually in mossy leaf litter and on buried twigs.
FREQUENCY:	Common and often found in large numbers.
SEASON:	Late autumn. It will survive early frosts.

LIKE ITS RELATIVE, the Horn of Plenty (p.83), this mushroom seems to wear an invisibility cloak. After staring at an apparently barren patch of leaf litter for a minute or so you will suddenly notice a single mushroom and then another and another until you realise that you cannot really put your foot down without treading on one. This is one of those joyful moments that all mushroom hunters love. Its other close relative, the flamboyant Chanterelle (p.46), is much less reticent. The Trumpet Chanterelle has a thinner flesh but holds its shape well in cooking and looks great in soups and stews.

It is also one of the best mushrooms for drying as it will reconstitute completely after 15 minutes of soaking. Trumpet Chanterelles are seldom attacked by slugs and bugs and they have the happy trick of coming up in the same place year after year. I have one spot (one very well hidden spot before you ask) where I have picked them for more than 20 years.

Beware of getting carried away and absent-mindedly picking any of the small brown toadstools that habitually grow in similar habitats. If you check each mushroom for the bright yellow stem all will be well.

P.S. Learning how living organisms are related to one another is often a rather startling enterprise, as any child who has just found out that dolphins aren't fish could tell you. The fungi seem to be inordinately fond of such surprises. The Chanterelle group of mushrooms may look more or less like any other group of mushrooms, but it is, in fact, only distantly related. Its nearest cousins are *Clavulina cristata*, which resembles coral, and (if the DNA analysis can be relied on) a fungus found on wood called *Tulasnella violea*, which looks, quite simply, like a coat of pink emulsion.

Trumpet Chanterelle

Velvet Shank

Velvet Shank *Flammulina velutipes*

CAP:	3–7cm. Orange, paler at the edge. Very slimy in wet weather.
STEM:	1.5–7cm by 0.3–1cm. Usually curved, yellow at the top, brown to black below and distinctly *velvety* when mature. Tough and fibrous.
GILLS:	Pale yellowish.
FLESH:	Thin, pale orange/yellow.
SPORES:	*White.*
HABITAT:	On the dead stumps of deciduous trees, notably elm. In large, dense, tiered clusters.
FREQUENCY:	Common.
SEASON:	Late autumn to winter.

THE VELVET SHANK is one of my favourite mushrooms, reliably appearing even when that other aficionado of early winter, the Blewit, has called it a day. This pretty group was photographed (and eaten) on Boxing Day. There had been a severe frost just a day or two before, but frost is no problem to this mushroom as it can survive being frozen solid. Sometimes it can even be found covered in a layer of snow. The flavour is excellent and rather unusual – distinctly sweet and malty – and the texture is slightly and pleasantly chewy, but not at all fibrous. It sautés well and holds its shape and colour in cooking. The Velvet Shank is another of those mushrooms that lends itself to pickling and preserving in oil (p.245), though the sliminess survives the pickling process and is not to everyone's taste.

You might, in fact, have eaten Velvet Shanks without knowing it as the cultivated Enokitake mushroom that is sometimes found in delicatessens is the same species. Grown on sawdust and other organic material in plastic bottles, they attain their unnatural pallor and bizarre form by being kept in the dark.

Like certain other species, the Velvet Shank enjoyed something of a heyday in the 1980s when Dutch elm disease filled the countryside with an abundance of tree stumps.

Beware of the poisonous species

that grow on wood. Since the Velvet Shank grows in the depths of winter, there is seldom much else around with which it might be confused. Even so, it is important that you familiarise yourself with those species that might make an appearance in mild winters. The most dangerous is the Funeral Bell (p.160), but the Sulphur Tuft (p.168) is superficially similar to the Velvet Shank and will give you severe problems. If you are unsure, take a spore print (p.24) – unlike these two nasties, the Velvet Shank has white spores.

Oak Milkcap *Lactarius quietus*

CAP:	5–8cm. Convex then flattened and sometimes with a small depression in the centre. Cap surface shiny/felt-like, dull orange with concentric **pockmarks** near the edge.
STEM:	4–7cm by 1–1.5cm. Same colour as the cap.
GILLS:	Cream with an orange tinge. Milk abundant, white to pale cream, mild to slightly gingery in taste.
FLESH:	Cream. Smells a bit oily or carroty.
SPORES:	Cream.
HABITAT:	Always under oak.
FREQUENCY:	Extremely common.
SEASON:	Autumn.

THIS IS A SADLY overlooked species that has suffered from an often repeated accusation of 'smelling of bed bugs'. I have never knowingly smelled a bed bug so I cannot comment on this, but would rather compare their smell to that of carrots – a much more positive view. The slightly bitter taste of the fresh mushroom largely disappears with cooking and the final flavour is of carrot with a hint of ginger.

Beware of the Fenugreek Milkcap (*Lactarius helvus*), p.145. Most inedible Milkcaps can be detected by their peppery taste but the Fenugreek Milkcap is the exception as it is both mild in flavour *and* poisonous.

Oak Milkcap

Horn of Plenty *Craterellus cornucopioides*

SHAPE: Like a very irregular black trumpet. Hollow right to the base. It is normally 6–10cm tall and up to around 4cm across. The inside is grey/brown to black and smoothly wrinkled. The outside is more grey.

HABITAT: Deciduous woods, chiefly beech and oak.

FREQUENCY: Uncommon, though locally abundant.

SEASON: Autumn.

ALONG WITH its close relative the Trumpet Chanterelle (p.78), the Horn of Plenty is a most retiring fungus that will often remain invisible, even when pointed out to you. Sometimes it stands out beautifully against bright green moss, but more commonly it will hide shyly in the leaf litter. If, however, you are lucky enough to spot one, stop just where you are and you will nearly always see many more, for it is in its abundance as much as in its shape that the Horn of Plenty earns its specific epithet.

It is well worth the effort of the hunt as, despite its outlandish appearance, the Horn of Plenty is a gourmet fungus sharing the top table with both the Cep and the Chanterelle. It is a happy companion of fish, particularly white fish, against which its colour provides a striking contrast. The delicate flavour is greatly intensified by drying.

The mushroom's funereal colours give rise to its alternative title: the Trumpet of Death – surely the most discouraging name for an edible fungus possible.

Horn of Plenty

The Miller *Clitopilus prunulus*

CAP:	3–8cm. Flat, wavy and often irregular in shape, white to cream with a texture like chamois leather. Rather soft and flaccid. Margin rolled under.
STEM:	2–4cm by 0.5–1cm. Same colour as cap.
GILLS:	White at first then *pink*, decurrent, often off-centre, thin and close together. *Can be peeled* away from the cap.
FLESH:	Smells very strongly of *raw pastry*.
SPORES:	Pale *pink*.
HABITAT:	Woodland, both broadleaved and coniferous.
FREQUENCY:	Very common.
SEASON:	Late summer to autumn.

I HOPE I HAVE convinced you that, with a little care, it is a fairly straightforward matter to tell most of the edible fungi from the poisonous ones. Most – but not the Miller. This looks so much like a seriously poisonous species, the Fool's Funnel (see below), that it was 20 years before I was able to summon up the courage to eat it. I collected it every year and I was 99.9 per cent certain I had got it right, but somehow that was never enough. The nineteenth-century mycologist Mrs Hussey bemoaned its reputation – 'neglected and despised in England, as one of that dreaded family, the Toadstools'.

While I cannot recommend the Miller as the ideal mushroom for the beginner, it is one that is well worth learning and I would be failing in my duty if I kept quiet about it. It is a delicious and very common mushroom. The powerful smell of raw pastry largely disappears when it is cooked, leaving a pleasant mushroomy taste.

The Miller grows in groups of half a dozen or so and for some reason (most probably parasitism) is fond of the company of Ceps. If you should find some, do take a moment to look around – there may be a particularly welcome bonus hiding nearby!

Beware of the Fool's Funnel (*Clitocybe rivulosa*), p.144. Fortunately, the Miller possesses several important characteristics that separate it from this villainous double and other dangerous *Clitocybe* species. It has pink spores, not white; gills that can easily be pulled away from the cap; a very strong smell of raw pastry; and a preference for woods, whereas the Fool's Funnel is a grassland species. With the Miller, be doubly sure to check that every expected characteristic is present. Also, remember that not all pink-spored species are edible, so do familiarise yourself with the Pinkgills (p.154).

The Miller on a wet day

Wood Blewit & Field Blewit

Wood Blewit *Lepista nuda*

CAP:	8–15cm. Convex, then flattened and wavy. Lilac, then brown but still with a hint of lilac, drying paler. Cold and damp looking.
STEM:	5–10cm by 1–3cm, often swollen at the base, lilac to brown and covered in paler lilac fibres, eventually brown.
GILLS:	Deep lilac, eventually fading as the spores mature.
FLESH:	Slightly rubbery, lilac. *Smells strongly aromatic/perfumed.*
SPORES:	Pale pink.
HABITAT:	All types of woodland, in hedges and sometimes in grass.
FREQUENCY:	Common.
SEASON:	Late autumn to early winter.
WARNING:	Must be cooked!

Field Blewit *L. saeva*

CAP:	8–15cm. Rounded, then flattened with a 'sharp' edge. Cream to grey/brown, paler when dry, extreme edge whitish for a long time. Usually feels a bit damp.
STEM:	3–6cm by 1.5–2.5cm (very short). *Intense lilac*, fibrous.
GILLS:	Similar colour to cap with a pink tinge on mature specimens.
FLESH:	Whitish to cream. *Smells spicy/perfumed.*
SPORES:	Pale pink.
HABITAT:	In mature grassland, often in well-defined rings.
FREQUENCY:	Uncommon, but may be locally abundant.
SEASON:	Late autumn, early winter.
WARNING:	Must be cooked!

THE FIRST HARD frosts bring the mushroom season to a shivering halt and plunge the mushroom hunter into a mild depression. The Ceps and Chanterelles are gone; Giant Puffballs a distant memory. But there is one group of mushrooms that prefers the cold and the damp of early winter and can raise the spirits of bereft foragers right into the New Year – the Blewits. By no means poor substitutes for the mushrooms of warmer times, Blewits are among the best and not to be missed. Their oyster-like slipperiness is quite extraordinary and truly different to other fungi, as is their faint beetroot

Wood Blewit

Field Blewit

Lepista sordida

Lepista luscina

flavour. Lightly sautéed, their delicate flavour and texture is realised, and to those blessed dyads of 'strawberries and cream' and 'ham and eggs' I think we must add 'Blewits and garlic'. Garlic goes well with most, if not all, mushrooms, but none so well as the Blewit. Of course, a little cream may find its way into the saucepan as well.

The unprepossessing Blewits only reveal their stunning looks after they have been picked, when the beautiful lilacs and purples of stem and gills can be seen. The nineteenth-century writer Mrs Hussey refers to them as 'Fair faced the Bluette'. They can look too good to eat – almost.

Also look out for a few other Blewits that taste just as good as our familiar pair. Occasionally you may find what appear to be rather undernourished Wood Blewits; these are likely to be *Lepista sordida*. They sometimes grow in dense, inextricable clusters in grass. My favourite rare Blewit, however, is *Lepista luscina*. Though considered uncommon, I know of it from several locations where it grows in huge rings. Though it lacks the distinctive lilacs

and blues of its cousins, it can be easily recognised by its spicy, flowery odour and the little brown dimples that form in rings on the cap. All Blewits are suspected of containing chemicals that can damage red blood cells. The chemical is unstable and is destroyed by cooking.

Beware of the Wood Blewit's slight similarity to some of the Webcaps. Two of the Webcaps may cause confusion: the common *Cortinarius purpurascens* and the beautiful and rare *Cortinarius violaceus*. Neither of these is poisonous and I have actually eaten *C. purpurascens*. However, several other Webcaps are deadly, and it may well be worth avoiding the entire genus. The tell-tale sign of any Webcap is the web of fibres connecting the stem to the cap edge. This is best seen on young specimens, though fibre traces can persist, clinging to the stem. If you are still uncertain, you can settle the matter with a spore print – Webcaps have rust-brown spores; Blewits, pale pink. The Field Blewit is much less problematic as the bright lilac stem and the pale cap and gills form a reassuringly distinct combination.

P.S. Most of the woodland fungi in this book are mycorrhizal. Blewits are quite different; they are saprotrophs living entirely on dead organic matter. This can be seen quite clearly if you pull a Wood Blewit out of the ground without trying to disengage it from its substratum – half the forest floor comes with it, all matted together by the mycelium of the fungus. The contribution of fungi to the wellbeing of the biosphere is little appreciated. Every year around one and a half trillion tons of cellulose, a material that only fungi can break down with any degree of efficiency, is produced. Without the fungi, the bulk of it would simply remain where it drops and life would soon become impossible for most organisms.

Horse Mushroom
& Macro Mushroom

Horse Mushroom *Agaricus arvensis*

CAP:	12–20cm. Almost spherical when young and unopened. Later, flattened convex. Creamy white and yellowing, especially when bruised. Smooth, sometimes a little scaly.
STEM:	8–12cm by 1.5–2.5cm. Cylindrical, sometimes club-shaped. Mostly smooth, but sometimes woolly just below the ring.
RING:	Large and pendulous with the typical *'cogwheel'* on the underside.
GILLS:	Pale cream, then pink, then brown.
FLESH:	White. Smells strongly of aniseed.
SPORES:	Purple/black.
HABITAT:	Pasture.
FREQUENCY:	Fairly common.
SEASON:	Late summer to autumn.

Macro Mushroom *A. urinascens*

Very similar to the Horse Mushroom except that the cap is scalier and sometimes grows to a massive 30cm diameter. The 'cogwheel' on the stem is less pronounced and the base of the stem is covered in woolly scales. Smells less aniseedy.

SINCE I SUSPECT that a good proportion of the 'Horse Mushrooms' collected for breakfast are, in truth, the almost identical and just as edible Macro Mushroom, I have dealt with them both together.

As a single specimen will easily fill a plate, a Horse or Macro Mushroom can constitute a meal all on its own. And what a meal it is; black, pungent and dripping with an inky juice. Simply brush some melted butter onto both the top and bottom of the cap, sprinkle with salt and grill hot and quick. Younger, unopened specimens have an unsurpassed sweet aniseed flavour and lack the bitterness of their older sisters. The stems are perfectly edible but a little fibrous for some palates, and are perhaps best in soups and stocks.

It is a providential custom of Horse and Macro Mushrooms to grow in 'family pack' quantities of around a half dozen, often in a ring. This ring,

Horse Mushroom

Macro Mushroom with faint 'cogwheel'

'Cogwheel' typical of this group of Agaricus

which turns the grass brown on the outside and lush green on the inside, can be visible for a good part of the year, even when there are no mushrooms growing. This enables the observant mushroom hunter to spot a potential dinner months beforehand! They have one other accommodating habit – that of a long season, from as early as Easter to as late as the first carol singers.

Beware of the Yellow Stainer (p.172), which can look superficially just like our Horse and Macro Mushrooms. It is worth taking extra care in studying in detail any *Agaricus* species you collect, because the Yellow Stainer is the most common cause of mushroom poisoning in this country. The Horse and Macro Mushrooms both bruise yellow, like the Yellow Stainer, but less intensely and not at all in the stem base. Also, the yellow persists, whereas it fades to brown after a few minutes with the Yellow Stainer. Finally make sure that your collection smells of aniseed, not antiseptic.

P.S. *Agaricus urinascens* has sometimes been called *A. macrosporus*, hence Macro Mushroom. This refers to the large size of the spores and, indeed, examining these under a microscope is the best way of identifying *A. urinascens* for certain. Well, there is one other way. Young specimens and fresh fully grown ones smell pleasantly of aniseed, but if you take them home and leave them for a day or two the smell suggested by the last part of its Latin name can be detected. While you will be very pleased to hear that this smell disappears with cooking, eating them as fresh as possible is a sensible goal.

Field Mushroom *Agaricus campestris*

CAP:	6–10cm. White and silky, fibrous, often with browner fibres in the centre, rounded then flat, cap *skin overhanging.*
STEM:	5–8cm by 1–2.5cm. Spindle-shaped and not bulbous at the base.
RING:	*Simple* and *fragile.*
GILLS:	Pink from very young, then brown as the spores mature.
FLESH:	Turns slightly *pink* when damaged.
SPORES:	Purple/black.
HABITAT:	Grassland, usually in rings.
FREQUENCY:	Locally common.
SEASON:	Summer to autumn.

FEW SIMPLE PLEASURES compare with that of picking your way across a mushroom field in the mist of an autumn morning, except perhaps the breakfast that follows.

When Continental Europeans speak of wild mushrooms, they mean anything with a cap and a stem that they can eat; the British, with their centuries-old aversion to fungi, think only of Field Mushrooms. This was the mushroom that my grandmother got chased out of a farmer's field for picking; this is the mushroom that people fondly remember there being many more of when they were young.

Like all fungi of the field, the Field Mushroom has declined due to modern agricultural practices and is an excellent example of the conservation culprit being habitat loss and not the innocent mushroom picker. Ploughing and reseeding of long-established grassland, the application of fertiliser and the loss of grazing to cereals and oilseed rape have all taken a serious toll and it has become quite a rare fungus in some parts of the country. It will require the return of more gentle farming practices to restore this wonderful resource to its past abundance.

Nevertheless, it can be found in quantity wherever there is old pasture and it has a particular enthusiasm for fields with horses. Occasionally found in small groups, but more often in rings, Field Mushrooms can sometimes be picked by the tens of kilograms and I have seen them sold at the roadside by farmers with an unexpected cash crop on their hands. The most famous glut occurred in 1976 after the rains that followed the serious drought of that year – fields turned white with mushrooms.

Field Mushrooms are such delicate and attractive fungi that it is a pity to let them get dirty, so I always trim the base of the stem. Simplicity is the key to

Field Mushroom

Pavement Mushroom

cooking them and any urge to fry some in bacon fat and serve them on toast should not be resisted.

Also look out for certain
other *Agaricus* species. Around 220 species are accepted by various authorities, from *A. abruptibulbous* to *A. zylophilus*, easily half of which are good to eat. By far the best known of these is *A. bisporus* – our familiar cultivated mushroom. A few more are covered elsewhere in this book, but identifying the more obscure species (i.e. most of them) is a job for the specialist. Quite a few of them are virtually indistinguishable from Field Mushrooms and can be eaten without fear.

Fragile ring of the Field Mushroom

One particular *Agaricus* that does deserve a mention here is the Pavement Mushroom (*A. bitorquis*), so named because of its extraordinary ability to punch its way through tarmac. It is,

unsurprisingly, a very solid mushroom, and is very good to eat if a bit chewy. The double ring on the stem together with the strongly inrolled cap edge in young specimens and very low stature make it easy to identify.

Beware of the Yellow Stainer (p.172). Despite its firm place in our culture,
the Field Mushroom is not really a species for complete beginners. Every year I speak to people who have been poisoned and it is almost invariably as a result of eating the Yellow Stainer in place of a Field or Horse Mushroom. Judging by the colourful and rather gruesome descriptions these people give of their symptoms, it would be well worth acquainting yourself with this treacherous impostor. Its key features are a long stem with a bulbous base, gills that are white when young, a large ring and a very strong yellowing on the cap edge and in the flesh of the stem base. It also has an unpleasant antiseptic smell, especially noticeable during cooking. In the Field Mushroom, the gills are always pink, the ring is thin and there is almost no yellow about it at all.

The Yellow Stainer will give you an unpleasant few hours, but that is all; far, far worse is the fate in store for someone mistaking a button Death Cap (p.140) or Destroying Angel (p.143) for a button Field Mushroom. Always be careful when picking immature specimens of any mushroom, as those all-important identifying characteristics may not have developed yet.

Shaggy Inkcap

Shaggy Inkcap *Coprinus comatus*

CAP:	12cm tall by 5cm. An elongated egg, curling up at the edges at maturity and turning to ink. Very shaggy, as you are entitled to expect. Pure white when young with a light brown patch on the top.
STEM:	10–20cm by 1–1.5cm. Cylindrical, hollow, white to pink, easily split into fibres.
RING:	Transient and fragile.
GILLS:	Extremely close together, cream at first then pink, then black.
FLESH:	Very thin.
SPORES:	Black.
HABITAT:	Grass, roadsides, often in disturbed ground.
FREQUENCY:	Extremely common.
SEASON:	Autumn.

THIS MUSHROOM demonstrates such a strange fondness for road verges and roundabouts that I sometimes wonder where it made a living before such things existed. It is a familiar and very distinctive mushroom and the only danger it presents comes from wandering around on busy dual carriageways when picking it. This was the very first wild mushroom I ever ate, but I cannot say that it is my favourite, tasting, as it does, of boiled polystyrene. However, many people say they like it, so maybe you will too.

Once Shaggy Inkcaps start to mature, the white flesh and gills redden and then go inky black, so pick only very young specimens that are white throughout. Not that they actually become poisonous with advancing age, but rather, like my Auntie Hilda, just more and more unpleasant.

Shaggy Inkcaps mature extremely quickly and because of this have the shortest sell-by date of any mushroom; it is therefore pointless trying to keep them for tomorrow's supper, even in the fridge. Eventually they reduce to the black ink from which they get their name by a process called 'auto-deliquescence' – a great word to use if you especially enjoy watching people's eyes glaze over.

Also look out for the Common
Inkcap (*Coprinopsis atramentaria*), p.170, which is shorter, fatter and grey and, despite its unequivocal name, rarer than the Shaggy Inkcap. It is edible but – and let's face it, this is a big 'but' for many of us – if you drink alcohol within a few hours of eating it, you will be poisoned. Life can be very unfair sometimes.

The Prince *Agaricus augustus*

CAP:	12–20cm, occasionally larger. Cream-coloured with brown fibrous scales.
STEM:	12–20cm by 2–3.5cm. Club-shaped, white, covered with white, ***brown-tipped***, shaggy fibres when young.
RING:	Large and pendulous with ***brown scales*** on the underside.
GILLS:	Free of the stem, white then brown, eventually chocolate.
FLESH:	White, yellowing. Smells of ***aniseed or almonds***.
SPORES:	Purple/brown.
HABITAT:	Woodland, parkland, more often with conifers.
FREQUENCY:	Uncommon.
SEASON:	Summer to autumn.

'AUGUST' means 'inspiring reverence or admiration'. Considering that The Prince can grow to a magnificent 25cm in diameter and is one of the most beautiful and delicious mushrooms you will ever eat, I think that 'august' is just about right. It is rather a pity, therefore, that it so seldom makes an appearance.

The Prince is one of the many mushrooms that tastes and smells of almonds. The chemical involved in the process is benzaldehyde, the same as that found in sweet almond oil. This mushroom grows fairly indiscriminately in all types of woodland, but does seem to prefer conifers.

The Prince

Wood Mushroom
& Blushing Wood Mushroom

Wood Mushroom *Agaricus silvicola*

CAP:	7–12cm. Rounded, eventually flat. Smooth. Bright white, yellowing with age. Bruising yellow when handled.
STEM:	5–10cm by 1–1.5cm. ***Base very swollen***. White, yellowing, especially when handled.
RING:	Pendulous with '***cogwheel***' markings underneath in younger specimens.
GILLS:	Grey/pink, then dark brown.
FLESH:	White, ***smells strongly of aniseed***.
SPORES:	Purple/brown.
HABITAT:	Oak and beech woods and also with coniferous trees.
FREQUENCY:	Fairly common.
SEASON:	Autumn.

Blushing Wood Mushroom *A. silvaticus*

CAP:	6–10cm, convex, then flattened, tawny-brown fibres forming larger scales on a paler background.
STEM:	6–10cm by 1–1.5cm, bulbous base, grey/white.
RING:	Pendulous when young, same colour as the stem and often with ***brown scales*** on the underside.
GILLS:	Pale, then pinkish, then dark ruddy brown.
FLESH:	Turns ***blood red*** when cut, then slowly dark brown. Thin in cap.
SPORES:	Dark brown.
HABITAT:	Coniferous woods, often in troops of a dozen or so.
FREQUENCY:	Common.
SEASON:	Autumn.

OF THE SEVERAL 'true' mushrooms (the genus *Agaricus*) that occur in woodland rather than pastures, these two are the most familiar. Despite the similarity of their names, they are not all that closely related and their taste is rather different. The white Wood Mushroom is a close cousin of the Horse Mushroom (p.90) with which it shares a sweet aniseed flavour and a disquieting tendency to bruise yellow (Yellow Stainer alert!). The Blushing

Wood Mushroom

Blushing Wood Mushroom

Wood Mushroom, which acquired its name from its habit of turning blood red when handled or cut, is considerably less substantial and you will need a good collection to make a decent meal. It is an altogether more nutty fungus in both cap colour and flavour. It has, on occasions, been referred to by the worrying name of *A. haemorrhoidarius*, and you will be pleased to hear that this is a reference to that startling colour change and not a warning of what it might give you.

Blood-red stem of Blushing Wood Mushroom.

Beware of the Yellow Stainer

group of toadstools (p.172). The fact that the Blushing Wood Mushroom goes blood-red when you cut it is a great encouragement as no Yellow Stainer does this. Just remember that the woodland version of the Yellow Stainer, the Inky Cap (p.172), also has dark fibrils on the cap, albeit distinctly grey ones. For collectors of the Wood Mushroom, however, great caution is needed to avoid confusion with the ordinary Yellow Stainer. It too is white and bruises yellow, but the smell (aniseed in the former and Elastoplasts in the latter) and colour change in the cut base of the stem (none and chromium yellow respectively) make identification certain.

It is well worth remembering that the Destroying Angel (p.143) is similar in shape to the Wood Mushroom, and is also white in cap and stem. It won't prove a problem to the careful forager because, unlike the Wood Mushroom, its gills are also pure white and it has a distinct volva at the base of the stem.

P.S. The way that fungi fall into natural groups or genera is an enormous help to the mushroom hunter desperately trying to make sense of the thousands of species that can be found. Well, further help is at hand. Many genera can be usefully split into smaller *sub*genera. The Brittlegills (or *Russula*), for example, can be divided up into lots of smaller groups depending on things like spore colour and cap colour, so if you know what the spore and cap colour are you will be very close to knowing what your specimen is called.

Agaricus is normally divided into the 'Flavescentes', which bruise more or less yellow, and the 'Rubescentes', which bruise more or less red. The Wood Mushroom and Horse Mushroom (p.90) are moderately yellowing fungi from the first group and the Blushing Wood Mushroom is an extremely reddening member of the second. Field Mushrooms redden mildly, Yellow Stainers yellow a great deal and so on. They can be divided up a lot more than this, but I am sure you get the idea.

Cep *Boletus edulis*

CAP:	12–25cm. Hemispherical to rounded, flattening at maturity. Various shades of ***brown, like the crust of a bread roll***, the extreme edge is often paler. ***Irregularly dimpled***, again just like a bread roll.
STEM:	6–15cm by 2–8cm. Usually very swollen, especially when young, grey/brown to white with a ***white network*** on the upper half.
TUBES:	Fine, white at first, then yellow, then green and spongy.
FLESH:	Firm and white throughout.
HABITAT:	Oak, beech, birch and coniferous trees. Prefers open situations.
FREQUENCY:	Common.
SEASON:	Summer to autumn.

IT IS A DANGEROUS business to judge a mushroom by its appearance, but the Cep, at least, is every last bit as good as it looks. The English name 'Penny Bun' neatly expresses its felicitous appearance. The Cep is the most prized of wild mushrooms and its collection is nothing short of an institution in several European countries. Long and unaccountably overlooked by the British, this mushroom is now highly prized here too, and every autumn the forests rustle to the sound of Cep hunters on the prowl.

The flavour is both subtle and rich, the texture both nutty and slippery. Being such a substantial mushroom, it does need more cooking than most; about ten minutes in the pan usually brings out the flavours and textures perfectly. The tubes on mature specimens are often peeled off by over-fastidious cooks who do not favour the frankly rather slimy texture of this component. I, for one, always leave them on. I work hard to find my Ceps and never waste any part of them – cap, tubes, stem, maggots – eat the lot, I say.

A young Cep looks so different from an old Cep that many people can hardly believe they are the same thing. While it is the firm, nutty young specimens that command the high prices, their middle-aged brothers have much more flavour. The elderly ones are best left

Tubes just maturing

The Cep

to release their spores, or, if you cannot resist them and they have not been too engaged in maintaining the mushroom fly population, used in soups.

A very rough guide is to look for Ceps with pines in Scotland, and with birch, beech and oak further south. As with many of the fungi, they seem to prefer open, park-like situations to the dark woodland depths, and a walk along a wooded path or roadside is most likely to meet with success. If you find a large number of Ceps, it takes a strength of personality beyond that given to most people to resist picking every last one. This is what I suggest: leave the babies and the elderly and pick two-thirds of the rest. It will be good for your karma.

Also look out for several Boletes that are close to the Cep and every bit as good to eat as their famous cousin. Unfortunately, they are rather rare and I cannot recommend eating them unless you're able to find them in some abundance. The closest is the appropriately named Dark Cep (*Boletus aereus*), found mostly under oak. More distantly related and not quite so tasty is the Oak Bolete (*Boletus appendiculatus*), with its beautiful 'oranges and lemons' coloration. The cut flesh blues slightly and the pores are bright yellow.

Beware of the very similar Bitter Bolete (*Tylopilus felleus*), p.175. While this aptly named toadstool is not at all poisonous, it would be most unwelcome at the dinner table. Its bitterness is quite extraordinary, and should one find its way into your *Ceps à la crème* you will have to throw the whole lot away. It is distinguished by the pinkish tinge taken on by the pores and the dark network on the stem.

P.S. The curse of the Cep hunter is not some dangerous look-alike species or even the unwelcome sight of another Cep hunter, but the humble maggot. Large specimens are seldom without these irritating competitors, and even young ones can become infested. Yet it is a great pity to despise these organisms, which have as much right to their dinner as we do. The most common maggots devoted to the annoyance of mushroom lovers are the fungus gnat larvae (*Mycetophilidae*) with their white bodies and dark heads. Most other fly larvae are whitish all over. If your maggots have legs, they are moth or beetle larvae. Larvae are generally found within the flesh of a fungus, but the 'fat-footed flies' (*Platypezidae*) feed between the gills. There are even some flies whose larvae feed on fungus larvae.

The ephemeral nature of most fruit bodies means that life cycles are necessarily short and many insect species manage to pack a whole lifetime into a very few days. Fruit flies (*Drosophilidae*) generally have the last bite of the cherry, living off the rotting gloop left by the disintegrated mushroom. My favourite maggot, however, is the gnat larva that harvests spores from bracket fungi by catching them in a slimy web, which it weaves underneath the tubes.

Dark Cep

Oak Bolete

Bay Bolete *Boletus badius*

CAP:	8–15cm. Hemispherical when young, viscid when wet but matt when dry, striking chestnut (bay!) in colour.
STEM:	5–10cm by 1–4cm. Very variable but narrow compared to Ceps, wrinkled and distinctly yellow/brown, paler at apex.
TUBES:	Pale yellow to greenish, bruising blue, pores small.
FLESH:	White to yellow, slowly bruising slightly blue/grey.
HABITAT:	Broadleaved and coniferous woods.
FREQUENCY:	Very common.
SEASON:	Autumn.

THE BAY BOLETE is a common, tasty and easily identified mushroom that is seldom prone to maggots. For the mushroom hunter it has it all. Its only downside is that, unlike mycologists, it does not improve with age. Pick only the reasonably young, firm specimens and avoid them in wet weather when they swell up like sponges and taste about the same.

Despite its benign character, the Bay Bolete was avoided by most nineteenth-century British mycophagists because it failed M.C. Cooke's 'golden' (and wrong) 'rule' for Boletes – 'don't eat them if they turn blue when cut'. The Bay Bolete lacks the meaty flavour of the Cep but is perfectly acceptable nonetheless. It also dries very well, a useful quality in a mushroom that can be gathered in such large quantities that reinforcements may be needed to carry your collection home.

Also look out for

a very common fungus called the Red Cracked Bolete (*Boletus chrysenteron*). It looks like a small Bay Bolete but is rather soft, the tubes are broader and greener, it has red on the stem and the cap surface usually has red cracks in it. A friend who was known for her fondness for road kill badger and garden snails, and whose frequent invitations to dinner always seemed to find me with a previous engagement, once collected a basketful of them. Her assessment, when I next saw her, that they tasted vile, I think we can take as definitive.

Red Cracked Bolete

Bay Bolete

Orange Birch Bolete
& Orange Oak Bolete

Orange Birch Bolete *Leccinum versipelle*

CAP:	8–15cm. Rounded, felt-like surface, dull orange. The *edge overhangs* the tubes.
STEM:	10–20cm by 2–5cm. Usually taller in relation to the cap than Ceps and slightly swollen at the base. Grey/white covered in woolly, *dark brown to black scales*.
TUBES:	Dull yellowish grey.
FLESH:	Whitish at first then faintly purplish grey and eventually black in parts.
HABITAT:	Under birch.
FREQUENCY:	Common.
SEASON:	Late summer to autumn.

Orange Oak Bolete *L. aurantiacum*

CAP:	10–20cm. Rounded, felt-like surface, bright orange-brown to brick red.
STEM:	10–20cm by 2.5–4cm. Pale at the top but the increasingly dense *russet* scales make it darker towards the bottom, sometimes blue-green at the base.
TUBES:	Cream to brown.
FLESH:	White at first, then faintly pink, green at the base and eventually turning grey to black.
HABITAT:	Under oak.
FREQUENCY:	Quite rare, so pick only when found in quantity.

THE *LECCINUM* species have tubes instead of gills and are close relatives of Boletes such as the Cep from which they are distinguished by their long scaly stems. The Orange Birch Bolete is by far the more common of the two and is distinguished by its grey stem. Both are solid mushrooms and take quite a bit of cooking, especially the stems, which need twice as long in the pan as the caps. Do not worry about the *Leccinum*'s tendency to go various shades of greens and pinks and blacks when cut – they are just trying to frighten you.

Also look out for one of the brown-capped *Leccinum* species, that constant companion of Birch trees, the

Brown Birch Bolete (*Leccinum scabrum*). This is pretty poor as edible mushrooms go, being rather tasteless and watery, but if you wish to try it, do pick the youngest and firmest specimens you can find. The Brown Birch Bolete has a brown cap and a long white/grey stem covered in dark brown scales, and the white flesh is unchanged when cut or slightly pink.

The Victorian mycologist Mrs Hussey certainly preferred the Orange Birch Bolete's 'trim grenadier' to the Brown Birch Bolete's 'dirty ruffian'. If we were left in any doubt of her opinion, she then goes on to call it a 'swarthy, shiny, scabrous, very vulgar individual'. I think it looks rather splendid, it is just a shame that its taste does not live up to its looks.

Orange Birch Bolete

Orange Oak Bolete

Brown Birch Bolete

Scarletina Bolete *Boletus luridiformis*

CAP:	10–20cm. Dark brown with a velvet texture and hemispherical when young, later convex to flat, more leathery and a lighter brown.
STEM:	5–12cm by 2–4cm. Swollen at base. Bright orange/red made up of thousands of little raised *orange dots* against a yellow background.
TUBES:	Yellow/green, turning bright blue on cutting. Pores bright red.
FLESH:	Very firm when young. Yellow, *immediately turning dark blue* on cutting. The blue fades after a while.
HABITAT:	Woodland, mostly beech and oak, occasionally pine.
FREQUENCY:	Common.
SEASON:	Late summer to autumn.
WARNING:	Poisonous raw, but perfectly safe when cooked!

IF THERE IS ANY mushroom that seems to come with a health warning it must be this one. With its blood-red pores and stem, and bright yellow flesh that turns instantly an intense blue on cutting, it is surely shouting 'Don't eat me!' But this colourful relative of the Cep is harmless and very good to eat. Having such a fearsome appearance, it is one that tends to be left alone by the average mycophile, so if you are brave enough there is a feast waiting for you.

I am afraid there are a few caveats. It is one of those that *must* be cooked before eating; it is known to be indigestible to a few, so try just a little the first time; and there are one or two Boletes that are not at all edible with which it could conceivably be confused.

I seldom bother with the larger specimens, which are usually soft and full of maggots, choosing instead the young ones with their distinctive velvet cap. These have a firm texture, like the Cep, and a pleasant, nutty flavour. It is a great pity that the blue disappears with cooking – it would be great fun to be able to serve blue 'toadstools' to nervous friends.

Mature Scarletina Bolete

Young Scarletina Bolete

Beware of other Boletes with bright red colours on the stem and pores. The first check is to cut the flesh to see that it is lemon-yellow turning instantly and intensely blue (this is a good thing). The second check is to ensure that the stem is covered with orange-red dots and not a red net. The best-known, though very rare, poisonous Bolete is the scarily named Devil's Bolete (*Boletus satanas*), p.177, which is easily distinguished by its dingy white cap.

P.S. When considering something merely as an item of food, it is easy to lose sight of the fact that one is eating an organism of surpassing complexity and wonder. The Boletes, and many other fungi as well, produce their spores not on the surface of gills like, say, Field Mushrooms, but inside tubes. Now, these tubes may be 30mm long but less than half a millimetre internal diameter. The spores are formed on the inside surface of these tubes, in fours, on little stalks at the end of long cells called basidia. They are then propelled, by a mechanism that has taken a hundred years to understand, into the middle of the tube where they can float downwards and eventually out into the world. As you will appreciate this is a very delicate mechanism and the fungus goes to great lengths to keep its tubes absolutely vertical so that the spores don't stick to the sides.

The Boletes are no slackers when it comes to producing spores in this way, but the prize for outrageous fecundity must go to *Ganoderma applanatum*, a large bracket fungus, which can produce spores at the rate of 500,000 per minute, a rate it can keep up for several months at a time.

Slippery Jack *Suillus luteus*

CAP:	8–12cm. Broadly rounded to flattened.
	Date-brown, covered in slime, which dries to a sticky skin.
STEM:	5–10cm by 2–3cm. Pale whitish yellow.
RING:	Large, white and membranous, darker below, granular.
TUBES:	Pale yellow, very small.
FLESH:	Firm, white to yellow.
HABITAT:	Under two-needle pines such as Scots pine.
FREQUENCY:	Common.
SEASON:	Autumn.
WARNING:	Must be peeled and cooked!

THE PIRATICAL sounding Slippery Jack is the best of an otherwise poor bunch that is the genus *Suillus*. While its taste is too faint and its texture too uninteresting for it to form the centrepiece of any dish, in the hands of a good cook and mixed with superior mushrooms it can be perfectly acceptable. With its enormous ring it is certainly a striking mushroom and very common wherever there is Scots pine. If you find a rather orange one under larch, then it will be the Larch Bolete (*Suillus grevillei*), which is also edible.

Slippery Jack has a very, very slimy skin that is mildly poisonous (or to put it another way, an excellent laxative) and needs to be peeled off and discarded. The stem is not particularly worth eating either. It might be best not to discard the tubes as well, as there will be almost nothing left if you do. All *Suillus* species contain quite a lot of water, so it is very important to reduce this as much as possible during the cooking process.

One of the best things to do with any of the *Suillus* species is to dry them and then pulverise the dried slivers in a food processor. The resultant powder can be added to soups and stews. Choose the youngest and firmest and, as they are so watery, dry them as quickly as you can. However, there is one place where the Slippery Jack comes nicely into its own and that is on a pizza.

Despite my faint praise, do give Slippery Jacks a chance; you might well like them.

Also look out for the Weeping Bolete (*Suillus granulatus*). It too grows under pines, often in large groups, and gains its name from the watery drops that appear at the top of the stem in young specimens. The ringless, pale stem, bright yellow pores and rather sticky orange cap make it easy to identify. It is less common than our Slippery Jack, but its superior flavour makes it well worth searching out. Again, it is important to peel the skin.

Slippery Jack

Weeping Bolete

Hedgehog Mushroom

Hydnum repandum

CAP:	3–10cm. Irregular in shape, rounded when young, then flat with a central depression. The colour and texture of fine chamois leather.
STEM:	2–7cm by 1–3cm. Joins the cap to form a general funnel shape. Same colour as the cap or paler.
SPINES:	Cream. Readily break off.
FLESH:	Pale cream. Smell is faint, slightly bitter.
HABITAT:	Woodland.
FREQUENCY:	Very common.
SEASON:	Late summer to early winter.

THE HEDGEHOG Mushroom is, for many reasons, the ultimate safe mushroom. It is common, very tasty and quite unmistakable. The kid-leather texture of the cap is clearly recognisable, even from some distance, and, once picked, its defining characteristic is

Hydnum rufescens

revealed – the little spines projecting from beneath the cap.

It is a reasonably close relative of the Chanterelle (p.46), as its texture and irregular funnel shape suggest, but it is paler and bears its spores on hundreds of little spines instead of on gills. It is also very nearly as delicious as the Chanterelle, with the added advantages of sometimes being more common and much larger. On the Continent, it has long been held in high esteem and, judging by the names it has been given – Little Goat, Sheep's Foot and Little Rake – a certain amount of affection.

It has very catholic views on habitat and can appear in just about any woodland setting where mycorrhizal trees such as oak, beech, birch, hazel and pine occur. Although it often grows in small patches of three or four, occasionally you will be lucky enough to find a ring of them. My best find was a ring that contained 1.5kg of perfect

Hedgehog Mushroom

specimens. Sometimes you get a real Hedgehog Mushroom year and they can be found in huge numbers. If they have one drawback, it is this: those little spines break off and get everywhere.

The uncooked mushroom is quite bitter but this disappears with cooking. The flavour has been likened to that of oysters to which I can only say – maybe. Its texture is one of the best of all the mushrooms and it keeps its shape and size well during the fairly long cooking that its dry nature demands.

Also look out for the Terracotta Hedgehog (*Hydnum rufescens*). This is so much like the ordinary Hedgehog Mushroom that it has long been debated whether it is a separate species or not. It is distinguished by its red tones and smaller size. There are several other toothed fungi but most of them are rare and poor eating. I once tried, with high hopes, a single, endangered Scaly Tooth (*Sarcodon imbricatus*), which someone had picked for me and which is reputed to be edible. It is not.

P.S. A few years ago an experiment was carried out in China in which some mice were, over a period of six months, given powdered Hedgehog Mushroom to test its reputation as a fatigue suppressant. Various biochemical tests showed that chemicals associated with tiredness were at lower levels and excreted at a faster rate in mice that had eaten Hedgehog Mushrooms than in mice that had not. A gruesome clincher that does little to enhance the status of scientists in the public perception was that in a swimming test 'experimental mice drowned after a longer period of time than the control mice'. I cannot ascertain if these results were confirmed, but perhaps Hedgehog Mushrooms are the breakfast of the future.

Common Puffball

Stump Puffball

Meadow Puffball

Common Puffball,
Stump Puffball & Meadow Puffball

Common Puffball *Lycoperdon perlatum*

SHAPE: 2–5cm in diameter. Rounded with a little bump in the centre and always with a definite stem. White when young, covered with easily broken brown/white spines that leave a mosaic pattern on the skin when broken off. Eventually brown and papery with a hole in the top for the spores to escape when mature. The flesh inside the thin skin is pure white when young, turning yellow then brown and dusty on maturity.

HABITAT: Woodland.

FREQUENCY: Extremely common.

SEASON: Autumn.

Stump Puffball *L. pyriforme*

SHAPE: Similar to the Common Puffball but is more pear-shaped, has much finer spines and is brown on top, even when very young.

HABITAT: Grows in dense clusters on old tree stumps, unlike any other Puffball.

FREQUENCY: Common.

SEASON: Autumn.

Meadow Puffball *Vascellum pratense*

SHAPE: Diameter up to about 4cm. The whole fruit body is usually ovoid when viewed from above. Even young specimens have a faint yellow tone. Minutely scurfy. The stem is less distinct and wrinkles at the base.

HABITAT: Meadows.

FREQUENCY: Common.

SEASON: Autumn.

WHILE THE GIANT Puffball (p.119) is the undisputed star of the Puffball world, there are a number of much smaller Puffballs that taste just as good and are very common. For once, the 'Common' appellation is accurate – the Common Puffball is the one you are most likely to come across. Its easily detached spines make it fairly simple to distinguish from other Puffballs, but with the Puffballs it is really not necessary to know which Puffball you have collected as they are all edible and all taste much the same.

I confess that though I like the little Puffballs, I usually walk past them if there is anything else around that is worth eating. The reason for this uncharacteristic self-denial is that, while their soft marshmallow interior is a delight, they are the very devil to peel. I know that some people cook them whole, but all I can say is that they must have very strong teeth. Having gone to the trouble of peeling your Puffballs, lightly fry them in a little butter, perhaps having dipped them in beaten egg and breadcrumbs first.

With all Puffballs, it is important to only pick young specimens that are pure white throughout when cut in half. Any sign of yellow or green and they should be discarded. They are not poisonous; they just taste like wet cotton wool with a dash of vinegar!

Beware of Earth Balls, which are similarly round and can commonly be found in the woods. Earth Balls have been implicated in the odd poisoning incident, but they are not seriously toxic and are easy to distinguish from Puffballs. The chief reason for avoiding them is that they have much the same culinary virtues as tree bark – none at all. Unlike Puffballs, Earth Balls are never pure white inside; the youngest have yellow flesh, the mature purple black. If that isn't enough to reassure you, just check the skin, which is thin on Puffballs and thick and leathery on Earth Balls.

P.S. Latin names are handed out by taxonomists with little concern for the feelings of the organism involved. We have contrived to give ourselves the very respectable '*Homo sapiens*', which means 'thinking man'. Our Meadow Puffball (*Vascellum pratense*) – 'Little vase that lives in a meadow' – doesn't do too badly either. However, the Stump Puffball (*Lycoperdon pyriforme*) was not so lucky. 'Pear-shaped thing that farts like a wolf' is not a name one would choose for oneself.

Puffballs are so-called because they 'puff' out their spores when squeezed. When mature, the spores sit in a cotton wool-like structure waiting for a drop of rain to land on the papery skin and puff the spores out through the little hole in the top. This, of course, is what the unfortunate Latin name refers to, though I have been unable to find out what wolves have to do with it. The Meadow Puffball is less sophisticated and the skin on its top simply breaks down to leave a little vase open to every drop of rain that might simply splash the spores into the air.

Giant Puffball *Calvatia gigantea*

SHAPE: Usually about 30cm in diameter, though occasionally much bigger. The largest one recorded was 84cm in diameter and weighed 22kg! When young, it has a pure white, kid-leather skin and the undifferentiated flesh is white and spongy throughout. There is no visible stem but the base wrinkles towards the fine mycelial strand that connects to the mycelium in the soil.

HABITAT: Pasture, nettle beds, sometimes rich soil in woods.

FREQUENCY: Occasional.

SEASON: Summer to autumn.

IF THERE IS ONE edible fungus that cannot possibly be mixed up with anything inedible, it just has to be the wonderful Giant Puffball. (Although I did once clamber into a field to try to pick a white duck.) Few things make the heart leap as much as spotting a ring of this enormous and supremely distinctive fungus in a meadow or on a distant hillside.

My best ever find was of 23 Giant Puffballs, all in one field and all in perfect condition. I picked half a dozen, which I then shared with friends, and virtuously left the rest to mature and produce their spores.

Giant Puffball

Giant Puffball

The texture of a Giant Puffball is rather similar to tofu, but I am pleased to report that the flavour is much, much better. ('Tofu' means 'rotten beans', which really says it all as far as I am concerned.) For a normal 30cm-diameter Puffball, it is worth cutting it in half and returning one half, in a plastic bag, to the fridge where it will keep for several days. The soft absorbent flesh is more suited to the frying pan than the stew pot, where it can become tasteless and soggy. I like them best in an omelette. Cut off the thin skin, slice the flesh about a centimetre thick, break up the slices into smallish pieces and fry both sides in butter with a little salt (it really needs the salt). When golden brown, pour in some beaten egg and you will soon be enjoying one of the world's greatest omelettes.

As Giant Puffballs start to mature, the flesh goes green and sweats profusely. Eventually, all the water is lost and the mature brown spores are suspended in a cotton wool-like mesh. Incidentally, this 'capillitium', as it is called, and the spores it holds have a clever knack of never getting wet, allowing the spores to be slowly released over a period of up to a year. We, of course, are only interested in the immature specimens, which are pure white throughout. If they feel dry and give a solid ring when tapped, they are likely to be okay. If you are unsure, just leave them in peace to produce their spores. Sometimes, if I find a maturing specimen in a vulnerable position (usually a field of cows), I rescue it and remove it to a hedgerow or adopt it and take it home to the safety of my garden. When the spores have matured, I wait for a windy day and give it a good kick; it's the least I can do.

They are most at home in rich soil in old grassland, but I have found them in nettle beds, ancient silage pits, hedges and even compost heaps. Giant Puffballs are so conspicuous that it is difficult to judge how common they really are. I give them the benefit of the doubt and pick just one or two.

P.S. The whole purpose of fruit bodies is to produce spores; this is something that Giant Puffballs do with Herculean single-mindedness. I haven't taken the time to check the assertion that a single average Puffball will produce no fewer than seven trillion spores, but it is in line with what is known about other large fungi. What I have done, and I realise I should get out more, is calculate what seven trillion spores would look like if they were each the size of a baked bean. Well, if you took four of the huge Millennium Stadia in Cardiff you could fill them to the roof. You would also have a particularly fine piece of installation art.

The immediate question, of course, is why are we not up to our necks in Puffballs? There are several answers: fewer than one spore in a thousand is viable; they are very fussy about where they grow; they have to face competition from other fungi; they are eaten by micro-organisms and invertebrates; and their mycelium may well be growing happily in that field down the road but just hasn't fruited yet.

Cauliflower Fungus *Sparassis crispa*

SHAPE: A more or less rounded mass of thin, branching, twisted lobes arising from a thick central stem. Almost white to creamy yellow, sometimes with a dark edge. Typically 30cm across, but occasionally much larger.

HABITAT: At the base of pine trees.

FREQUENCY: Fairly common, though scarce in some years.

SEASON: Late summer to autumn.

NOT EVEN THE most nonchalant of mushroom hunters can repress a whoop of delight at the sight of a Cauliflower Fungus resting at the base of a pine tree. For once, nature has supplied us with a fungus that both tastes very good indeed and comes in banquet-sized packages. It has a strong nutty/mushroomy flavour and can hold its own in a greater variety of dishes than just about any other

Wavy lobes

mushroom. It is at home in frittatas soups and stews and happy to be baked braised and sautéed. Actually, there is a limit even to this highly adaptable species as I discovered when I tried to make a sweet milk pudding with it once – it was quite awful and the memory of it has haunted me ever since.

The Cauliflower Fungus can appear at the base of the same pine tree year after year. Still, I always feel guilty picking a whole one so unless I am throwing a dinner party for the entire village I usually just slice off what I need for tea.

The only fungus that looks remotely like it is the edible, if sometimes indigestible, Hen of the Woods (*Grifola frondosa*) – not to be confused with the Chicken of the Woods! It has a mass of small caps that are grey/brown on top and white below.

If there is one drawback with the Cauliflower Fungus, it is the amount of time needed to extricate pine needles pine bark and earwigs. I minimise this effort by simply not worrying too much; there is just no point in being too precious about this sort of thing.

Cauliflower Fungus

Chicken of the Woods

Laetiporus sulphureus

SHAPE:	More or less semi-circular layered brackets, 10–40cm across. Upper surface velvety, zoned bands of **bright orange and yellow**, edge rounded and bright yellow. Lower surface bright yellow with very small pores. All these colours fade with age.
HABITAT:	On oak trees and some other trees.
FREQUENCY:	Common.
SEASON:	Spring to autumn.
WARNING:	Must be cooked, upsets some, avoid any growing on yew!

THERE IS NO FUNGUS that stirs people's imagination like Chicken of the Woods. Perhaps it is the intriguing name, or perhaps its amazing colour. It has a pleasant flavour, even if it is a little 'fungus-y' for some palates. The combination of mild flavour and soft fragility make it something of a fungal 'tofu', but the 'chicken' part of its name is no misnomer and it can replace chicken in many recipes.

Chicken of the Woods is extremely easy to identify and as such it is a safe bet. Unfortunately there is a problem – it doesn't agree with everyone. There are many credible reports of it causing dizziness, hallucinations and gastro-intestinal problems in a relatively small proportion of those who eat it. To minimise your chance of suffering any such misfortune, I suggest that you pick only specimens that are young and fresh, avoid any that do not grow on broad-leaved trees, make sure that the fungus really is thoroughly cooked and when you first eat it, try just the smallest of amounts.

Mostly they are found on living (though soon to be dead!) oak trees, but fruit bodies on willows, poplar, yew (do not collect any that grow on yew as they are known to be poisonous!) and some others are not uncommon. Rather than removing the whole thing from the tree, I just cut off some of the softer, milder flesh from the edge.

Beware of *Phaeolus schweinitzii*,

a large bracket fungus found at the base of conifers. It would take an inexcusable lack of concentration to confuse Chicken of the Woods with anything unpleasant, but *Phaeolus schweinitzii* does bear a passing resemblance. It is not poisonous, but you really wouldn't want to eat one. It is vaguely the same shape and it does have quite a bit of yellow about it. It is easily distinguished, however, because it also has a lot of brown and it is as hairy as a badger.

Chicken of the Woods

Jelly Ear *Auricularia auricula-judae*

SHAPE: Cup-shaped when young, becoming irregularly lobed and uncannily ear-like on maturity. ***Very rubbery***. Red-brown. Inner surface smooth and shiny, outer surface scurfy.

HABITAT: Dead elder tree branches, and rarely on holly and other small trees.

CONSIDERING THAT Jelly Ears of one sort or another are cultivated at the rate of nearly half a million tons per year, it may seem surprising that few British mushroom hunters ever bother with them. The Jelly Ear, however, is something of an acquired taste. The undistinguished mild flavour and its unassailable crunchiness (I casseroled some for eight hours once and they stayed as crisp as when they were when picked) has assured them a place in Chinese cuisine, but has proved something of a challenge to western palates. A plate of boiled or fried Jelly Ears may be an unappetising prospect, but used with discretion in a spicy soup or stew where they can absorb the surrounding flavours, their unfamiliar qualities become clear assets.

The Cloud Ear (*Auricularia polytricha*) is the closely related cultivated species that can be bought in dried form from Oriental emporia. Our own native species, the Jelly Ear, is a very common fungus that is nearly always found on the dead branches of elder trees. The Jelly Ear, or Jew's Ear as it is often called (after the unlikely story that Judas Iscariot hanged himself on an elder tree – they are too springy for that grim purpose), is the most reliable of all the fungi; if I need some I just go to one of my local Jelly Ear trees and pick them. Only during the coldest and driest times of the year do they fail. If you acquire a particular liking for this fungus, it is worth drying some (p.243); 15 minutes of soaking in warm water will reconstitute them completely.

Beware of some of the Cup Fungi

(from the *Peziza* family), as they can also look like ears, and are often similar in colour. They are all inedible, but easily distinguished by their brittle rather than gelatinous flesh, and by always growing on soil. There are many other Jelly fungi but none of them look like ears and none of them are known to be poisonous.

Jelly Ear collection

Jelly Ear

Beefsteak Fungus *Fistulina hepatica*

CAP:	15–25cm across and 6cm thick. Dark liver-coloured, rubbery. Exudes a watery blood-like latex, especially when cut or squeezed.
TUBES:	Cream-coloured when young and easily separated from one another.
FLESH:	Red and marbled with white veins when young. Tastes acidic.
HABITAT:	On oak, rarely sweet chestnut.
FREQUENCY:	Common.
SEASON:	Autumn.

ONE REASON that fungi have for so long been treated with suspicion is their tendency to look like body parts – occasionally unmentionable body parts. Nowhere is this odd talent better demonstrated than in a young Beefsteak Fungus, which looks so very much like a tongue it is surprising that it was never adopted by proponents of the Doctrine of Signatures as a cure for stammering. As it ages, it starts to look more like a piece of liver (though if you saw it in a butcher's shop you would probably decide on lamb chops for tea that night), and it is from this appearance that it earns its name '*hepatica*'. At any stage, the cut flesh has a marbled, fibrous texture just like a rather fatty piece of braising steak and will exude copious amounts of a fluid easily mistaken for blood (you can clearly see a drop of this 'blood' on the leaf in the picture opposite). Altogether a thoroughly meaty fungus.

But does it live up to all this savoury promise? Well, not entirely. Its strongly acidic flavour, especially noticeable in young fruit bodies, is quite unlike the subtle, mild flavours we are used to with most mushrooms and will appeal only to those with more robust palates. If the acidity is too much for you, then soaking it in milk for 24 hours will certainly help. The rather rubbery texture survives the cooking process largely intact and is not to everyone's taste, so another possibility is to stew the sliced flesh with shallots and water for 20 minutes or so and to use only the ensuing gravy-like sauce, discarding the fungus itself. I am reminded of the good Dr Johnson's advice on the preparation of cucumber: 'A cucumber should be well sliced, and dressed with pepper and vinegar, and then thrown out, as good for nothing.' While I think that he would have said much the same about the Beefsteak Fungus, perhaps you ought to give it a chance. At least it is impossible to mix up with anything else and it provides an amusing way of frightening vegetarian friends at dinner parties.

Beefsteak Fungus

P.S. The Beefsteak Fungus is a cause of brown rot in oak and chestnut. As parasites go it is very well behaved, and will live quietly within the heartwood of the tree, gradually removing the structurally important cellulose to leave the brown lignin. Eventually it will make a career change from mild parasite to saprotroph, and proceed to hollow out the tree, releasing nutrients for the tree to recycle. If this process is, literally, cut short and the oak felled for timber, the planked boards will have a rich brown colour quite unlike the pale straw tones of uninfected oak and is referred to as 'brown oak'. Sometimes the infection has only taken partial hold and the result is the beautiful 'tiger-stripe oak'. You may have seen wooden bowls, usually of beech, at craft fairs and such like where the wood displays a pattern of black lines and irregular circles known as spalting. These are caused by fungal colonies spreading outwards in a roughly spherical manner and meeting another colony advancing in the other direction. The black lines mark the ensuing battle.

Summer Truffle *Tuber aestivum*

SHAPE: 2.5–9cm in diameter. Irregularly rounded, sometimes with hollowed-out areas. Surface consists of shiny black pyramidal warts. Flesh white at first then yellow-brown, marbled. When mature, smells strongly of Truffle!

HABITAT: In calcareous soil under a variety of trees, notably beech, hazel and oak.

FREQUENCY: Uncommon, though probably very under-recorded.

SEASON: Summer to early winter.

WITH EITHER great good fortune or a good deal of hard work it *is* possible to find Truffles in Britain. Although Truffle hunting has been an occasional occupation of the English countryside in the past, Truffles have never enjoyed anything like the adulation they receive in France and Italy. The noted French Truffle writer Jean-Marie Rocchia says that the Summer Truffle is found '… even in Southern England, where it is supremely disdained by the subjects of Her Gracious Majesty'.

As most people in this country will happily walk past a group of Ceps without a second glance, it is hardly surprising that few concern themselves with the rare and subterranean Summer

Hollowed Truffle

Truffle. Pursuit of this elusive quarry has not been encouraged by the fact that the British Isles lack the Périgord Truffle and the White Truffle, both of which are orders of magnitude ahead of our Summer Truffle in both taste and price.

But how do you find them? My favoured method is to wait for someone who has discovered a handful of them, perhaps while digging over a rose bed near a beech hedge, to bring them along to ask for my expert opinion. I will say that I have no idea what they are but that if they leave them with me I will study them most diligently and let them know the results of my cogitations in due course.

Slightly more reliable is to simply find a suitable spot and scratch around in the hope of finding something. By far the best place to look is in open beech woods on chalky soil. There should be little in the way of ground cover, such as ivy and bramble, as Truffles dislike, and even suppress, surface vegetation, and their presence can sometimes be inferred from these exceptionally bare patches of ground. The little diggings of

Summer Truffle

squirrels searching for a snack can also provide a clue and I have even found partially nibbled Truffles just lying on the forest floor.

Start scraping away the soil close to the foot of a tree and work outwards for a metre or two. You will not need to dig deeply as Truffles seldom grow more than a few centimetres below the surface and will even push the soil up above them as though trying to burst through. Scratching away at the soil around a tree is very destructive of the mycelium of any of the fungi that may be there, including Truffles, so it is not a practice that I recommend you to use, except occasionally and then only on a small part of the area around each tree.

I once asked an Italian Truffle hunter if he used pigs to find Truffles. He said, with palpable derision, that only the French used pigs and then he spat on the ground. However, pigs can be used to find Truffles, though there are several drawbacks, not least of which is convincing the animal that you deserve the Truffle more than it does. Pigs are very large creatures and your powers of persuasion may not be up to the challenge. Much more sensible is to follow the Italians and use a dog. The main qualifications for being a Truffle hound are a good nose, a sweet temper and a manageable size. Something with a bit of spaniel in it is likely to fit the bill. Training a dog to find Truffles is actually not too difficult; contrary to popular belief, there is no need to have smeared Truffle paste onto its mother's teats when it was a pup, though you can if you want. Get hold of some dimethyl sulphide or (and I guess you are pleased to hear that there is an 'or') some Truffle oil and smear it on some small potatoes. Bury them for an hour or so, offer the smell to the dog and encourage it to locate the hidden potatoes (this is the hard part, but most dogs are very clever animals and should understand what is expected of them). When your dog finds the potato, reward him or her with fulsome praise and a treat. Alternatively, put some Truffle oil inside a cut-open tennis ball and play a game of 'catch', which should be allowed to develop into a game of 'hunt the tennis ball'.

If you are lucky or determined enough to find any Truffles, you could do no better than slice them onto scrambled egg.

Also look out for some of the other species of true Truffle in Britain, of which there are around 15. All of them are edible, though they are seldom large enough to be worthwhile. Pictured on p.130 are some small Hollowed Truffles (*Tuber excavatum*). This species is collected on the Continent and is used to make Truffle pâtés and oils. Hollowed Truffle is one of the Truffles that has a smooth surface.

P.S. Years ago, the British Mycological Society organised what can only be described as a pilgrimage to the various centres of the Italian Truffle industry. This memorable expedition has provided a lifetime's supply of anecdotes for its 20 or so participants, but apart from the searing embarrassment of once receiving a full, and unexpected, civic reception – mayor, town hall, brass band, the lot – while unshaven and wearing an anorak, the memory that stays with me most is that of the perfumed streets of Alba. In shop windows, on the plates of pavement diners and singly on little tables nervously attended by their owner, the White Truffles of Alba filled the air with their scent. The smell is intense, heady and overwhelming.

The White Truffle produces the most complex cocktail of aromatic chemicals, followed closely by the Périgord Truffle. Our own Summer Truffle lacks the more intriguing of these and so is less revered; but it does contain that most important of all the Truffle aromatics – the brain-numbingly smelly dimethyl sulphide.

Truffles produce their strong smells for a good reason. They belong to the ascomycetes – a group of fungi that disperse their spores by forcibly shooting them from the microscopic sausage-shaped structures in which they form. Living underground is in many ways a good lifestyle choice – it is safe, moist and relatively warm – but there is a serious drawback: there is nowhere to shoot your spores to. To circumvent this seemingly intractable problem, the mature Truffle produces a strong smell that attracts various animals, which proceed to devour it. In due course, the animals deposit the spores elsewhere and, with luck, a new Truffle mycelium is established.

Morels

Morchella esculenta

CAP: 6–10cm, irregularly rounded and deeply pitted like a honeycomb, hollow. Pale yellow to brown to grey.

STEM: White, hollow, grooved at base.

HABITAT: Copses, scrubby woodland, waste ground, gardens.

FREQUENCY: Uncommon.

SEASON: April and May.

WARNING: Poisonous raw, but perfectly safe when cooked!

M. elata

Generally similar to *M. esculenta* but with a pointed cap, which is grey/brown when mature. Most commonly found in forest bark mulch. It, too, must be cooked.

Morchella elata

SPRING FAMOUSLY brings many joys, but few match the sight of a group of Morels basking in the pale April sun. I spent a decade searching out this most thrilling of fungi. Every spring I would scour the New Forest, taking a special interest in the old forest fire sites, which Morels are said to favour, in the hope that this time my efforts would be rewarded. Years later I discovered that there is no record of Morels ever having been found in the New Forest and that I had been wasting my time. Hey ho.

What I did not know is that Morels are urbanites. They have, for the most part, given up their country ways and gone to live the high life in the big city. And so it is that every Morel I have ever found has been in someone's garden – in rose beds, in lawns, on compost heaps, on old Charlie's allotment and, most prolifically, in forest bark mulches. Even when Morels are found in natural locations, it is frequently on disturbed ground (that they like forest fire sites is quite true) and usually in unprepossessing locations.

The Morel you are most likely to find, *M. elata*, is the one that has taken to growing, sometimes in huge numbers, on forest bark mulches in municipal flowerbeds and domestic rose gardens. This species has a way of blending into the background and it can take a while to spot every one. It is not as tasty as *M. esculenta*, but it is still a great treat.

All the hollows and pits in a Morel provide excellent shelter for a variety of bugs, so you may have to spend some time serving eviction notices. On the other hand, their vernal habit means they are mercifully free of maggots.

As is witnessed by the imaginative prices they command in delicatessens, Morels have a very high epicurean standing. I am not too sure how well deserved this is as the flavour is really rather mild, but nevertheless they are strikingly beautiful fungi and it would be a pity not to treat them with some respect. I therefore favour recipes that preserve their good looks, like the one on p.196. However, should you be lucky enough to fill a couple of baskets with Morels, it would be worth drying and crushing a few (p.243). Powdered Morel is a fantastic thing to have in the kitchen as that mild flavour becomes highly intensified and can give a good mushroomy punch to any dish.

It is important to note that Morels are quite poisonous when raw, so, please, absolutely no salads and no lightly tossed stir-fries!

Beware of the False Morel (*Gyromitra esculenta*), p.178. Although it is a related species, the resemblance to real Morels is only superficial – instead of having a honeycomb structure, the cap surface is convoluted. It is fairly uncommon in Britain, but still worth knowing about because it can be deadly.

P.S. The domestic use of forest bark has turned the rather rare *M. elata* into a relatively common fungus, with 90 per cent of British finds occurring since 1985, when forest bark became popular. Why it should be so happy to grow on forest bark in people's gardens but not in forest bark in forests is something of a puzzler. It may be another example of 'stress fruiting', where fungi, running out of food, produce their reproductive organs (mushrooms) on the now-or-never principle. Experiments in Morel cultivation have found that if a single mycelium is grown in a medium half of which is rich in nutrients and half of which is not, then nutrients would be drawn from the rich part to feed Morels that start to grow in the poor part. (Do try to pay attention, there will be a test later.) This is exactly what we have when a nutrient-rich mulch is spread over a nutrient-poor soil. That my best ever find occurred where the mulch was on top of a weed-suppressing membrane of no nutrient value whatsoever seems to support my theory. As for where the spores come from, well, they're everywhere.

Morel

Poisonous Species

Poisonous Species *contents*

As not all fungi have been tested for their toxicity, it is difficult to say how many of the 4,000 or so larger fungi that grow in this country are poisonous. My guess of around the 400 mark would give a random picker a one in ten chance of poisoning themselves. Don't do this. Fortunately, only around 20 are deadly poisonous and of these fewer than half are at all common. Less fortunately, the Death Cap (p.140), which causes a good 90 per cent of all fatalities due to fungal poisoning in Europe, is quite a common fungus. It is a toadstool I see three or four times a year and if you want to go mushrooming you really must learn what it looks like.

There are obviously nothing like 400 species considered here, but some groups (genera) of fungi contain many poisonous members and it is often sufficient to discuss just one of them accompanied by a warning to avoid some or all of its cousins. Nevertheless, if your specimen is not mentioned here this does not mean you can eat it! You must also have *positively* identified it as an edible species. The meanings of the ominous-looking 'X's are clear enough with an 'XXX' reserved for the deadly species.

Fungi can poison people in a whole range of fascinating ways and full and colourful details are provided with the appropriate species. The worst toxins are those that actually damage cells of the body. It is into this category that the Death Cap falls. The 'mildest' are those that simply cause gastrointestinal upset though it may not seem all that mild at the time. In addition, there are some that interfere with body chemistry. Muscarine, for example, stimulates the production of body fluids and coprine prevents the body from dealing effectively with alcohol. Finally, there are the toxins that produce primarily psychological effects, such as the one in the so-called Magic Mushroom (p.167).

In addition to the poisonous species, I have included one or two that, if not actually poisonous, would be unwelcome at the dinner table. The knowledge contained in the following pages is among the hardest earned in human history and we owe a huge debt to the many nameless martyrs who provided it.

Incidentally, I am occasionally asked what is the most deadly of all the fungi. The obvious answer is the Death Cap, but there is another species that has many, many more deaths on its conscience. It is called *Saccharomyces cerevisiae*, better known as brewer's yeast, and it produces a deadly toxin called ethyl alcohol.

Finally, do remember that even the most edible of fungi are poisonous if they have gone bad, so collect only the freshest of specimens and eat them as soon as you can.

Death Cap *Amanita phalloides* xxx

CAP:	5–12cm. Smooth and flatly convex at maturity. Sickly green, darker in the middle (the colour can be washed out in wet weather). Of particular importance for identification are the ***innate fibres*** radiating out from the centre of the cap.
STEM:	7–15cm by 1–2cm. Paler than the cap with an olive/grey mottled appearance. Swollen at the base and sitting in a distinct bag or ***volva.***
RING:	Large and pendulous with grooves on the top.
GILLS:	White, not touching the stem.
FLESH:	Pure white. Smells unpleasant, sickly, rancid.
SPORES:	White.
HABITAT:	It grows, usually in widely spaced groups of half a dozen or so, under oak and beech and in general mixed woods.
FREQUENCY:	Occasional.
SEASON:	Autumn.

I HAVE BEEN rather scathing in this book about using English names for fungi, but if any fungus needs one and deserves the one it gets, it is the Death Cap. A single specimen is quite enough to despatch you into the next world. Untreated, Death Cap poisoning has a 50 to 90 per cent mortality rate, and

Dull green with innate fibres

even with all that modern medicine can do it is fatal in 20 per cent of cases, tragically rising to around 50 per cent with children. It is responsible for 90 per cent of deaths by fungus so if you only ever learn to recognise one toadstool, then let it be this one.

The Death Cap is by no means uncommon; I usually find it three or four times a year, so it is no use just hoping that it won't cross your path. If you spend much of your time mushrooming, then one day you will find one. Death Cap fatalities in Europe and Russia run at a handful every year; in the UK it is around one per decade with just one or two non-fatal cases of poisoning every year. These are tiny percentages but of course if it is you, it is 100 per cent.

Death Cap

It is customary in books on fungi to delight the reader with a gruesome description of the fate awaiting anyone unfortunate enough to consume a Death Cap, and I see no reason to depart from tradition. Here goes. The first symptoms have a relatively long incubation period of around 8 to 12 hours, a characteristic that is important in diagnosis. The symptoms suffered are gastrointestinal in nature, and they consist of abdominal pain, vomiting and cholera-like diarrhoea. The resulting fluid loss can cause lowered blood pressure, accelerated pulse, shock and leg cramps. This lasts for 12 to 24 hours, occasionally longer, and is followed by a period of recovery that also lasts 12 to 24 hours. But all this time the poison, amanitin, has been doing its terrible work and the signs of hepatic failure – pressure-sensitive liver, jaundice, intestinal bleeding and psychological disturbance – become evident, followed, in severe cases, by coma and death.

Loss of liver and kidney function ensures that a little of the poison goes a long way, so it helps to have only eaten a small amount in the first place, though it helps a great deal more not to have eaten any at all. There is no real cure, although high doses of penicillin and silybin (an extract of milk thistle!) have proved to be beneficial. Stomach washes and activated charcoal to remove the toxins from the stomach are employed, as are diuretics and blood treatments, such as haemodialysis. Apart from this, it is a matter of maintaining the body's electrolyte balance, general nursing care and hoping for the best.

I hope I have suitably frightened you about this fungus, but please do not become too paranoid about it; it is quite

Death Cap

False Death Cap

Destroying Angel

safe to handle one as long as you don't lick your fingers, and you must wash your hands before eating anything. Should you decide to collect one, and I am concerned as to why you would wish to do so, remember not to get it anywhere near other fungi – even the shed spores are deadly.

In its most typical form this is one of the easiest of all species to recognise, with several distinct characteristics.

Dingy green caps, white rings on the stem and white bags at the base should all make the mushroom hunter pause for reflection. It is only when the fungus is damaged, very young or appears in its white form (a rare variety) that mistakes can understandably be made. The young 'button' Death Cap, when the whole fungus is covered with a white membrane, is particularly dangerous as it looks just like a button mushroom.

Also beware of other members of the *Amanita* genus, for, apart from *Amanita rubescens* and *A. fulva*, no Amanita should be eaten. Most of them are harmless, but many are rare and difficult to identify. At least one, the completely white Destroying Angel (*Amanita virosa*), is known to be every bit as deadly as the Death Cap. This beautiful whited sepulchre is quite rare in the south, but may be found with greater ease in Scotland.

Just as the edible species seem to have a poisonous or inedible double, the Death Cap has the False Death Cap. This is not poisonous, but the smell of raw potatoes does not inspire. It is distinguished from its evil twin by the smell, the yellow cap and by the 'gutter' around the top of the swollen base in place of the loose bag.

Fool's Funnel *Clitocybe rivulosa* **xx**

CAP:	3–5cm. Flattened to slightly depressed. Cap edge inrolled for a long time. Dirty white with a definite *frosted* look like the icing on a Belgian bun.
STEM:	2–4cm by 0.5–0.8cm. Same colour as the cap, darker with handling.
GILLS:	Slightly decurrent, crowded, whitish to pale ochre.
FLESH:	Thin. Smells faintly mealy.
SPORES:	White.
HABITAT:	Pasture.
FREQUENCY:	Common.
SEASON:	Summer to late autumn.

THIS COMMON toadstool is seriously poisonous, even deadly. It contains high levels of the sweat-inducing toxin muscarine, and has sometimes been called the Sweating Mushroom.

The Fool's Funnel lives in small troops in grass and has the unhelpful habit of sometimes growing near the tasty, edible Fairy Ring Champignon (p.54). Fortunately, it does not look anything like it, although it is the same size. More worrying is its similarity to one of my favourite mushrooms: The Miller (*Clitopilus prunulus*), p.84.

There are several other poisonous little white *Clitocybe* species. They are all more or less funnel-shaped and have decurrent gills.

Fool's Funnel

Fenugreek Milkcap *Lactarius helvus* x

CAP:	6–12cm. Convex then flattened, often with a small central depression. Surface felt-like, later a little scaly, rather a dull greyish brick, later yellowish.
STEM:	5–12cm by 1–3cm. Similar colour to cap.
GILLS:	Pale ochre. *Milk watery*, mild or slightly bitter.
FLESH:	Mild smelling when fresh, but smelling strongly of spicy stock cubes when dry.
SPORES:	Pale cream.
HABITAT:	In damp, mossy birch and pine woods.
FREQUENCY:	Uncommon.
SEASON:	Autumn.

LIKE THEIR cousins the Brittlegills, the Milkcaps can give warning of their poisonous nature by being very hot to the taste. The Woolly Milkcap and the Peppery Milkcap, for example, are unlikely to poison anyone because they are simply too hot to eat. Unfortunately, unlike the Brittlegills, the Milkcaps contain a rogue species that is poisonous even though it is mild in flavour. The poison is of the gastrointestinal variety and will give anyone who eats it an unpleasant few hours.

The Saffron Milkcap and its associates, all of which exude a bright orange milk, are very easily distinguished from the Fenugreek Milkcap, but the other Milkcap in this book – the Oak Milkcap (p.82) – requires more concentration. The most noticeable characteristic of the Fenugreek Milkcap is the strong smell of rather spicy stock cubes in dried or drying specimens. It is also fairly uncommon and found in damp pine and birch woods, not with oak.

Fenugreek Milkcap

The Dapperlings *Lepiota spp.* **xxx**

I will not describe any particular *Lepiota*, but sum up their main features.

CAPS:	Usually 6cm or less, the central patch is surrounded by concentric immovable scales. Umbrella-shaped, often with a central boss.
STEMS:	Often shaggy/fleecy.
RINGS:	Sometimes distinct, sometimes just a vague ring zone.
GILLS:	White and free of the stem.
SPORES:	White.
HABITAT:	Usually in *woods*, occasionally in parks and pasture.
SEASON:	Summer to autumn.

AS AROUND one-quarter of the 40 or so Lepiotas contain the same poison, amanitin, as the Death Cap I have consigned the entire genus to outer darkness. The worst of a bad bunch is the Star Dapperling (*Lepiota helveola*), or possibly it is the Deadly Dapperling (*L. bruneoincarnata*), or maybe the Fatal Dapperling (*L. subincarnata*) which is pictured here. These and others have been implicated in a number of serious poisonings, including the occasional fatality. As the toxin is the same, the succession of symptoms is the same and I refer anyone who wants a good scare to the Death Cap entry (p.140) for the full gory details.

Lepiota species are quite distinctive, but they are still occasionally picked in error. The main concern for the mushroom hunter is their distinct similarity to *Macrolepiota* species, the eminently edible Parasols (p.75). The most straightforward way to avoid

any Lepiota is to ensure that no open Parasol that you pick is less than 12cm in diameter. Most Lepiotas, including all the deadly ones, are less than 7cm in diameter and the only larger one, the rare *L. ignivolvata*, is not poisonous. Also make sure that your Parasols have good large rings that can be slid with reasonable ease up and down the stem. I met someone only recently who had picked and eaten some Dapperlings thinking they were young Parasols. It was a terrible mistake to make. She spent a week desperately ill in bed and was very lucky to survive.

One final consideration is that Dapperlings tend to have warm russet, orange or even pink colours, whereas Parasols are more chestnut in tone.

The other Dapperling pictured here is *L. magnispora*. As far as I know it is harmless, but I include it because it shows so well some of the characteristics of this dangerous genus.

Fatal Dapperling

Lepiota magnispora

Fly Agaric

Fly Agaric *Amanita muscaria* x

CAP:	10–20cm. Bright red and sometimes orange. Covered in pure white, movable spots (the remnants of the veil that covered the young fruit body).
STEM:	8–20cm by 1–2cm. White and faintly fleecy, base swollen and with fleecy bands.
RING:	Simple, pendulous.
GILLS:	White. Not touching the stem.
FLESH:	White.
SPORES:	White.
HABITAT:	Pine and birch.
FREQUENCY:	Very common.
SEASON:	Autumn.

THE FLY AGARIC is the consummate toadstool – beautiful, magical and deadly. Except that it is not deadly and, despite its fearsome reputation, it is not seriously poisonous at all. It does contain trace amounts of muscarine, but it would take about 70kg of Fly Agaric to cause any serious damage, a challenging meal for even the hungriest mushroom hunter. Its fairy tale beauty is in no doubt, however, and neither is its magical quality. The 'magic' comes from a substance called ibotenic acid, which turns into the powerful psycho-active drug muscimol. The symptoms start half an hour to three hours after ingestion and may include nausea and other physical symptoms. The psycho-logical effects are not entirely unlike those caused by an excess of Chablis – including euphoria, difficulty speaking, confusion and sleep. As a bonus, one can look forward to feelings of floating,

exaggerated movements, cramps, tremors and also muscle spasms.

These all sound rather too scary to me, but the Fly Agaric is commonly used as a recreational mushroom and there are some highly colourful reports of its use in north-eastern Asia from the eighteenth and nineteenth centuries. The famous ethnomycologist, Wasson, relates the practices of the robust Koryak people who exchanged reindeer skins for dried Fly Agarics from Russia. The Fly Agarics were scarce and highly prized but 'fortunately' (and I do use the word with considerable hesitation), muscimol is an eminently 'recyclable' compound and is excreted in the urine intact. The revellers would therefore carefully collect their urine and consume it in order to give themselves a 'second go', or maybe a friend (presumably a very close friend) their first. Cheers!

Panther Cap *Amanita pantherina* **XX**

CAP:	7–12cm. Chocolate brown with fine, **white fleecy scales**, fine striations on the edge.
STEM:	6–10cm by 1–2cm. White, swollen base with a distinctly **rimmed volva** like a little flower pot.
RING:	White. **Lacks grooves** on upper surface.
GILLS:	White, not touching the stem.
FLESH:	White.
SPORES:	White.
HABITAT:	Broadleaved woodland.
FREQUENCY:	Fairly uncommon, though locally abundant.
SEASON:	Autumn.

THIS IS THE neatest toadstool you will ever see. Dapper even. But one should never judge a fungus by how good it looks and this is a seriously poisonous species. It contains the same toxins, including the hallucinogenic ones, as its close cousin the Fly Agaric (p.149), but in concentrations that are high enough to cause dangerous physical symptoms in many and even death in someone weakened by heart disease.

The problem with the Panther Cap is two-fold: it is occasionally mistaken for the edible Amanitas and it is known to attract those collecting for purely 'recreational' purposes.

The Panther Cap is the bane of the careless Blusher collector (p.64). The similarity is superficial, but a lapse in concentration could see a Panther Cap finding its way into the mushroom basket. Its distinctly brown cap (which never shows any sign of pink), the white rather than pink/grey spots and the lack of grooves on the upper surface of the ring make differentiation certain, but a systematic check must always be made when picking Blushers.

The most problematic species, at least for those who like to indulge in extreme mushrooming, is the common and reputedly edible Grey Spotted Amanita (*Amanita spissa*). This looks almost *exactly* like the Panther Cap, but can be quickly distinguished by the fact that it *does* have little grooves on the top of the ring. Relying on one small detail is just not enough for me, but if you like the excitement of having your life hanging by a thread, then you could do worse than collect Grey Spotted Amanitas.

The Panther Cap is sometimes gathered for its mind-altering qualities, but as hallucinogenic mushrooms go this is a very poor choice. It is one of the few 'magic' mushrooms that is known to have caused fatalities and, as the active ingredients vary enormously depending on when and where they were picked, the effects are totally unpredictable.

Panther Cap

The Sickener *Russula emetica* x
& Beechwood Sickener *R. nobilis* x

CAP:	4–8cm. Bright red.
STEM:	5–8cm by 1–2cm. White.
GILLS:	White to pale cream, brittle.
FLESH:	White, pink below peeled cap. Very hot and acrid (spit it out!).
SPORES:	White.
HABITAT:	Sickener in coniferous woods, Beechwood Sickener in beech woods!
FREQUENCY:	Common.
SEASON:	Autumn.

THIS PRETTY PAIR is common in coniferous and beech woodlands respectively. No Brittlegill is particularly dangerous, but the intense acridity of many of them, including these two, is too much for most stomachs, which promptly complain in the colourful way they know best. Apparently, and I really don't intend to check this, parboiling can make many, if not all, of the acrid Brittlegills both palatable and safe.

While the safest way to avoid the two Sickeners is to avoid all red Brittlegills, some of them are, in fact, mild in taste and perfectly edible. The Brittlegills are notoriously difficult to identify but the simple test of nibbling a piece and spitting it out if it tastes hot is enough to settle the matter (this *only* works with Brittlegills!). The nineteenth-century Italian mycologist Vittadini is reported by Badham to have, unsportingly, fed them to his dogs and, observing no ill effects, fried up five good specimens and ate them. They were, he says, still acrid and unpleasant to the taste, but he suffered no more than 'praecordial uneasiness' and flatulence. Whatever the first of these is, I doubt if I would like it any more than I would the second.

P.S. The peppery taste of some of the Brittlegills and Milkcaps comes from a group of chemicals called the sesquiterpenes. If you have ever eaten a ginger biscuit, you will have eaten sesquiterpenes before. The flavour of ginger comes from a trio of these compounds – though, oddly, not its pungence.

There is reason to believe that the sesquiterpenes are synthesised chiefly after the fungus has been damaged, as is witnessed by the time it sometimes takes to taste them. It is very likely that they form a defence against attack by insect larvae; a defence that also works well against humans!

Beechwood Sickener

The Beechwood Sickener's pure white gills

Livid Pinkgill & Silky Pinkgill

Livid Pinkgill *Entoloma sinuatum* x x

CAP:	7–15cm. Convex then flattened/wavy. Cream to dirty grey/brown with age. Innate fibres radiating outwards.
STEM:	5–12cm by 1–2.5cm. Fairly cylindrical, sometimes with a swollen base. White, then off-white. Innate fibres run the length of the stem, slightly scaly.
GILLS:	*Pale yellow at first*, then pink as the spores mature.
FLESH:	White and firm, smells mealy.
SPORES:	Pink.
HABITAT:	Broadleaved trees.
FREQUENCY:	Uncommon.
SEASON:	Autumn.

Silky Pinkgill *E. sericeum* x

CAP:	5–7cm. Rounded then flattened, dark brown drying paler, *innate silky fibres*.
STEM:	2.5–6cm by 0.3–0.6cm. Brown, whitish below, fibrous.
GILLS:	Pink. Edge irregular.
FLESH:	Brown, smells mealy.
SPORES:	Pink.
HABITAT:	Pasture.
FREQUENCY:	Common.
SEASON:	Autumn.

THE LIVID PINKGILL is a splendid-looking toadstool that grows in large rings or groups in deciduous woods. Although believed to be responsible for 10 per cent of all poisonings, I cannot imagine which mushroom it is that people mistake it for, unless it is the barely edible Clouded Agaric; perhaps it just looks tasty. It is not clear what toxins it contains, but it does cause serious gastrointestinal symptoms, which include severe stomach cramps. It has also been associated with liver damage that might be fatal. Though again I do not know what one would mistake it for, the Silky Pinkgill is also worth knowing because it can cause vomiting and is a common denizen of fields and meadows.

There are several other Entolomas, but none are worth eating and most are known to be poisonous or are under suspicion. They all have flesh-pink spores that often colour the gills a fainter pink.

Livid Pinkgill

Silky Pinkgill

Deadly Fibrecap *Inocybe erubescens* xxx

CAP:	4–8cm. Conical with a central boss, cream with brown *radial fibres*, **reddening** with age, often *split* at the edge.
STEM:	4–8cm by 1–1.5cm. Slightly darker than cap, reddening, fibrous, slightly swollen at the base.
GILLS:	Buff at first with a white edge, then darker brown as the spores mature, reddening.
FLESH:	White.
SPORES:	Brown.
HABITAT:	Broadleaved trees, usually beech, can stray into neighbouring pastureland.
FREQUENCY:	Rare.
SEASON:	Summer.

I SUPPOSE the archetypal poisonous toadstool must be the Fly Agaric with its bright red cap and white spots (p.149). While it is indeed poisonous, its evil reputation is largely undeserved and comes more from its startling appearance than its actual toxicity. The little-known Deadly Fibrecap, on the other hand, contains no less than 100 times as much of the deadly muscarine as does the Fly Agaric. Furthermore, anyone who eats a Fly Agaric can hardly

Deadly Fibrecap

say they haven't been warned, whereas the Deadly Fibrecap is altogether more subtle in appearance and can fairly easily be mistaken for several of the collectable mushrooms.

Muscarine affects the peripheral nervous system and it produces an interesting range of symptoms of a 'productive' nature including sweating, lacrimation (tears), excessive urination, excessive salivation, vomiting and diarrhoea. It also, more dangerously, slows the heart and constricts the lungs. The effects wear off after an eventful 6 to 24 hours. The good news is that muscarine poisoning is seldom fatal and can be easily treated with atropine, which presents us with an intriguing possibility. Atropine is the deadly toxin found in Belladonna, so *in theory*, if you ate Deadly Fibrecap followed by Deadly Nightshade, you would be fine. Never, ever try this at home!

The chief concern with the Deadly Fibrecap is that when it is young, it is white to cream-coloured and so looks rather similar to a button mushroom. As a consequence, confusion with Field

Lilac Fibrecap

Mushrooms (p.93) and, given its early summer appearance, the St George's Mushroom (p.62), is conceivable. The Deadly Fibrecap does always grow with trees, but a field alongside a wood might well produce them, too. Do not become too alarmed, however. Its similarities with edible species are superficial and the differences profound; it is only the reckless that will succumb.

Also beware of *all* the Fibrecaps, as every one is believed to be poisonous. Apart from the Deadly Fibrecap and the two discussed below, they fall into the 'Little Brown Toadstool' category, and are unlikely to tempt the average mushroom hunter. However, they could be collected in error while gathering small mushrooms like the Trumpet Chanterelles (p.78) or The Deceivers (p.66).

The most common of the Fibrecaps are the White Fibrecap (*I. geophylla*) and the Lilac Fibrecap (*I. geophylla* var. *lilacina*). The latter is bright lilac and could be mistaken for the Amethyst Deceiver (p.66). All of the Fibrecaps have caps made up of fibres radiating out from the centre. Often the cap edges are split. The spore print is snuff brown.

Deadly Webcap & Fool's Webcap

Deadly Webcap *Cortinarius rubellus* **xxx**

CAP: 3–8cm. Conical or convex. Rusty/orange with fine scales.

STEM: 5–12cm by 0.5–1.5cm. Swollen at base. Paler than the cap, covered in a zigzag band of yellowish scales.

GILLS: *Broadly spaced*, rusty yellow.

FLESH: Pale yellow, staining rust in parts. Smells of radish.

SPORES: Rust brown.

HABITAT: Under pine and spruce.

FREQUENCY: Rare. Most commonly found in Scotland.

SEASON: Late summer to autumn.

NOTE: The Fool's Webcap (*C. orellanus*) and other dangerous members of this genus are similar, but the simple rule is to never eat any *Cortinarius* species.

IN 1952 THERE WAS a terrible mass poisoning in Poland. One hundred and two people were poisoned and eleven of them perished. The fungus that had wrought such havoc had undoubtedly caused untold suffering before, but it had evaded suspicion because of the very long delay – two to seventeen days – before its very serious effects became evident. This time it had, as it were, gone too far, and *Cortinarius orellanus*, the Fool's Webcap, was unmasked as a killer.

It is uncommon in Britain, as is the closely related Deadly Webcap, pictured opposite, which is just as dangerous. Some years ago the Deadly Webcap poisoned a trio of young people who were holidaying in Scotland. One of them recovered, but the other two, having suffered irreparable kidney damage, required transplants to restore them to reasonable health. There are one

or two other species, such as *C. gentilis*, in this dangerous group, all of them members of the sub-genus *Leprocybe*.

The toxic syndrome is referred to as 'orellanus syndrome'. It is very similar to the Death Cap's 'phalloidin syndrome', which likewise assaults kidney function. The symptoms, expressed after the very long latent period (which evidently does not encompass any early gastrointestinal disturbance) are appetite loss, thirst, headache, vomiting, diarrhoea and shivering. Total kidney failure may follow and death soon afterwards.

The genus *Cortinarius* is very large and its members notoriously difficult to identify. It contains no fungus of even moderate culinary worth, but it does contain several deadly poisonous ones and a large number that live under a cloud of suspicion. I once managed to eat the Bruising Webcap (*C. purpurascens*), but it was not the most uplifting

Deadly Webcap

experience – the faint but distinctive hydrogen cyanide flavour of bitter almonds is not one to be looked for in a mushroom; I shall not be repeating the experiment. It is worth having nothing to do with any of them.

As a genus, *Cortinarius* is quite easy to recognise as long as you are able to examine a young specimen. Instead of a ring from the stem to the cap edge, there is a web of fibres. This 'cortina', as you can see from the picture of the anonymous specimen pictured to the right, is clearly visible on immature fruit bodies, although spore-stained remnants of it can be seen stuck to the stem or cap edge on the more elderly. The youngsters sport either a white cortina or sometimes a blue cortina, a fact that I find endlessly amusing.

White cortina

Funeral Bell *Galerina marginata* **XXX**

CAP:	2–7cm. Convex. Rusty brown, drying distinctly paler in the middle and/or at the edge. Margin slightly striate.
STEM:	3–9cm by 0.3–0.8cm. Similar colour to the cap or paler, darker below. Smooth.
RING:	Membranous ring.
GILLS:	Reddish brown.
FLESH:	Brown. Smells unpleasant.
SPORES:	Rust brown.
HABITAT:	In troops on dead wood, most often coniferous, but also broadleaved.
FREQUENCY:	Fairly common.
SEASON:	Autumn.

CONSIDERING the common occurrence and extremely poisonous nature of this toadstool, it is surprising that it is made so little of in the popular literature. Indeed, it has been described as being just unpalatable. In the 1960s, the presence of amatoxins in some *Galerina* species was detected and the treacherous character of this genus established. Amatoxins, the same deadly poisons found in the Death Cap, may come in lower concentrations in *G. marginata*, but meal-size portions of 100–150g of the fresh fungus are enough to cause death.

When I first began mushroom hunting I would often come across a species called *Kuehneromyces mutablis*, which was recommended by the few books I possessed as an edible species. I am pleased that it never took my fancy as my books gave no warning that it is almost identical to the Funeral Bell, and the two can only be differentiated by the most careful examination.

Some grassland species of *Galerina* are also poisonous and the downfall of the careless 'recreational' collector. The rule that Little Brown Toadstools should be avoided is a good one.

P.S. If you spend much of your time reading books on mushrooms, you may have come across the names *G. autumnalis* and *G. unicolor*. Now, taxonomists (the people who name living organisms) come in two notoriously argumentative flavours: the 'lumpers' and the 'splitters'. At the moment, the lumpers are ahead of the game and these two toadstools are both now considered to be our *G. marginata*. But there are good reasons for believing that there are three separate species after all and the splitters may yet rule the day. For our simple purposes, however, the situation is straightforward enough – don't eat them. Any of them.

Funeral Bell

Funeral Bell in detail

Poison Pies *Hebeloma spp.* x

I will not describe any particular *Hebeloma*, but sum up their main features.

CAP: Typically 2–7cm but one or two are larger. Convex. Russet to clay brown, sometimes sticky when moist.

STEM: Often swollen at the base, white to cream-coloured, fibrous and often powdery. One or two have a ring.

GILLS: Not touching the stem. Clay brown, white edged. Droplets often form **dark patches** on the gill edge.

FLESH: Pale, sometimes smells of radish or bitter almonds.

SPORES: Rusty brown.

HABITAT: Mixed woodland.

FREQUENCY: Very common.

SEASON: Autumn.

POISON PIE is a nicely appropriate name for these gastrointestinal irritants. Their alternative name, Fairy Cake Mushrooms, is misleading to the point of irresponsibility. They may well be the smelliest of all fungi, with the various odours of radish, aniseed, flowers and chocolate reported.

Common in every type of woodland, often in large troops, their sometimes pale cap and brown gills could lead the unwary forager to mistake them for an ordinary mushroom. The genus *Hebeloma* contains over 70 species, none of which are welcome in the kitchen and most of which look pretty much like the one pictured on the right.

My favourite exception to this impenetrable uniformity is the Rooting Poison Pie, which has a ring on its taprooted stem and smells strongly of aniseed. Its already poor reputation as an edible fungus received a mortal blow when it was discovered where that taproot on the stem usually went: to the underground latrine of a mole.

Bitter Poison Pie

Typical Poison Pies complete with water drops

Brown Roll Rim *Paxillus involutus* **xxx**

CAP:	7–15cm. Generally funnel-shaped and usually with a central umbo at first. A variety of dingy-looking browns, viscid in wet weather. The cap edge is distinctively *rolled under*, except on aged specimens. Cap margin with *broad grooves*.
STEM:	3–7cm by 0.7–1.5cm. Cream-coloured and darker below.
GILLS:	Very decurrent, crowded, brown, bruising reddish. Easily separated from the cap.
FLESH:	Ochre.
SPORES:	Rusty brown.
HABITAT:	Woodland, most often with birch.
FREQUENCY:	Extremely common.
SEASON:	Late summer to autumn.

THE BROWN ROLL RIM is an oddity. While it can poison you in two quite separate ways, one of them occasionally deadly, it is still considered an edible species by some. Eaten raw it causes gastrointestinal disorders, but the guilty toxin can be removed by cooking and no ill effects will be felt. However, after the fungus has been eaten a number of times, another effect can come into play and haemolytic anaemia may occur. This may result in collapse, abdominal pain, vomiting and diarrhoea, along with renal symptoms, such as kidney pain and blood, or to be precise, haemoglobin, in the urine.

The Brown Roll Rim does not poison its victims but rather induces a severe allergy to itself in a process referred to as immunohaemolytic anaemia. Slowly, and largely without symptoms, it forms antigens in the blood serum until one meal too many is taken and catastrophic large-scale destruction of red blood cells occurs. Susceptibility varies from one person to another and the period of grace may stretch over years.

For a long time it was generally considered to be perfectly edible, provided it was prepared carefully – preferably parboiled before cooking, with the water thrown away. Then in 1940, the distinguished German

Deeply decurrent gills

Brown Roll Rim

mycologist Julius Schaeffer, famous for his work on the genus *Russula*, inadvertently contributed more to the body of mycological knowledge than he had ever hoped. After eating a series of dishes of Brown Roll Rim he promptly died and is, as far as I can discover, unique in being the only professional mycologist in history to have died by mushroom poisoning.

In my opinion, this drab and downright disreputable fungus – the ones pictured here are exceptionally neat examples of their kind – usually looks as though it should be helping the police with their enquiries and why anyone would wish to eat it is beyond me. Nevertheless, it is still regularly eaten in Eastern Europe, most notably in Poland, where it is the third most common cause of fungal poisoning.

Since the demise of the unfortunate Julius Schaeffer, a number of further deaths have been attributed to the Brown Roll Rim and, despite occasional and irresponsible attempts at rehabilitation, it is now properly considered to be a deadly species. Nevertheless, I know that people, presumably of East European origin, have taken to collecting it in the UK and it is only a matter of time before disaster strikes.

Magic Mushrooms

Magic Mushroom *Psilocybe semilanceata* x

CAP:	1–1.5cm. Acutely conical with a distinct 'nipple' on the top. Date-brown when young, maturing to a pale lemon, darkening at the cap edge. The cap is covered by a rubbery and peelable membrane.
STEM:	3–8cm by 0.1–0.2cm. Rather wavy.
GILLS:	Deep purple-brown.
SPORES:	Dark brown.
HABITAT:	Short grass in pasture or on heathland.
FREQUENCY:	Common.
SEASON:	Autumn.

THE MAGIC MUSHROOM is a singular fungus in many ways, not least in that it is the only one in this book that it is illegal to pick. If you don't know what it looks like, you *can* pick it legally though since you have seen the picture opposite I'm afraid that this excuse is now closed to you. The law changed in 2005; prior to then it was legal to collect it though not to prepare it. This meant that if you put your collection on a shelf and they dried out of their own accord that was fine, but if you put them on a shelf with the *intention* of drying them out, that became a preparation and wasn't. Now it is considered a class-A drug in any form and its possession or sale is a serious matter.

The 'magic' ingredients are psilocybin and psilocin, the former being the most important. Some 6–20mg, amounting to 12 to 24 specimens, is quite enough to cause intoxication. The effect is similar to that produced by LSD – elation, confusion, paranoia, formication (no not that, for*m*ication, which is

the feeling of having things crawling under your skin), hallucinations and altered perception of space and time. These last for several hours, then wear off completely with no ill effects. Sometimes the experience is not at all a good one and people become locked, for a time, in a very frightening world. There is little evidence that Magic Mushrooms cause long-term damage, but excessive use over several years is unlikely to improve anyone's mental wellbeing.

For people who are determined to pick them, whatever the law says, the chief hazard is the possibility of picking something even worse and poisoning themselves as a result. While I do not wish to encourage dangerous experimentation, I must say that the Magic Mushroom is an extremely easy toadstool to identify. The key characteristics are the transparent rubbery membrane that covers the cap like a piece of cling film and the distinct nipple on the top.

Sulphur Tuft *Hypholoma fasciculare* xx

CAP:	4–7cm. Convex, sulphur yellow with an orange centre. Young specimens can have the remains of the partial veil attached to the edge.
STEM:	4–10cm by 0.5–1cm. Sulphur yellow turning foxy brown at the base.
RING:	Faint ring zone visible, usually dark with spores.
GILLS:	Sulphur-yellow, eventually black as the spores mature. Very crowded.
FLESH:	Yellow. Very bitter.
SPORES:	Purple-brown, almost black.
HABITAT:	Large and dense tufts on all sorts of dead wood.
FREQUENCY:	Extremely common.
SEASON:	Most abundant in the autumn to early winter, but often found earlier.

IT IS A POOR FUNGUS foray that does not encounter at least one group of Sulphur Tufts. This attractive toadstool appears in huge numbers on fallen logs and stumps and it is a great pity that it is not edible. The taste is extremely bitter and it causes quite serious gastrointestinal symptoms. It is highly distinctive and only by abandoning all caution could one pick

Typical sulphur-yellow gills

this species by mistake. Unfortunately, this is just what an Italian restaurateur did quite recently, hospitalising all his customers with his mushroom special.

There have actually been a few fatalities attributed to this toadstool. It is, however, more likely that a mixed 'mushroom' dish containing some other nasty, such as the Funeral Bell (p.160), was responsible. If this is the case the unfortunate victims were worse mushroom hunters than even our Italian restaurateur, having managed to collect and consume not just one but two poisonous toadstools.

There is actually another *Hypholoma* species, the Brick Cap (*H. sublateritium*), which I know is quite a popular edible species but to my mind is too close to its poisonous cousin to be worth the risk. It has a brick-red cap and lacks sulphur-yellow gills.

A troop of Sulphur Tufts

Common Inkcap

Coprinopsis atramentaria **X**

CAP:	8cm high by 4cm wide. Ovoid then expanding to roughly conical. Grey or grey-brown. Striate.
STEM:	5–15cm by 0.8–1.5cm. White.
RING:	Ring-like zone near the base.
GILLS:	Extremely close together, white/grey, then brown to black. Disintegrating at maturity.
SPORES:	Black.
HABITAT:	Pasture, parks and gardens.
FREQUENCY:	Common.
SEASON:	Autumn.

THIS IS THE only fungus in the book that enjoys the dubious honour of a place in both the edible (with the Shaggy Inkcap, p.97) *and* the poisonous sections. This comes about because it is edible, but poisonous if you eat it with alcohol. For sensitive individuals there may even be a reaction from the tiny

Common Inkcap

amount of alcohol absorbed through the use of aftershave or deodorant.

The Common Inkcap's duplicitous personality is due to a substance called coprine, which works its mischief by acting as an acetaldehyde-dehydrogenase inhibitor. This simply means that the liver becomes unable to break down alcohol completely and toxic levels of acetaldehyde build up in the body.

The symptoms are not life threatening. Unusually, for a poison of fungal origin there are no gastrointestinal problems. The chief effects are a feeling of hotness, reddening of the face and other parts of the upper body, tingling in the limbs and sometimes headache, sweating and shortness of breath. Sensitivity to alcohol can last for 72 hours, so you may be on the wagon for a while. As for what it tastes like, I am afraid that during the last 30 years or so my blood/alcohol ratio has not afforded me one single opportunity to find out.

Common Inkcap

Yellow Stainer & Inky Mushroom

Yellow Stainer *Agaricus xanthodermus* xx

CAP:	6–10cm, often flattened in the centre. White, sometimes grey, occasionally cracking, ***strongly yellowing*** when rubbed, notably so at the edge.
STEM:	5–12cm by 1–1.5cm, often ***long*** for the size of the cap. Base often swollen. White, ***bruising an intense yellow***, especially in the ***cut base***.
RING:	Large and complex, also yellowing when pinched.
GILLS:	White or pale in very young specimens (not pink as in the Field Mushroom). Mature specimens turn pink, then dark brown.
FLESH:	White but turns bright ***chromium yellow*** at the base of the stem and under the skin. The yellow ***turns brown*** after a few minutes. Smells unpleasant – carbolic.
SPORES:	Dark brown to black.
HABITAT:	Parkland, meadows, copses.
FREQUENCY:	Occasional.
SEASON:	Summer to autumn.

Inky Mushroom *A. moelleri* xx

CAP:	6–12cm, almost spherical when young, then flatly convex. A white background with grey/brown scales, darker in the centre. ***Strongly yellowing*** when rubbed, particularly at the edge.
STEM:	8–12cm by 1–1.5cm, usually ***long*** for the size of the cap. White, ***bruising an intense yellow***, especially in the ***cut base***.
RING:	Large and pendulous, yellowing when pinched.
GILLS:	White or pale in very young specimens, then pink, then dark brown.
FLESH:	The same as ***A. xanthodermus***.
SPORES:	Dark brown to black.
HABITAT:	Parkland, woods, copses.
FREQUENCY:	Occasional.
SEASON:	Summer to autumn.

Yellow Stainer

Stained cap edge

Inky Mushroom

THE YELLOW STAINER is no killer, but its similarity to Horse, Field and Wood Mushrooms (pp.90, 93 and 99) makes it the single most common cause of mushroom poisoning in Britain. Many people assume that all 'mushrooms' (*Agaricus* species) are edible and pick them without discrimination. A mycological friend of mine was called upon to give his opinion on what turned out to be Yellow Stainers because, as his overly determined enquirer complained, 'they keep making me ill'.

The Yellow Stainer's woodland cousin, the Inky Mushroom (p.172), is quite frequent both in woods and at the roadside and, with its dark scaly cap, is sometimes mistaken for a Blushing Wood Mushroom (p.99).

Unfortunately, the Yellow Stainer is a very variable species that delights in appearing in many forms. It frequently foxes even the most experienced mushroom hunter who may have admired his or her fine collection of mushrooms for a minute or two before realising their mistake. Sometimes it is pure white, sometimes grey/brown. There are smooth ones and scaly ones, long-stemmed and short-stemmed. The violent colour change is your most reliable guide, though even then you must examine the effect on a fresh young specimen. It is worth noting that the chromium yellow seen in the Yellow Stainer fades to brown after a few minutes, whereas the yellow bruising seen in the edible *Agaricus* species is paler and persistent.

The other excellent identification point is the smell of Elastoplasts. If you miss it when you pick them, the smell gets even worse during cooking and provides you with a final warning!

Yellow Stainers contain a cocktail of unpleasant chemicals, but the main toxic constituent appears to be phenol. Phenol is rare in nature and is a very nasty poison indeed. In the Yellow Stainer, concentrations are quite low, so only 'mild' gastrointestinal symptoms occur and the unfortunate sufferer is at least spared the neurologic, cardiovascular and renal depredations that result from greater exposure. I doubt, however, that the average victim of this impostor would agree with the use of the word 'mild'. I have met people who have been very ill indeed for 24 hours – and that's 24 hours, apparently, of sitting in a small room clutching a bucket. Some people, however, suffer only mildly and others still say they can eat it with impunity. One authority suggests that the phenol is largely created during cooking, which would make it an exception to our rule that wild mushrooms should be cooked first. The possibility that they would be fine in salads is not something I have any intention of checking.

I was brought some rather elderly specimens once by someone who had managed to poison his entire family. They looked rather unusual and turned out to be the closely related but extremely rare *A. pilatianus*. When I informed him that he had poisoned everyone with one of Britain's rarest mushrooms he was thrilled.

Bitter Bolete *Tylopilus felleus*

CAP:	8–12cm. Beige to brown, *suede-like* at first.
STEM:	7–10cm by 4–6cm. Usually swollen at the base. Ochre, paler at the top, covered in a *brown* net.
TUBES:	White at first, then distinctly *pale pink*.
FLESH:	Whitish, unchanging, *intensely bitter*.
HABITAT:	Under broadleaved and coniferous trees.
FREQUENCY:	Occasional.
SEASON:	Late summer to autumn.

ALTHOUGH THIS toadstool is not poisonous, it is well worth getting to know because of the devastation it will inflict on any dish into which it finds its way. As bitter as gall, this charlatan looks very much like the Cep (p.102) and has ruined many a meal; just one, or even a quarter of one, will make an entire dish quite impossible to eat. It imitates the Cep in size, in shape and to some extent even colour. Yet it is on colour differences that we must rely to identify it.

The cap is a duller brown than the Cep; the tubes and pores are pale pink in mature specimens but, unfortunately, whitish in young ones, just like the Cep; the stem is ochre in colour, pale at the apex and covered in a *brown* net. Of course, if you are still not sure, you can always nibble a bit, then you will be left in no doubt at all.

Bitter Bolete

Devil's Bolete

Devil's Bolete *Boletus satanas* xx

CAP:	15–25cm, convex, dingy white.
STEM:	7–10cm by 5–10cm. Very swollen at the base. Bright yellow at the top, ochre at the base, blood red in the middle and covered with a red net.
TUBES:	Dark yellow/green, pores small and blood red, more orange at the margin.
FLESH:	White, yellow in places, slowly turning *light blue*. Smells strongly of rotting flesh.
HABITAT:	Under beech and oak on chalky soils.
FREQUENCY:	Very rare.
SEASON:	Summer.

THE DEVIL'S BOLETE is rare enough to be on a Red Data List, so it is not likely to prove a frequent hazard to the mushroom hunter. Of course, should anyone actually manage to find and eat this endangered species, both dinner and diner would be that much the poorer.

It is very distinctive in appearance and mature specimens are reputed to smell sufficiently of rotting meat to take one's breath away if they have been kept in a box. Despite its portentous name, the Devil's Bolete is unlikely to cause anything more than severe gastrointestinal distress though, like many fungi, it is more poisonous raw.

While there are several other Boletes that look at least a bit like it, none of them are considered edible and confusion with these species is not an issue. The only Bolete I recommend that has any red on it – the Scarletina Bolete (p.110) – is distinctive in having a brown velvet cap and yellow flesh that goes violently blue on cutting. The Devil's Bolete is probably the toadstool that, in the nineteenth century, gave other bluing Boletes a mostly undeserved bad name. The blue reaction is 'simply' due to the enzymatic oxidation of yellow pigments.

For any organism, getting your name on a Red Data List is a sure-fire way of becoming relatively common – naturalists suddenly take an interest in your wellbeing and start finding you everywhere. Whereas the Devil's Bolete was once only known from two or three sites, it has now been recorded in over 30. Recently there was a find of around 250 fruit bodies in a single location; as with so many things they may be rare but if they find a spot they like, they can grow like weeds. The Devil's Bolete is still only really known from southern England, where it grows in open, sunny and south-facing locations, usually under beech, less often under oak.

False Morel *Gyromitra esculenta* XXX

CAP:	7–12cm. Irregularly rounded with brain-like convolutions. Yellow/brown to reddish brown.
STEM:	Up to 5cm long. Irregular, whitish to flesh-coloured.
HABITAT:	In sandy soil under pines.
FREQUENCY:	Uncommon.
SEASON:	March to April.

THIS IS THE PUFFER FISH of the fungal world. Raw or poorly prepared it is deadly, yet with proper treatment it is, by all accounts, delicious. I cannot corroborate this as I have not tried it, and eating a dish of False Morels is not on my to-do list. Here is why.

Although the poisonous agent is quite different to that in the Death Cap (p.140), the symptoms are similar and follow the same protracted path. There is a latent period of 6 to 12 hours, after which an unpleasant two- to six- day gastrointestinal phase begins, sometimes accompanied by psychological disturbances. After this there is likely to be a period of recovery, but by this time liver damage and sometimes haemolysis (destruction of the red blood cells) has occurred. In very serious cases, delirium, coma and death from circulatory or respiratory collapse follow within two or three days. Mortality is around 14 per cent.

There is considerable variation in people's susceptibility to the toxin, as is demonstrated by one well-documented incident in which four people out of a family of six suffered no symptoms while the other two were taken ill, one of whom died. This variable immunity is thought to be due to an inherited ability to metabolise the poison. The chemistry of the toxin involved in False Morel poisoning is horribly complicated but, simply put, the acid in people's stomachs reacts with gyromitrin to produce monomethyl-hydrazine, better known as rocket fuel.

Despite this, large quantities of False Morel are collected each year in Europe, though the sale of fresh specimens is banned in several countries.

The treatment I mentioned earlier is simply a matter of boiling it twice and discarding the water each time, although this is not without hazard as the kitchen can become filled with rocket fuel vapour. Drying them first (p.243) also renders them safe. If you really, really want to try the False Morel, you can buy it in tins in delicatessens.

Assuming you are not going to collect False Morels intentionally, they are still worth knowing about because of their similarity to, obviously enough, real Morels (p.133). Morels have a honeycomb structure whereas False Morels have convolutions, like a loosely screwed-up piece of brown paper.

False Morel

Recipes

When it comes to wild mushrooms I must confess to being
rather a lazy cook or, at least, not a terribly adventurous one. A gentle sautéing is all I usually bother with; at most I might add those old familiars – garlic and cream.

I do not think that there is anything wrong with this light approach. It is, after all, one of the most delicious ways to cook mushrooms, especially if you are trying a new, unfamiliar species and you want to experience its flavour as fully as possible, unchallenged by other ingredients.

Yet now I have learned that a good mushroom dish is not a matter of pointless elaboration but rather a way of enhancing and exploiting the qualities of a particular mushroom. It was Hugh and River Cottage that converted me. I had always had trouble with Parasols. Sautéed they can become soggy or tough. Then one day Hugh presented me with Deep-fried Parasols with garlic mayonnaise (p.236) and my moment of revelation had come.

Nevertheless, a great many of the recipes that follow still rely on a base of simply sautéed mushrooms – so it really pays to get that method just right. Fried mushrooms can be very disappointing if they're not done properly. Heart-breakingly disappointing.

While there are a few notable exceptions, mushrooms contain an awful lot of water. The moment they arrive in the frying pan this water is released and unless you like boiled mushrooms (and you really don't), it has to be removed – not by wastefully discarding it, but by evaporation. The juices soon reduce to a delicious glaze and the whole is then caramelised in the oil and butter. The basic mushroom-sautéing method is outlined in the first recipe of this section (p.184), but here is a fuller explanation of the principles behind it.

- Using a roughly half-and-half mixture of oil and butter for frying is a good idea. Butter gives an incomparable flavour but can burn easily. The oil will stop this and, if you use a decent olive oil, contribute some savoury flavour of its own. (Don't use a cold pressed oil though, as this also burns at a low temperature.)
- The bigger your pan, the more easily and quickly liquid will evaporate from it, so go for a large frying pan if you can. If you only have a small one or if you have a lot of mushrooms, cook them in batches. You don't want the uncooked mushrooms to form a layer more than one mushroom deep in your pan.
- Once you've added the mushrooms to a hot pan, throw in some salt and pepper too. Mushrooms need salt more than any other food and are quite forlorn without it.
- Use a medium heat to start with so that the water is released without burning the mushrooms, then increase it as the water starts to bubble.

- Keep cooking, stirring occasionally, until all the released moisture has evaporated, by which time the mushrooms are likely to have shrunk considerably. Continue until the mushrooms start to develop golden-brown patches. You now have a panful of mushrooms, ready to eat.

I should add that the amount of water contained by different types of mushroom – and even by the same types on different days – varies considerably, which means it is impossible to give precise cooking times. With very moist fungi, such as the Bay Bolete, it is sometimes worth removing the mushrooms from the pan for a few minutes and reducing the liquid on its own for a while to avoid overcooking. In contrast, with dry and firm fungi like Hedgehog Mushrooms and Chicken of the Woods, it can actually make sense to add a little water to extend the cooking time so the mushrooms don't brown or dry out on the outside before they are tender in the middle.

None of these details should obscure the fact that mushrooms are really very forgiving ingredients. Unlike fish and the finer cuts of meat, you do not need a thermometer and a stopwatch to get things just right, and while mushrooms should not be cooked to death it does little damage to leave them in the pan for a few minutes longer than originally intended. Some of the firmer mushrooms, like the Cep, need more cooking than their more delicate brethren – about ten minutes should do it – while others, such as the tiny Fairy Ring Champignon, can be ready in just two.

Another thing you can be pretty relaxed about is the actual choice of fungi for a given recipe. Nearly all the recipes here can be prepared with nearly any type of mushroom – which is fortunate if you're gathering your own as foraging strictly to order is a rare talent. There are exceptions, of course: Parasols and Puffballs would be poor ingredients for any type of stew, for instance, and the slippery Wood Blewit is unsuited to deep-frying. Notes at the beginning of each recipe indicate which mushrooms are likely to be most or least successful, but don't be afraid to experiment and improvise. The ideas that follow have certainly helped me expand my mushroom-cooking repertoire and plain old mushrooms on toast is now a thing of the past. Well, almost.

The recipes in this book have been a great joint effort by the River Cottage team. I cannot remember how each one came into being; a good number, of course, are Hugh's, some were created or donated by Gill and Dan, the resident River Cottage chefs, and some were suggested by Nikki and Helen on our editorial team. A few seemed to appear from nowhere at the last minute inspired by the fungi we had to hand. I had minimal involvement except in one important respect. When the recipes were tested and photographed I tasted all the finished dishes. Well somebody had to do it.

Fried mushrooms on toast

This is the simplest recipe in the book, but may well be the one you turn to most often. You're unlikely to meet a mushroom that doesn't respond well to this treatment so, if in doubt, get the frying pan out. The quantities here are for one, but, of course, you can easily scale the recipe up. If you're frying large quantities of mushrooms, it's best to do them in batches, or it will take ages for the liquid they release to evaporate.

Works with: just about anything.

Serves 1

150–200g wild mushrooms
 – either one variety or a mixture
1 tbsp olive oil
A knob of butter
1 small garlic clove, peeled and
 finely chopped

Salt and freshly ground pepper
Thick slice sourdough, granary or
 other good bread
1 tsp chopped flat leaf parsley
A squeeze of lemon juice (optional)

Clean and trim the mushrooms. Leave small ones whole, but cut any that are larger than a walnut into slices or chunks.

Heat the olive oil and butter in a frying pan over a medium heat, add the garlic and let it sweat for a minute or so, without colouring. Add the mushrooms and some seasoning. As they begin to release their juices, increase the heat under the pan so the liquid bubbles away. Keep cooking, stirring frequently, until the mushrooms are soft, all the liquid has evaporated and the mushrooms are starting to colour – how long this takes depends very much on the type of mushroom you're using.

While the mushrooms cook, toast and butter your bread. When the mushrooms are done to your liking, stir in the parsley and, if you like, a squeeze of lemon juice. Taste and adjust the seasoning, then pile onto your hot toast and eat straight away.

Scrambled eggs
with shaved Truffles

Should you find yourself in possession of a Summer Truffle, treat it with enormous respect. Use it with restraint, in only the simplest recipes, and with only the finest ingredients to partner it. To make your black jewel go as far as possible, begin by putting it in an airtight box with a few eggs and leaving it for a day or two so that its perfume subtly infuses them. You can then use a little of the Truffle for this recipe, and a little more, perhaps, for the Roast chicken with Truffles (p.241).

You probably don't need a recipe for scrambled eggs – everyone has their own favourite method – but here's a quick run-down anyway.

Serves 2
4 eggs
Salt and freshly ground black pepper
A large knob of butter
A few shavings of Truffle

Break the eggs into a bowl or jug. Season with salt and freshly ground black pepper and beat lightly with a fork. Heat a saucepan over a low heat and add a large knob of butter. When the butter is foaming, add the eggs. Stir gently, keeping the heat very low, as the egg cooks. The slower you cook the egg, the creamier and richer it will be. When the egg is nearly all set, with just the merest film of wetness still visible in places, remove from the heat. Give it another stir, then heap on to hot, buttered toast. Shave some of your Truffle very finely using a special Truffle shaver, or a mandoline, or cut it into slivers with a very sharp knife. Scatter over the eggs and serve immediately.

Salad of raw mushrooms

There are few fungi that are safe to eat raw, so this is a dish to make with the most flawless, freshly picked specimens of just a few species. Like all very simple dishes, it demands the very best ingredients so, as well as perfect mushrooms, you need a really good, peppery extra virgin olive oil, some dewy fresh herbs and perhaps a sliver or two of a fine aged Parmesan or Cheddar. An alternative to a top-notch olive oil would be a simple, slightly mustardy vinaigrette – and this would be a good option if you want to serve the mushrooms with a green salad.

Works with: Ceps, Field Mushrooms, Horse Mushrooms, Brittlegills.

Serves 2 as a starter

200g flawless, very fresh mushrooms
2 tsp very finely chopped herbs –
    flat leaf parsley, chives, chervil or
    wild sorrel would be good
Extra virgin olive oil
Flaky salt and freshly ground
    black pepper
A few shavings Parmesan or top
    notch Cheddar (optional)

For the vinaigrette (optional)
2 tbsp olive oil
2 tbsp sunflower oil
1 tbsp white wine
    or cider vinegar
½ tsp Dijon mustard
A pinch of sugar
Salt and freshly ground black pepper

If you want to use the vinaigrette, make it first by simply whisking together all the ingredients.

Clean and trim the mushrooms and slice them very thinly. Arrange them, overlapping the slices slightly, on two plates. Scatter on the herbs, trickle on the olive oil (or the vinaigrette, if you're using it), then sprinkle with a little flaky salt and black pepper. Add the Parmesan or Cheddar, if you like, then serve the mushrooms straight away.

Wild mushroom omelette

Any kind of mushroom can be used in an omelette and will taste delicious, but the more delicately textured varieties, such as Chanterelles, give particularly elegant results. This recipe enriches the eggs for the omelette with a good shot of melted butter, but this isn't essential.

Works with: pretty much any mushroom – large or meaty ones should be sliced first.

Serves 1 hungry forager, or 2 for lunch with bread and a salad
100g mushrooms
50g butter
Salt and freshly ground pepper
4 eggs
2 tsp chopped parsley

Clean and trim the mushrooms and cut into smallish pieces.

Set an omelette pan, or another good, non-stick pan, around 25cm in diameter, over a medium heat. Add about one-third of the butter. When it's foaming, add the mushrooms, with some seasoning. Sauté for 4–5 minutes or until all the liquid the mushrooms release has evaporated and they are starting to colour in the butter. Transfer them to a warm plate and set aside somewhere warm.

Beat together the eggs lightly, along with some seasoning. Melt the remaining butter in the mushroom pan over a medium heat, then pour most of it out of the pan and into the beaten eggs. Whisk it in lightly. (If you don't want to do this, just use a small knob of butter to grease the pan.)

Pour the eggs into the hot pan. As they cook, move the mixture around with a spatula or fork, pulling cooked egg up from the bottom of the pan and allowing runny egg to come into contact with the heat. Tip and tilt the pan a little at the same time. When the omelette is just set, but still slightly runny on top, pile the mushrooms on to one half of it. Scatter on the parsley. Remove the pan from the heat. Flip the un-mushroomed side of the omelette over onto the mushroomed side, and slip the whole thing out on to a warmed plate. Serve straight away, just as it is, or with a green salad to follow.

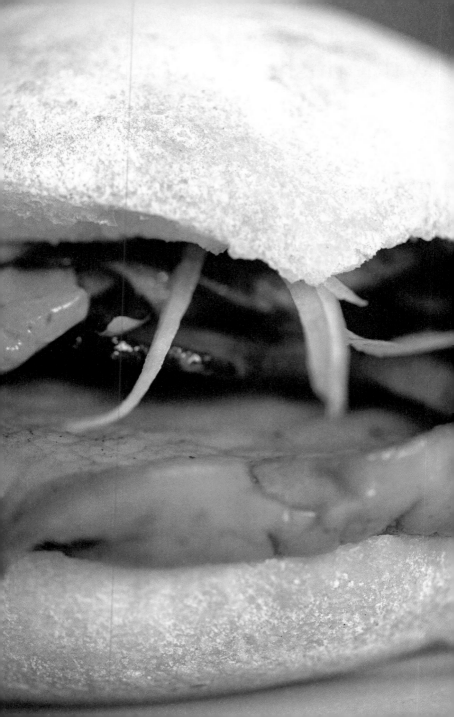

The Puffburger

This is an incredibly satisfying bit of fast food. You could make it with large, flat Field Mushrooms or something similar but, to be honest, it would be quite a different dish. The dense, savoury flesh of a Puffball, enhanced by being fried in bacon fat, is uniquely delicious.

Serves 2

1 tbsp oil or lard
4 rashers streaky bacon
4 slices Puffball, skin removed and cut into slices about 2cm thick, trimmed to roughly the same size as the baps
Salt and freshly ground black pepper

2 good soft baps
A few salad leaves – dressed, if you like, with a little vinaigrette (combine 3 tbsp olive oil with 1 tbsp wine, sherry or cider vinegar and season with salt, pepper and a pinch of sugar)

Put a frying pan over a medium heat, add the fat, then add the bacon and cook until it is as crisp as you like it. Remove the bacon and keep it warm. Add the slices of Puffball then turn them over immediately, to stop the first side absorbing all the fat, and fry for about 3 minutes, until golden. Flip them over again and fry the other side for the same amount of time. Season the Puffball. Cut open the baps, add two slices of bacon to each, then some of the dressed leaves, then a couple of slices of Puffball. (Some have been known to add ketchup at this stage.) Close the baps and serve straight away.

Asparagus
with St George's Mushrooms

The late spring discovery of a few creamy white St George's Mushrooms should be a cause for great celebration, as they are excellent, firm-textured fungi. As luck would have it, their appearance tends to coincide perfectly with the beginning of the British asparagus season. Combining these two delicious, highly seasonal ingredients in a very simple dish is an awfully good idea.

Also works with: the only other fungi you're likely to find during asparagus season are Morels and the occasional Horse Mushroom, both of which could be used in this dish.

Serves 2 as a light lunch
About 200g St George's Mushrooms
Salt and freshly ground black pepper
12 asparagus spears, trimmed
1 tbsp olive oil
50g butter

Clean, trim and halve the mushrooms (or quarter them if they're large).

Bring a saucepan of water to the boil, add a little salt, throw in the asparagus and cook for 3–4 minutes, until just tender, then drain them. Alternatively, you can steam the spears.

Heat the olive oil in a frying pan over a medium heat, add the mushrooms and sauté gently until they are tender and the liquid they release has evaporated. St George's Mushrooms need a fair bit of cooking and don't contain that much water, so keep the heat low to avoid drying them out before they're cooked through. Add the steamed asparagus spears to the mushroom pan, along with the butter. Season with salt and pepper, toss around once or twice, then transfer to warmed plates and serve at once, with bread and butter. A crusty white roll is rather good.

Steak, mushroom
& blue cheese sandwich

A good sandwich is no mere stopgap but something to marvel at before devouring in a cutlery-free frenzy. This is one for the real sarnie enthusiast because it does involve a little cooking, but it's worth the effort. Of course, it will be very special if you've gathered the mushrooms from the wild, but cultivated Portbells or other open-capped mushrooms will be fine. Don't stint on the steak. Some thin-cut sirloin, rib-eye or rump, with a decent bit of marbling, is essential to do the other ingredients justice. If blue cheese is not your thing, goat's cheese, Gruyère, Cheddar – or no cheese at all – work well.

Works with: any firm, meaty mushroom.

Serves 1 (amply)

A good handful of mushrooms
1 small baguette, or half a large one
1 tbsp olive oil
Salt and freshly ground black pepper
225g sirloin, rib or rump steak,
   about 1cm thick

Cold unsalted butter
1 tsp thyme leaves
100g mature blue cheese, such as
   Dorset Blue Vinney, Gorgonzola or
   dolcelatte, thickly sliced

Trim and clean the mushrooms, and slice them thickly if they are sizeable specimens.

Put the bread to warm in a low oven (or use a just-baked baguette that's still warm). Meanwhile, set a large frying pan over a high heat. When it's really hot, add the oil. Season the steak, put it in the pan and fry for about 20 seconds each side, if you like it rare, or more if you like it medium.

Remove the steak from the pan and leave it in a warm place to rest. Reduce the heat under the pan, add a little butter and then the mushrooms, some seasoning and the thyme. Sauté until all the liquid the mushrooms release has evaporated and they are starting to take a bit of colour.

Remove the bread from the oven. Open it up, butter thickly and then lay on the steak. Spoon over the mushrooms and any juices left in the pan, then finish with the blue cheese. Press the sandwich together firmly with the palms of your hands and dig in. This is particularly good with a pint of Guinness.

Oyster Mushrooms
with lemon & thyme

This is so simple, but incredibly tasty, the mushroom juices and butter making a lovely rich sauce. The mushrooms are delicious served on their own, just piled on hot toast, but also make a very good partner to some simply grilled fish or chicken. Alternatively, try them with a lemon zest mash. To make this, just boil some floury potatoes and mash them with a little warm milk and melted butter, a couple of tablespoons of extra virgin olive oil and the grated zest of a lemon.

Also works with: pretty much anything, except Puffballs.

Serves 2
150–200g Oyster Mushrooms
50g butter
Salt and freshly ground black pepper
2–3 tsp roughly chopped thyme
Juice of 1 lemon

Clean and trim the mushrooms. If they're large, tear them into pieces. Otherwise leave them whole.

Melt half the butter in a large saucepan over a medium–high heat. When foaming, add the mushrooms, season with salt and fry them briskly, being careful not to burn the butter. When the mushrooms are soft and golden, throw in the thyme, the lemon juice and plenty of black pepper. Add the rest of the butter and, as soon as it has melted, the mushrooms are ready to serve, piping hot.

Chicken breast
with Morels, marsala & cream

The average *Morchella esculenta* (the finest of the Morels) is the size of a small fist, so you'd only need a few for this dish, and they would have to be cut into several pieces. If you're using bought, dried Morels, which are likely to be a different species and imported from the Continent, they'll be much smaller.

Serves 2

150–200g Morels
2 tbsp olive oil
2 boneless, skin-on chicken breasts
Salt and freshly ground black pepper
A knob of butter

1 small onion, peeled and finely
   chopped
2–3 tbsp marsala
200ml chicken stock
150ml double cream

For fresh Morels, clean and trim them, and cut into halves or quarters. For dried ones, put them to soak in the chicken stock (heated up). Give them 20 minutes or so, then strain, reserving the stock. Preheat the oven to 180°C/Gas Mark 4.

Add the olive oil to an ovenproof pan, large enough to take both chicken breasts comfortably. Place on a medium–high heat. Season the chicken all over with salt and pepper. When the pan is hot, add the chicken, skin down, and fry for a minute or so. Flip the breasts, cook for another minute, then flip skin-side down again and put in the oven for about 10 minutes, until about three-quarters cooked. Return the pan to the hob on a low heat, and transfer the chicken to a warmed plate.

Add the butter and onion to the pan. Fry gently for 5 minutes, until the onion starts to soften. Turn up the heat to medium and add the Morels. Fry for another few minutes, until the Morels are just about cooked, then add the marsala, then the stock, and boil until the liquid has reduced by half. Add the cream, then return the chicken to the pan, skin-side up, and simmer for a few minutes until the chicken is just firm when pressed and the sauce is reduced and thickened. If the sauce looks right and the chicken is not cooked, add a little more liquid and keep simmering. If the chicken is cooked and the sauce a little loose, remove the chicken and simmer the sauce until ready.

For an extra-special finish, turn the chicken a few times in the sauce and put it, skin-side up, under a hot grill to create a rich glaze. Serve with sautéed potatoes and wilted spinach or steamed broccoli.

Venison
with Fairy Ring Champignons

The slightly nutty flavour of Fairy Ring Champignons works brilliantly in this dish. They certainly give Chanterelles (for which this recipe was originally devised) a run for their money.

Also works with: Chanterelles, Hedgehog Mushrooms, Deceivers and Winter Chanterelles (generally found in November, just in time for the venison season).

Serves 4

A few handfuls of Fairy Ring
   Champignons
10 peppercorns
2 bay leaves
4 juniper berries
2 pinches flaky sea salt
500g piece of trimmed venison loin

1 tbsp olive oil
100g unsmoked bacon or
   pancetta, diced
1 tbsp white wine (optional)
25g butter
Salt and freshly ground black pepper
1 tbsp chopped parsley

Preheat the oven to 200°C/Gas Mark 6.

Clean and trim the mushrooms. Put the peppercorns, bay leaves, juniper berries and sea salt in a coffee grinder or spice mill. Grind to a fine powder and scatter over the whole venison loin and rub it in lightly. Heat a medium-sized, ovenproof frying pan over a high heat, and add the olive oil. When it's hot, add the venison. Sear it, turning it so each surface gets a chance to meet the heat, until well browned on all sides. Transfer the pan to the oven and cook for 10 minutes.

Remove the meat from the pan and set aside on a plate to rest for 20 minutes. This is important, as it allows the juices in the meat to settle, making it more tender and juicy when you come to carve it. It also gives you time to cook the mushrooms.

Put the pan back over a medium heat. Throw in the bacon and cook until it just starts to crisp. Add the prepared mushrooms, toss them well with the bacon, and cook for 2–3 minutes, or until tender. Add a little wine if you like, but really only a splash – and let it bubble away to almost nothing. Add the butter to the pan and stir it in to the mushrooms as it melts. Season to taste and sprinkle over the parsley.

Spoon the mushrooms and bacon onto four warmed plates. Slice the venison and arrange alongside the mushrooms and serve with a mixed green salad.

Palourdes
with Chanterelles

Here's a recipe that you'll also find in *The River Cottage Fish Book*, on the basis that mycophiles deserve to know about it just as much as piscophiles.

Little palourde clams – or cockles, which would work just as well here – can be gathered at any time during the Chanterelle season (from August right up to late autumn, depending on where you are and what the weather's doing). This dish is a lovely, simple combination of those two delicious wild ingredients and incredibly quick to put together.

Serves 1–2

About 200g fresh Chanterelles
1 garlic clove, peeled and
    finely chopped
2 knobs of butter
2 tbsp white wine

24 palourde clams, purged by
    being left in a bucket of
    cold fresh water overnight
Freshly ground black pepper

Clean and trim the Chanterelles. If they are really big, cut them in half or quarters.

Put the garlic and a knob of butter in a lidded wide pan over a medium heat. When it's sizzled for a minute, add the wine. When the wine is bubbling, add the palourdes and cover the pan. Let them steam for 2–3 minutes, or until almost all the shells are open. Remove them from the pan and pick the meat from inside the shells, making sure you collect any juice from the shells as you go, returning it to the pan. Return to the heat and boil the liquid until it's reduced to about 1 tablespoon.

Heat a clean frying pan over a medium heat. Add another knob of butter and allow it to bubble, then throw in the Chanterelles. Sauté gently for 2–3 minutes, just until they soften, then add the palourde clams and toss them together with the mushrooms. Add the reduced palourde liquor and season with pepper – salt won't be necessary. Serve straight away, on a warmed plate, with bread and butter.

Warm salad of roast squash
& fried mushrooms

A more elegant and satisfying autumn dish you could not wish for. There are few mushrooms that wouldn't work well here.

Works with: almost anything.

Serves 2 as a light lunch, or 4 as a starter

½–1 medium squash (about 1kg) –
   butternut or Crown Prince is ideal
12 sage leaves, roughly bruised
4 garlic cloves, peeled and
   thickly sliced
150ml olive oil, plus 1 tbsp
Salt and freshly ground black pepper
250g mushrooms
50g butter
A small bunch of wild rocket

200g softish blue cheese such as
   Cashel Blue or Oxford Blue,
   cut into chunks

For the vinaigrette
3 tbsp olive oil
1 tbsp wine, sherry or cider vinegar
Salt, freshly ground black pepper
   and a pinch of sugar

Preheat the oven to 200°C/Gas Mark 6.

Peel and deseed the squash and cut into 2.5cm chunks. Put these in a roasting tin with the bruised sage leaves, the garlic, 150ml olive oil and a generous seasoning of salt and pepper. Roast the squash for 35–45 minutes, stirring once or twice, or until soft and coloured at the edges. Leave until warm but not cold.

Meanwhile, clean, trim and slice the mushrooms. Whisk together the ingredients for the vinaigrette.

Put 1 tablespoon olive oil and the butter in a large frying pan over a medium heat. Add the mushrooms, season lightly with salt and pepper, and sauté for 4–5 minutes or until the liquid they release has evaporated and they're starting to turn golden. Leave to cool slightly but not completely.

The salad should be 'tiede' or warm room temperature, definitely not fridge cold, or even larder cold. In a large mixing bowl, gently combine the cooked squash, mushrooms, rocket and cheese. Lightly dress with the vinaigrette. Toss this all together and serve.

Mushroom pâté

If you think mushroom pâtés are always going to be a disappointment, then you've been eating the wrong ones. This very simple, deliciously garlicky version is based on a recipe from Julie Davies, of Crai Organics, who developed it using the organic Shiitakes she cultivates. It works just as well with other mushrooms, fresh, dried, wild or cultivated. If you have any of the pâté left over, try stirring it into a little hot béchamel sauce or some cream to make a delicious mushroom sauce.

Serves 10–12 as a canapé
250g mushrooms
30g butter
3–4 garlic cloves, peeled and
   finely chopped

250g cream cheese
Salt and freshly ground black pepper

Clean and trim the mushrooms and chop them finely.

Heat the butter in a large frying pan over a medium heat. Drop in the mushrooms and garlic and sauté, stirring frequently, for 10 minutes, or until all the moisture the mushrooms release has evaporated. Leave to cool for a few minutes.

Blitz the mushrooms in a food processor until smooth, then add the cream cheese and blitz again until well blended. Season to taste then leave to cool completely. Refrigerate for at least an hour for the garlic flavour to develop. Serve in generous dollops on crostini, or triangles of toast. This pâté keeps very well in the fridge for up to a week.

Mushroom soup

Mushroom soup should not be an also-ran, a repository for a haul of past-it, second-rate fungi that you wouldn't otherwise eat. However, it is actually a very good way of using mushrooms that don't look perfect, especially since these are often more mature specimens, which have lots of flavour. This particular soup is very smooth and creamy, but finished with a few whole, sautéed mushrooms. This gives a nice bit of texture as well as some individual mushroom flavours.

Works with: anything.

Serves 4–6

About 500g mushrooms –
    mixed or all of one type
35g butter
2 tbsp olive oil
1 leek, trimmed and sliced
1 small potato, peeled and diced
1 large onion, peeled and chopped

2 garlic cloves, peeled and chopped
1 tsp thyme leaves
Salt and freshly ground black pepper
1 litre mushroom stock, or vegetable
    or chicken stock, or a combination
100ml double cream
1 tbsp chopped parsley

Clean the mushrooms in the normal way, but don't be too fastidious about the trimming. As long as the stalks are clean and grit-free, they can go in to the mix. The same goes for slightly damaged or broken caps. Set aside 100g of the most aesthetically pleasing fungi to finish the soup with, and roughly chop the rest.

Put a large saucepan over a medium heat. Add about 25g of the butter to the pan with 1 tablespoon olive oil and, when foaming, add the leek, potato, onion and garlic. Cook for 10–15 minutes, or until soft but not coloured. Add the chopped mushrooms and the thyme and season with a little salt and pepper. Cook for a further 5 minutes. Pour over the stock, bring to a simmer and cook for 10 minutes.

Purée the soup in a blender until smooth and creamy. Return it to the pan, add the cream and bring back to a gentle simmer.

Meanwhile, in a separate small frying pan, heat the remaining butter and olive oil over a medium heat. Slice the reserved mushrooms (unless they're really small) and fry them until tender and starting to colour, making sure any liquid they release evaporates. Serve the soup in warmed bowls, topped with the sautéed mushrooms and some chopped parsley.

Mushroom loaves

These look really impressive and yet are very simple to cook. They make a great light lunch or supper, or a very generous starter.

Works with: pretty much anything.

Serves 4

4 large white crusty bread rolls – not too light and flaky, though	Salt and freshly ground black pepper 75ml white wine
100g butter	150ml double cream
350g mixed mushrooms	1 tbsp mixed chopped parsley
1 large leek, trimmed and finely sliced	and chives

Preheat the oven to 200°C/Gas Mark 6.

Slice a 'lid' off the top of each roll and scoop out most of the soft crumb from inside (use this to make breadcrumbs for another dish). Melt 75g of the butter and brush the hollowed-out rolls, inside and out, and the lids, with it. Place them on a baking sheet and bake for 5–10 minutes until golden and crisp. Turn off the oven, open the door and leave the rolls inside to keep warm.

Clean and trim the mushrooms and cut into fairly small slices.

Heat the remaining 25g butter in a large frying pan over a medium–low heat, add the leek and sauté gently until soft. Add the mushrooms and a pinch of seasoning and increase the heat a little. Cook, stirring frequently, until the mushrooms have released all their liquid, and it has evaporated. Add the wine and let it bubble away until the liquid has disappeared, then add the cream. Simmer gently for 5 minutes or so until thick – you don't want the mixture to be runny. Stir in the herbs and check the seasoning. Spoon the mushroom mixture into the hot, crisp rolls, put the lids on and serve straight away with some tender salad leaves.

Consommé
with dried mushrooms

Many fungi recipes are earthy, gutsy and rustic – and none the worse for that. This one, on the other hand, is the very soul of elegance. It's also quite unusual in that it works better with dried mushrooms than fresh. You could augment it with a few vegetables: finely diced carrot added with the mushrooms, for instance, or sliced spring onions thrown in at the end, but don't be tempted to add too many extra ingredients: you want the flavour of the mushrooms to shine through unchallenged. Dried Ceps are the perfect mushroom to use, but any well flavoured, sliced dried mushroom will do.

Works with: any dried, well flavoured mushroom.

Serves 4

50g dried, sliced mushrooms
800ml good clear beef or chicken stock
50ml white wine
1 tbsp olive oil

100g very small pasta, such as
   risoni or tiny pasta shapes
Salt and freshly ground black pepper
A little chopped parsley

Put the mushrooms in a bowl and pour over enough boiling water to cover them – around 200ml. Leave for about 20 minutes, then strain them, reserving the liquid. Pass this through a funnel or sieve lined with a coffee filter or some muslin, to remove any grit, then add it to the stock and white wine in a large saucepan. Bring to a simmer.

Meanwhile, heat the olive oil in a frying pan over a medium heat. Chop the soaked mushrooms fairly small, add them to the pan and sweat them gently for a few minutes before adding to the stock. Bring the stock to a simmer, then add the pasta and cook for 10 minutes or so, until the pasta is done. Taste and season accordingly, then ladle into soup bowls, scatter with just a little chopped parsley, and serve.

West Country stroganoff

This is so called because it was first cooked using Somerset cider, Devon cream and Dorset mushrooms. However, it would of course be best made with the local equivalents wherever you live. Winter Chanterelles are excellent in this dish, but by no means the only option, and also a mixture of types would work well.

Works with: Trumpet Chanterelles, Winter Chanterelles, Blewits, any Bolete, Blushers, Tawny Grisette, The Miller.

Serves 3–4

400–500g mushrooms
1 tbsp groundnut or
   sunflower oil
2 onions, peeled and thinly sliced
A large knob of butter
Salt and freshly ground black pepper

2 fat garlic cloves, peeled
   and finely chopped
150ml medium cider
150ml double cream
A squeeze of lemon juice
1 tbsp chopped parsley

Clean and trim the mushrooms and cut into walnut-sized chunks.

Heat the oil in a large frying pan over a medium heat. Add the onions and fry gently until starting to soften – about 10 minutes. Turn up the heat, add the mushrooms and knob of butter and fry, stirring, until the mushroom liquid has evaporated and everything starts turning golden. Season lightly, and toss in the garlic. Just as the garlic begins to colour, pour in the cider and stir well, then pour in the cream. Simmer for 5–10 minutes until the sauce is reduced and thickened. Add a squeeze of lemon juice. Taste and adjust the seasoning. Serve, with the chopped parsley scattered over, on a baked potato, or with rice.

Braised mushrooms
on pearl barley

Use large, dark-gilled Field Mushrooms or Horse Mushrooms for this – or organic cultivated mushrooms, such as Portobellos. Their substantial texture is delicious against the nutty grains of the barley and their inky juices contribute lots of flavour to the wine-infused sauce. If pearl barley is not to hand, you could serve them on a risotto (p.227) or on a mound of well seasoned, wet polenta.

Serves 4

For the barley
1 tbsp oil
A small knob of butter
1 onion, peeled and finely chopped
350g pearl barley
Up to 1.5 litres vegetable, mushroom
  or chicken stock (or use a mix of
  stock and water)

For the mushrooms
500g large Field or Horse Mushrooms
2 tbsp olive oil
A knob of butter
1 garlic clove, peeled and chopped
Salt and freshly ground black pepper
1 tsp chopped thyme
100ml red wine
200ml vegetable or chicken stock

Start with the barley. Heat the oil in a large-ish saucepan over a medium heat. Add the onion and cook for about 10 minutes, until soft and golden. Meanwhile, put the barley in another pan, cover with cold water, bring to the boil, then drain and rinse with cold water. Add the barley to the onions, stir it in, add about 1 litre of stock and bring to the boil. Turn down the heat to a simmer and cook, stirring often, for 45–75 minutes. After 40 minutes it should be tender but still chewy, whereas 75 minutes should render it pretty soft. As the barley cooks, add more stock or water – add it gradually because you don't want liquid left in the pan when the barley is cooked. Stir the knob of butter into the cooked barley and season well.

Meanwhile, clean and trim the mushrooms and slice them thickly. Heat the oil and butter in a deep frying pan over a medium heat. Throw in the garlic and cook for just a minute, without letting it colour, then add the mushrooms and seasoning. Cook, stirring from time to time, until they have shrunk to about half their original volume, and released their juices. Add the thyme, wine and stock. Bring to the boil, lower the heat and simmer for about 15 minutes, or until the mushrooms are very tender and the liquid has reduced by about half. Check the seasoning. Spoon the barley into warmed dishes, top with the mushrooms and their juices, and serve.

Cauliflower Fungus cheese

Cauliflower Fungus can look pretty daunting but, in fact, it's not difficult to prepare – treating it as you would an actual cauliflower is a pretty good approach. That is just how the idea for this dish came about and it turned out to be a delicious way to cook this spectacular-looking wild food.

Serves 4–6 as a side dish

About 1kg Cauliflower Fungus –
    either 1 whole small one,
    or part of a larger one (p.122)
1 small onion, peeled and grated
1 carrot, peeled and grated
500ml whole milk

1 bay leaf
Salt and freshly ground black pepper
50g butter
75g plain flour
100g mature Cheddar, grated
1 tsp English mustard

Preheat the oven to 180°C/Gas Mark 4.

Use a sharp knife to cut the Cauliflower Fungus into golf ball-sized florets. Work through the body, discarding any discoloured or damaged areas together with the tough core. You now need to get rid of all the unwelcome extras – pine needles, earwigs, etc. – that the fungus will inevitably contain. You might be able to do this with a thorough brushing, but you will probably need to wash the florets. Rinse them under the tap rather than soaking in water, and be as gentle as you can.

Put the grated onion and carrot in a small saucepan with the milk, the bay leaf and some black pepper. Bring almost to boiling, then set aside to infuse for 10 minutes before straining the milk into a warmed jug. Discard the bay leaf and vegetables.

Melt the butter in the milk pan (you don't need to wash it) over a medium heat and stir in the flour to get a loose roux. Cook this gently for a couple of minutes, then gradually add the warm, seasoned milk, stirring well after each addition to prevent lumps. When all the milk is added and the sauce is thick and smooth, bring it to a simmer and cook gently for just a minute. Add most of the cheese (reserving a little for the topping) and the mustard and stir well so the cheese melts into the sauce.

Place the prepared cauliflower fungus in a large mixing bowl, pour over the cheesy sauce and fold together with a large spoon (or use your hands). Spoon the mixture into a buttered, ovenproof dish. Sprinkle over the remaining cheese and bake for 15–20 minutes until bubbling and golden brown. This is particularly good served with steak or a piece of boiled bacon. It also makes a nice starter on its own.

Braised pheasant
with wild mushrooms, shallots & bacon

Wild mushrooms always go well with game – and their seasons coincide neatly too – and you can use various different species of either here. If pheasant isn't available, try partridge or rabbit, for instance. Wood Blewits, as shown in the photo, are a good mushroom choice but this dish would also be excellent with Velvet Shanks, Deceivers, Winter Chanterelles or Saffron Milkcaps – all more unusual species that hold their shape during the long cooking.

Works with: almost anything, except Puffballs and Parasols.

Serves 2

150–200g mushrooms
2 tbsp sunflower or groundnut oil
1 pheasant, jointed into four pieces
A little plain flour
Salt and freshly ground black pepper
6 thick rashers streaky bacon,
   roughly chopped
12 baby shallots or
   pickling onions, peeled

A knob of butter
2 fat garlic cloves, peeled
   and thinly sliced
2 glasses red wine
About 250ml game, chicken or
   mushroom stock, or water
1 tbsp chopped parsley

Preheat the oven to 120°C/Gas Mark ½.

Clean and trim the mushrooms, and cut them into halves or quarters.

Heat the oil in a flameproof casserole dish over a high heat. Toss the pheasant pieces in the flour, shaking off any excess, then season them with salt and pepper. When the oil is hot, but not smoking, add the pheasant pieces, skin-side down. When they're a deep golden brown, turn them over, and add the bacon, shallots and mushrooms. Fry the whole lot, scraping and stirring as best you can, until everything has taken some colour. Toss in the butter and garlic, let it sizzle and foam, then pour in the wine and scrape up all the lovely caramelised bits from the bottom of the pan.

Add enough stock or water to nearly cover the pheasant, bring just to the boil, put the lid on and then transfer to the oven for about 1½ hours, until the meat is very tender and beginning to fall off the bone. Taste the juices, season if necessary, stir in the parsley and serve with mash or a baked potato.

Rabbit & mushroom
puff pies

This is one of those forager-friendly recipes where almost any mushroom can be used. However, these pies are particularly good made with smaller fungi such as Deceivers, Winter Chanterelles and Fairy Ring Champignons. Hedgehog Mushrooms would be another good choice, not least because 'rabbit and Hedgehog pies' sound very intriguing. You could, though, use almost any game meat here. Pheasant works very well, for instance.

If you're in a hurry, you can skip the marinating and just flavour the meat by adding some garlic, bay and juniper to the pan as you brown it. Then again, if you have plenty of time you can make a sauce for the pies using the marinating liquid. Strain it, add another 150ml port and boil until reduced by half. Add 150ml stock, reduce by half again, then add a few tablespoons double cream and simmer until thick and rich.

Works with: anything except Parasols and Puffballs.

Serves 4

4 tbsp ruby port	50g butter
2 bay leaves, torn	25g plain flour
1 garlic clove, bashed	250ml double cream
1 tsp crushed juniper berries	Salt and freshly ground black pepper
About 800g boned-out rabbit (or hare, pheasant, pigeon or venison meat) from the saddle or leg, free of tendon or sinew	2 tsp chopped parsley
	300g puff pastry
	1 tbsp olive oil
	1 egg, beaten, to glaze
500g mixed mushrooms	

Combine the port, bay leaves, garlic and juniper, mix in the rabbit or other game and leave to marinate for an hour or two. Take the rabbit from the marinade, shake off the liquid, and cut the meat into thick slices.

Clean, trim and roughly slice the mushrooms.

Melt the butter in a large frying pan over a medium heat, add the mushrooms to the pan and cook gently for 4–5 minutes. Sift in the flour, and work it well in to the butter and mushrooms. Add the cream, turn down the heat and simmer gently for about 5 minutes, or until thick. Season with salt and pepper, add the parsley and leave to cool.

Roll out half of the pastry and cut into four thin discs, approximately 15cm in diameter, then roll out the rest and cut into four discs about 10cm in diameter. Put the larger discs in shallow saucers and spoon on the mushroom mix, leaving a wide rim at the edge.

Heat the olive oil in a large frying pan over a high heat. Add the sliced rabbit and fry it just until sealed and golden on the outside. Arrange the meat on top of the mushrooms on the pastry discs. Bring the edges of the pastry up over the filling, moisten the edges with water or a little milk, put the smaller discs on top and seal. Use a fork to crimp the edges together. Chill for half an hour.

Preheat the oven to 200°C/Gas Mark 6.

Transfer the pies to an oiled baking sheet, brush with the beaten egg and make slits in the top for steam to escape. Bake for 30 minutes, or until crisp and golden. Serve accompanied by some simply steamed seasonal veg – wilted spinach or shredded cabbage, perhaps – and some new or mashed potatoes.

Two mushroom tarts

A good mushroom tart is a very fine thing and there is no end to the possible variations on the theme. With a pastry case and a savoury egg custard being the two constants, you can create a filling with whatever you choose. Two excellent recipes follow, both combining specific mushrooms with aromatic and salty ingredients to delicious effect. Take these as templates and create your own tart filling with ingredients you have to hand. If the process of making and baking a pastry case seems a little too time consuming, consider the very easy, puff-pastry-based tart on p.222.

Cep, pancetta & thyme tart

This works really well with fresh Ceps but a combination of fresh and dried gives an even better flavour.

Also works with: for any tart, favour dryish mushrooms such as Hedgehog Mushrooms, Chanterelles, Winter Chanterelles or Charcoal Burners.

Serves 6

For the shortcrust pastry
250g plain flour
A pinch of salt
125g cold butter, cut into small cubes
1 egg, separated
About 50ml cold milk

For the filling
25–50g dried Ceps
Around 200g fresh Ceps

150g pancetta, cut into lardons
1 tbsp chopped flat leaf parsley
1 tbsp thyme leaves
A knob of butter
1 large onion, peeled, halved
    and sliced
2 whole eggs, plus 2 egg yolks
200ml full-fat milk
200ml double cream
Salt and freshly ground black pepper

To make the pastry, put the flour, salt and butter in a food processor and pulse until the mix reaches a breadcrumb consistency. With the machine running, add the egg yolk, followed by the milk, which should be added in a gradual stream. Watch carefully and stop adding the milk as soon as the pastry comes together. Turn out on to a lightly floured surface and knead into a smooth ball. Wrap in cling film and chill for half an hour.

Preheat the oven to 170°C/Gas Mark 3.

Roll out the pastry thinly and use to line a 25cm-diameter, loose-bottomed tart tin. Leave the excess pastry hanging over the edge. Prick the base all over with a fork, line with greaseproof paper and baking beans, put the tin on a baking sheet and bake for 15 minutes. Remove the beans and paper and return the pastry to the oven for 10 minutes. Then lightly beat the egg white and brush some of it over the hot pastry. Return it to the oven and bake for a final 5 minutes. This helps to seal the pastry and prevent any filling leaking out. Trim off the excess pastry using a small, sharp knife.

Turn up the oven to 180°C/Gas Mark 4.

Pour on enough hot water to just cover the dried Ceps and leave them to soak for 15 minutes. Swish them about in the bowl a few times to help loosen any grit (though if they are your own dried mushrooms, they really should not be gritty). Remove the Ceps with a fork, drain on a piece of kitchen paper, then chop them up roughly.

Pour the soaking liquid through a funnel lined with a coffee filter paper into a small saucepan. Set it over a high heat and boil until reduced to 100ml. Remove from the heat and reserve.

Clean, trim and slice the fresh Ceps.

Heat a large frying pan over a fairly high heat, add the pancetta lardons and fry until they are just starting to colour. Add the dried and fresh Ceps, along with the parsley and thyme. Cook until all the moisture the mushrooms release has evaporated, and they are starting to colour, then tip the mixture into a bowl.

Add the butter to the same pan, add the onion and fry over a medium heat until soft and just coloured. Combine with the pancetta and Ceps.

Beat the eggs and egg yolks with the milk, cream and the Cep liquor. Season with salt and pepper.

Fill the baked tart case with the Cep mixture (don't press it down too firmly), then pour over the custard. Make sure there aren't too many bits of Cep poking up out of the custard as these will dry out as the tart cooks.

Cook the tart in the oven for about 30 minutes or until golden on top and with only the hint of a wobble left in the middle. Leave to rest for at least 20 minutes before eating.

Parasol, leek & goat's cheese tart with walnut pastry

This follows the same basic method as the Cep tart, and is a lovely, earthy, autumnal dish. If you don't like walnuts, use the shortcrust pastry on p.218.

Serves 6

For the walnut pastry
60g walnuts
250g plain flour
A pinch of salt
125g cold butter, cut into small cubes
1 egg, separated
About 50ml cold milk

For the filling
200–300g closed or just-opened
    Parasols or Shaggy Parasols

50g butter
1 leek, trimmed, halved
    lengthways and finely sliced
2 whole eggs, plus 2 egg yolks
200ml full-fat milk
200ml double cream
Salt and freshly ground
    black pepper
100g hard goat's cheese, grated

First make the pastry. Preheat the oven to 170°C/Gas Mark 3. Put the walnuts in a food processor and chop them very finely. Then add the flour, salt and butter and proceed in exactly the same way as for the shortcrust pastry on pp.218–19. Roll out the pastry and use to line your 25cm-diameter, loose-bottomed tart tin, before baking as described on p.219. Turn the oven up to 180°C/Gas Mark 4.

Discard the Parasols' stalks, which can be fibrous, then clean and trim the caps and cut into slices about 5mm thick. Put half the butter in a large frying pan on a medium heat. Add the Parasols and a little seasoning and fry gently. They will shrink alarmingly, then, after their moisture has evaporated, they will turn golden and smell wonderfully nutty, even a little chickeny.

At the same time, melt the remaining butter in a lidded second pan, add the leek and cook gently. Stir every now and then, keeping the lid on between stirs, until soft but still bright green – about 10 minutes. Leave the mushrooms and leeks to cool.

Beat the eggs and egg yolks with the milk and cream, season with salt and pepper (allowing for the saltiness of the cheese) and stir in the mushrooms, leeks and cheese. Tip this mixture into the tart case and bake for about 30 minutes, until patched with gold on top and just a little wobbly in the middle. Leave to rest for at least 20 minutes before serving. This is also very good cold.

Easy wild mushroom tart

This is the simplest of tarts, and a good option if you don't have the time or inclination to make your own pastry. You can use any mushrooms you fancy and the whole thing takes little more than half an hour, start to finish.

Works with: just about anything.

Serves 2 as a starter or snack

About 200g mixed wild mushrooms
25g butter
Salt and freshly ground black pepper
1 garlic clove, peeled and finely
  chopped
Breadcrumbs made from 1 thick slice
  stale white bread, crusts removed

Finely grated zest of ½ lemon
1 heaped tbsp grated Parmesan
250g bought puff pastry or
  home-made rough puff pastry
1 tbsp finely chopped parsley
1 egg, beaten

•

Preheat the oven to 180°C/Gas Mark 4.

Clean, trim and slice the mushrooms.

Heat the butter in a small frying pan and add the mushrooms and a pinch of salt. As the mushrooms start to soften, throw in the garlic and fry gently for another 2–3 minutes or so. You want the mushrooms to be tender but not coloured and their liquid evaporated. Remove the pan from the heat and stir in the breadcrumbs, lemon zest, Parmesan, parsley and a few grinds of black pepper.

Roll out the pastry into a rough circle, no more than 5mm thick. Use this to line the base only of a 20cm-diameter tart tin or ovenproof frying pan and trim off the excess. Heap the mushroom mixture into the pastry, leaving a couple of centimetres uncovered around the edge – this will make a nice puffed-up, crisp, golden rim to the tart. Brush this edge with the beaten egg and bake for around 20 minutes, until the pastry is puffed up and golden. Serve hot or cold.

Pizza bianca
with mushrooms

Pizza bianca is a very simple pizza without tomato sauce. Given sweetness and softness with a topping of golden caramelised onions, it is a wonderful vehicle for a few, precious wild mushrooms as you don't need very many to create a big impact, visually and taste-wise.

Works with: just about anything, but perhaps the more colourful the better – try Chanterelles and Horns of Plenty (shown here), or Hedgehog Mushrooms and Blewits as well as Amethyst Deceivers or Waxcaps.

Serves 4

For the pizza dough
5g dried yeast
125g plain flour
125g strong white bread flour
5g salt
1 tbsp olive oil

For the topping
100–200g mushrooms
A large knob of butter

Flaky sea salt and freshly
   ground black pepper
3 tbsp olive oil
750g onions, peeled and
   very thinly sliced
2 heaped tsp fresh thyme leaves
A few tbsp crème fraîche
   or 1 ball buffalo mozzarella, sliced
Extra virgin olive oil

First make the dough: dissolve the yeast in 160ml warm water and leave for 10 minutes or so until it starts to froth. Meanwhile, combine the two flours and the salt in a large bowl. Add the yeast liquid and the oil, mix together into a rough dough, then turn out and knead on a floured surface for 5–10 minutes until silky and elastic. Leave it to rise in a warm place until doubled in size (at least 1 hour).

Meanwhile, prepare the mushrooms by cleaning and trimming them, then slicing thinly. Heat the butter in a large frying pan over a medium heat, add the mushrooms and a pinch of salt and fry gently until soft but not coloured. Remove them from the pan.

Add the olive oil to the pan. Add the onions, and a good pinch of salt, and cook gently on a low heat, stirring occasionally, for about half an hour until soft, golden and translucent.

Preheat the oven to 250°C/Gas Mark 9 and put in a baking sheet to heat.

Once the dough has doubled in size, knock it back and cut it in half. Use a rolling pin, or your hands, or both, to roll and stretch one half into a thin piece that will cover your baking sheet. Take the hot baking sheet from the oven, scatter it with a little flour or, even better, some cornmeal, fine polenta or semolina, and lay on the dough. Spread half the soft onions over the dough, scatter over half the mushrooms, then half the thyme, then add a few dollops of crème fraîche, or half the mozzarella. Scatter over some flaky salt and a few twists of black pepper, trickle on some extra virgin olive oil and bake for 10–12 minutes, until the base is crisp and golden brown at the edges. While it's cooking, roll out the second piece of dough, and prepare in the same way, so it's ready to go as soon as the first is cooked. Serve hot, in big slices.

Variation: Mushroom, ham & chard pizza

This alternative topping is slightly more substantial but just as delicious.

100–200g mushrooms	**8 chard leaves, stalks removed,**
A large knob of butter	**torn and washed**
Flaky sea salt and freshly	**8 slices air-dried ham**
ground black pepper	**1 ball buffalo mozzarella, sliced**
	Olive oil

Make the dough as on p.225. Preheat the oven to 250°C/Gas Mark 9.

Clean, trim and slice the mushrooms. Heat the butter in a frying pan over a medium heat, add the mushrooms and a pinch of salt and fry gently until soft but not coloured. Remove the mushrooms from the pan, throw in the chard and cook for 30 seconds, just to wilt it a little.

Knock back the risen dough and use half of it to make your first pizza base with the method above.

Arrange half the mushrooms, ham, chard and mozzarella as artfully or artlessly as you like over the top, grind over some pepper and scatter on a little flaky sea salt, then trickle with a lick of olive oil. Bake for 10–12 minutes until the base is crisp and golden brown and the mozzarella sizzling. Repeat with the remaining dough and topping ingredients.

Wild mushroom risotto

The earthy flavour of mushrooms always works wonderfully in a risotto, and you can use almost any kind in this recipe. We like to use a real medley in ours: Ceps, Oak Milkcaps, Brittlegills, Bay Boletes, Hedgehog Mushrooms and Chanterelles. A mixture of fresh and dried mushrooms would work well too and the soaking liquid from rehydrated dried ones is a great addition to the stock.

We like to spoon the mushroom medley over the finished risotto, rather than stir it in: it makes for a nice clash of intense mushrooms with mildly fungal, creamy risotto. But if you like the idea of mixing everything up, go right ahead!

Works with: almost anything.

Serves 2

Around 300g fresh mushrooms,
  or a mixture of fresh and dried
75g butter
2 tbsp olive oil
4 shallots or 2 small onions,
  peeled and finely chopped
1 large garlic clove, peeled
  and finely chopped

Up to 750ml chicken, vegetable
  or mushroom stock
150g arborio or other risotto rice
Around 100ml white wine
Salt and freshly ground black pepper
2 tbsp chopped flat leaf parsley
2 tbsp double cream
50g grated Parmesan,
  plus extra to serve

If you're using any dried mushrooms, pour on just enough hot water to cover them and leave for 10–20 minutes. Strain them, reserving the liquid. If it looks gritty, pass it through a coffee filter, then add to the stock.

Clean and trim the mushrooms, and cut or slice them into fairly small pieces.

Melt about 15g of the butter with 1 tablespoon olive oil in a large, heavy-based saucepan over a medium heat. Add the onions and garlic and sauté gently for about 10 minutes, until soft – don't let them colour.

Meanwhile, bring the stock to a gentle simmer in a saucepan. Then turn down the heat very low – you need to keep the stock hot while you add it to the risotto.

Add the rice to the buttery onions and stir in well. Cook for a minute or two, then add the wine and let it simmer until absorbed.

Turn down the heat a little under the risotto pan. Add a ladleful of hot stock to the rice and let it cook, stirring from time to time, until nearly completely absorbed. Repeat with a second ladleful. Keep going, adding the stock gradually and stirring frequently, for about 20 minutes. By this time you should have used nearly all the stock, and the rice should be tender, with just the tiniest hint of bite left in it.

While the rice is cooking, heat a small knob of butter and 1 tablespoon olive oil in a large frying pan. Add the mushrooms and some seasoning and sauté for about 10 minutes until they are tender. Make sure that any liquid they release evaporates. Stir in the chopped parsley and keep the mushrooms warm while the rice finishes cooking.

When the rice is done to your liking, scatter the remaining butter, cut into little cubes, over the surface, along with the cream and the Parmesan. Turn off the heat and cover the pan for two minutes, then stir in the melted butter and cheese. Season well with salt and pepper. Check the consistency. If you like your risotto quite loose and wet, you can always add a little more hot stock now.

Spoon the rice into warmed dishes, spoon the mushrooms and any juices over the top, and serve with more grated Parmesan.

Pappardelle
with Ceps, sage & pancetta

Fresh homemade egg pasta, cut into thick ribbons, makes a wonderful vehicle for meaty slices of Cep. You can, of course, use a good shop-bought pappardelle instead, but find a fresh variety, made with egg, if you can – its tender texture will really make the dish.

Also works with: any Bolete and just about anything else, except perhaps Parasols, which would go soggy.

Serves 3–4

1 quantity pasta dough, as per the ravioli recipe on p.233
Around 750g Ceps (more, if you've got them)
2 tbsp olive oil
150g pancetta or streaky bacon, cut into smallish dice

10 sage leaves, finely shredded
1 garlic clove, peeled and finely minced
Salt and freshly ground black pepper
A knob of butter
Grated Parmesan, to serve (optional)

Make the pasta dough, following the recipe on pp.233–5. Trim the thin, freshly rolled sheets of pasta into lengths of about 20cm, then cut each into strips 2–3cm wide. Dust very lightly with flour and leave on a tea towel or hang up to dry – you can drape them over a coat hanger, or lay them on a flour-dusted tea towel hung over the back of a chair. Repeat with all the pasta. You can leave it for an hour or so, or use it straight away. Put a large pan of water on to boil.

Clean and trim the Ceps, cut them in half, then slice each half thinly.

Heat 1 tablespoon olive oil in a large frying pan, add the pancetta and cook until well coloured. Add the Ceps, sage and garlic, toss them with the pancetta and cook for a further 4–5 minutes or until the mushrooms' liquid has evaporated and they're starting to colour. Season with salt and pepper. Turn off the heat but keep warm.

Generously salt the pan of boiling water, drop the pappardelle into it and cook until al dente – probably no more than 2 minutes. Drain the pasta, tip it into the pan with the Ceps and pancetta, and add a good knob of butter and another tablespoon of olive oil. Toss well and serve on warmed plates. Parmesan is optional – the more Ceps you have, the less you need.

Boletus lasagne

This is a River Cottage classic, a variation on a porcini (Cep) lasagne cooked for Hugh many years ago by Mauro Bregoli of The Old Manor House restaurant in Romsey. It's a great way to make a really good meal from a relatively scant haul of mushrooms, as three or four good Ceps is enough for a lasagne to feed six. Any type of Bolete will work in this dish, or a combination of several different mushrooms. The lasagne you see here was made with Ceps, Bay Boletes and Slippery Jacks. You can use ready-made lasagne sheets but, if you have the time to make your own fresh pasta, it will contribute a lovely, tender quality and a superior flavour.

Works with: any Bolete, Wood Blewits, and large, firm Field Mushrooms.

Serves 6

For the béchamel sauce
500ml whole milk
½ onion, peeled
1 bay leaf
50g butter
50g plain flour
A pinch of grated nutmeg
Salt and freshly ground black pepper

For the lasagne
4–6 large firm Boletes – Ceps
   for preference
50g butter

4 tbsp olive oil
2 garlic cloves, peeled and finely
   chopped
Fresh pasta made with 200g flour,
   2 eggs and 1 tbsp oil (p.233), cut
   into sheets the same length as your
   dish, or 250g fresh lasagne sheets
75g Parmesan, grated
75g hard goat's cheese, such as
   Woolsery, grated (or use all Parmesan)
4–6 very thin slices of air-dried ham
   (enough to make one good layer in
   the middle of your lasagne)

Begin with the béchamel sauce. Put the milk in a saucepan with the onion and bay leaf and bring to just below simmering. Set aside to infuse for 30 minutes. Melt the butter in a separate pan over a medium heat, stir in the flour to make a roux and cook for a few minutes. Now gradually add the hot milk, stirring after each addition to prevent lumps. When all is added, bring the sauce to a simmer and cook for 1 minute. Season with nutmeg, salt and pepper. The finished sauce should be a thick pouring consistency; add a little more hot milk if necessary.

Clean the Boletes and cut into fine slices. Since they aren't cooked before being added to the lasagne, they need to be thin enough to cook through easily, but not so thin that they disintegrate: about 3–4mm thickness is about right. If you have large Boletes, cut the stalk from the cap, slice the cap and then slice the stalk diagonally.

Melt the butter with the oil in a small saucepan. Stir in the garlic and then take off the heat. Preheat the oven to 190°C/Gas Mark 5. You are now ready to assemble your lasagne.

Brush the bottom of a large square or rectangular oven dish with some of the warm garlic and oil mixture. Put a layer of lasagne on the bottom then brush with more of the garlic oil. Pour a thin layer of béchamel, just a couple of tablespoons, over the pasta (you don't want to overwhelm the subtle mushroom flavours with too much sauce), then add a layer of sliced mushrooms. Brush with more of the oil mixture, then season with a twist of pepper and a sprinkling of the two cheeses. The cheese is simply a seasoning, it's not meant to form a thick layer, so keep it light.

Add another trickle of béchamel, then repeat the layering (lasagne, oil, béchamel, mushrooms, oil, pepper and cheese). Now add a layer of air-dried ham, top with béchamel, then repeat lasagne, oil, béchamel, mushrooms, oil, pepper and cheese, béchamel. Finish off with a final layer of pasta, a final, thick layer of béchamel and a final sprinkling of cheese.

Bake for about 25 minutes until nicely browned on top. Serve with a green salad.

Mushroom ravioli
with lemon & parsley butter

The filling for these elegant pasta parcels requires mushrooms with plenty of flavour. Horse Mushrooms and rehydrated dried Ceps is a particularly tasty combination.

Also works with: Chanterelles, Fairy Ring Champignons, Morels, Hedgehog Mushrooms, Horn of Plenty, Scarletina Boletes.

Serves 4

For the filling
350g mushrooms
1 onion, peeled and cut into quarters
1 garlic clove, peeled and halved
A large knob of butter
Salt and freshly ground black pepper
1 tsp chopped thyme
100ml white wine
75g soft, mild, rindless goat's cheese
   (or use ricotta or another
   soft white cheese)
25g grated Parmesan

For the pasta dough
300g '00' pasta flour
A pinch of salt
3 eggs
1 tbsp olive oil

For the butter
100g unsalted butter
Grated zest of ½ lemon
1 tbsp finely chopped flat leaf parsley

Clean and trim the mushrooms and break them into pieces.

Put the onion and garlic in a food processor and chop very finely. Heat the butter in a large frying pan and add the onion mixture, with a good pinch of salt and pepper. Fry, stirring frequently, until the onion is soft and most of the liquid has evaporated. Meanwhile, put all the mushrooms in the processor and chop them very finely. Add them to the pan with the onions, throw in the thyme, and cook for at least 15 minutes, stirring often, until you have got rid of all the mushrooms' moisture. Add the white wine, stir it in and cook until the liquid has evaporated. Then transfer the mixture to a dish and leave to cool. When it is cool, stir in the goat's cheese and Parmesan. Taste the mixture and add more seasoning if necessary.

To make the pasta, put the flour, salt, eggs and oil into a food processor and process until they just come together in a crumbly mass. Tip onto a lightly floured surface and knead for 5–10 minutes until smooth. The dough will seem dry and stiff but

don't worry, it will soften a little as it chills. Wrap in cling film and chill for at least half an hour. Cut the pasta dough into four pieces and use a pasta machine to roll each one out. Dust one piece with a little flour and roll it through on the thickest setting. Fold in half and repeat, then repeat twice more. Then keep rolling the pasta through, gradually adjusting the machine so the pasta gets thinner and thinner. Dust with a little more flour if it starts to get sticky. You want the pasta thin enough that you can just about see the colour of your skin through it – probably at setting 5 or 6 (the second or third thinnest) on your machine.

To make the ravioli, use an 8cm cookie cutter to cut circles from the pasta sheets. You should get 24 ravioli from this recipe, so you'll need to cut 48 circles. Have a bowl of water and a pastry brush to hand, and a tray covered with a lightly floured tea towel. Put a blob of filling in the centre of one pasta disc. Dab a little water around the edge, top with a second pasta disc, and press the edges together to seal – work around the edge with your finger so no air is trapped inside. Place on the floured tea towel and repeat with the remaining pasta and filling. If you're not cooking the ravioli straight away, cover and refrigerate for up to 2 hours.

When you're ready to cook, put a very large pan of water on to boil. Prepare the lemon butter: melt the butter in a small saucepan over a very low heat, stir in the lemon zest and set aside to infuse.

When the pan of water is boiling, salt it generously. Depending on the size of your pan, you'll have to do this in two or three batches, maybe even four. So put 12, eight or six of the ravioli carefully into the boiling water. When the water returns to the boil, cook for 3 minutes, stirring once or twice so the ravioli don't stick together. Fish them out with a slotted spoon, letting the water drip off them, then transfer to warmed dishes. Repeat with the remaining ravioli. Stir the chopped parsley into the lemon zest-infused butter, spoon over the ravioli and serve straight away.

Variation: Mushroom piroshki, pasties or calzone

The intensely flavoured mushroom filling can also be folded inside pastry discs to make delicious little mushroom pasties, or piroshki as the Russians would call them. Either rough puff or shortcrust pastry will work. Alternatively, you can use small balls of pizza dough (p.225), rolled out very thinly, filled with the mix, and folded over, to make little wild mushroom calzone.

Deep-fried Parasols
with garlic mayonnaise

All the kinds of mushrooms could be given the deep-fried-in-breadcrumbs treatment but we honestly feel none will beat the Parasols. Their texture is excellent – almost chicken-like – and deep-frying is the perfect cooking method for them as it stops them turning into the wet rags you can end up with if you try to sauté them. Dipped in homemade garlicky mayonnaise, they really are wonderful. For best results, choose firm, heavy Parasols with their caps still closed, nearly closed or at least only recently opened.

Also works with: any *Agaricus* species, large thick-capped mushrooms only.

Serves 6 as a starter

For the garlic mayonnaise
1 very fresh egg yolk
1 anchovy fillet
1 garlic clove, peeled and
    finely chopped
½ tsp English mustard
1 small pinch each of salt, sugar
    and freshly ground black pepper
½ tbsp cider vinegar or lemon juice
100ml olive oil
150ml groundnut oil

For the Parasols
About 400g Parasols
Groundnut oil, for frying
2 tbsp plain flour
Salt and freshly ground black pepper
1 egg
100g fairly fine, fresh
    white breadcrumbs
Flaky salt and lemon wedges,
    to serve

Start by making the mayonnaise. Put the egg yolk, anchovy, garlic, mustard, salt, sugar, pepper and vinegar or lemon juice into a food processor and process until smooth. Combine the two oils in a jug. With the processor running, start pouring in the oil in a very thin trickle. When the oil starts to emulsify with the yolks, you can add the oil a little faster. By the time you've added all the oil, you'll have a thick, glossy mayonnaise. Adjust the seasoning and, if it seems too thick, thin it slightly with a little warm water. Cover and refrigerate until needed.

Remove the stalks from the Parasols and clean the caps well with a brush. Break the caps into segments – larger ones into eight, smaller ones into quarters.

Pour groundnut oil into a deep, heavy-based saucepan to a depth of at least 5cm. Heat it up to 180°C, or until a cube of white bread dropped in turns golden brown

in about 50 seconds. Meanwhile, put the flour in a small bowl and season. Put the egg in a second bowl and beat lightly. Put the breadcrumbs on a plate.

Dust each piece of Parasol with flour, dip in the egg, then roll in the breadcrumbs, patting them on well. Drop a few carefully into the hot oil and fry for 2–3 minutes until golden brown. Scoop out and drain on kitchen paper. Continue until all the Parasols are cooked. Serve straight away with the garlic mayonnaise, some flaky salt and some lemon wedges.

Mushroom tempura

A lacy, crunchy tempura batter – much lighter than a traditional British batter – is a lovely coating for the more delicate members of the mushroom family. Don't try it with big, thick chunks of dense mushroom, as the water contained in them will make the batter soggy, but go for small pieces of thin, light fungi. You do need to be organised, getting your sauce and your mushrooms prepared before you even think about mixing the batter, and then frying the tempura quickly so you can get the whole lot to the table still piping hot. It's important also to leave the batter itself just barely mixed so it's thin, with plenty of lumps. This ensures a lovely, light, crunchy texture.

Works with: tender, delicate mushrooms such as Chanterelles, Oysters, Yellow Swamp Brittlegills or Oak Milkcaps.

Serves 4 as a starter

For the dipping sauce
2 tbsp soy sauce
2 tbsp mirin
½ garlic clove, peeled
and finely chopped
½ hot red chilli, deseeded
and finely chopped

For the mushrooms
About 300g mushrooms
Groundnut oil, for frying

For the batter
1 egg yolk
250ml ice-cold water
125g plain flour
Fine sea salt

Make the dipping sauce first. Put all the ingredients in a small pan, bring to the boil, then remove from the heat and leave to infuse. Prepare and trim the mushrooms. You want them in bite-sized pieces, so cut them up as necessary. Preheat the oven to 120°C/Gas Mark ½.

Heat about 8cm depth of oil in a deep frying pan, until it reaches 180°C (test with a cube of white bread – it should turn golden brown in about 50 seconds).

Meanwhile, prepare the batter: in a bowl, beat the egg yolk lightly, and add the cold water. Sift the flour into another bowl, then stir the cold egg mix into it very briefly – you want the ingredients barely combined, the batter should be lumpy. It also needs to be thin, to ensure a light, crisp coating, so add more water if necessary. When the oil is hot, dip a mushroom into the cold, lumpy batter and drop it into the hot oil. Repeat with just a few more mushrooms (too many and the temperature

of the oil will drop) and cook for a couple of minutes until they are crisp (the batter should barely colour). Scoop out with a wire basket or 'spider' and transfer to a kitchen paper-lined plate. Scatter with fine salt straight away then transfer to the oven – or pass straight to your waiting guests. Cook the rest of the mushrooms in the same way, working as quickly as you can. Serve them piping hot, with the dipping sauce in one or two little bowls.

Roast chicken with Truffles

This is a lovely way to cook chicken, using just a little bit of Truffle to delicately perfume the breast.

Serves 4–5

100g soft butter
1 heaped tsp chopped thyme,
  plus an extra sprig
Salt and freshly ground black pepper
1 small but plump roasting chicken,
  weighing about 1.5–2kg

4–6 thin slices fresh English Truffle
8–10 small, whole shallots, unpeeled
  but rinsed clean
2 bay leaves
½ glass of white wine

Preheat the oven to 220°C/Gas Mark 7.

Beat the softened butter with the chopped thyme and season well.

Take off any string or elastic trussing from the chicken, place the bird in a roasting tin and spread out its legs from the body. Enlarge the opening of the cavity with your fingers, so hot air can circulate inside the bird.

Ease the skin of the breast away from the flesh by pushing your fingers gently down under the skin. Take great care not to tear it. You don't need to go all the way down, just create a large pocket of skin over the breast. Press half the thyme butter into this pocket, smearing it over the flesh of the breast, then carefully place the slivers of Truffle over the butter so they lie flat between skin and breast.

Smear the remaining butter all over the outside of the bird, and season it well. Put the whole shallots inside the bird (if they won't all fit, just put some in the tin), along with the bay leaves and sprig of thyme.

Roast for 20 minutes in the hot oven. Then baste the chicken, turn down the oven to 180°C/Gas Mark 4, pour the wine into the tin (not over the bird) and roast the bird for another 30–40 minutes, depending on its size. Open the oven door, turn off the oven and leave the bird for 15–20 minutes. This is usually enough time to roast a small chicken through without burning the skin. Check by pressing a skewer into the meat between the leg and the body: the juices should run clear.

Carve the bird in the tin, letting the pieces fall into the buttery pan juices, along with the cooked shallots, and letting the fresh juices from carving mingle with the rest. Then take the tin to the table and serve. A green salad is the only accompaniment you will need.

Mushroom stock

This makes a fantastic base for mushroom soups, stews, risottos and sauces, but can be used in all manner of other dishes where you need a good backbone of savoury flavour. There's little point being specific about quantities – use what you have, but it's not really worth making this stock with less than 500g mushrooms. You can use any fungi, wild, dried or cultivated, and this is an excellent and thrifty way to take care of excess mushrooms not needed for other dishes, clean stalks and other trimmings, and the more elderly or knocked-about fungi from your foraging trips. Don't, however, use anything that feels slimy or smells unpleasant.

Butter, lard or any other fat that's solid
   at room temperature
Mushrooms and mushroom trimmings
Onions, peeled and sliced – about
   one-sixth the weight of your mushrooms
1 leek, carrot and stick of celery
   (not essential, but desirable),
   all chopped fairly small
A bay leaf and/or a sprig of thyme

Heat a good knob of fat in a large frying pan, add a batch of mushrooms and fry until all their liquid has evaporated and they're golden brown. Repeat with all the mushrooms then put them in a stock pot with the onions, vegetables and herbs. Bring to the boil, reduce to a simmer and cook, with the lid on, for an hour or so.

Leave to cool until hand-hot but not scalding, then pass through a large sieve lined with muslin. Leave to cool completely, then refrigerate. When the stock is cold, remove the layer of solid fat that will have formed on top. Pour the stock slowly into a storage container, discarding any sludge at the bottom you don't like the look of. Store, covered, in the fridge, for up to three days, or freeze.

Preserving mushrooms

Whether you are fortunate enough to have a glut of mushrooms, or you simply don't want to use all the ones you've just gathered straight away, it's very handy to have a few preserving techniques up your sleeve. Almost without exception, a mushroom in good condition that's been properly preserved will perform just as well in a recipe as a fresh one. There are cases where preserved mushrooms are positively desirable, in fact. The Cep tart on pp.218–19 benefits from some dried mushrooms, which have a particularly concentrated flavour, while the oil, salt and vinegar used for pickling give mushrooms a unique, highly seasoned quality that makes them ideal for appetite-whetting canapés or antipasti.

Drying

This is perhaps the most popular way of preserving mushrooms, and the easiest. It works with just about any fungi, and enhances the flavour of most. Dried mushrooms can very quickly be rehydrated for cooking, but can also be powdered and added to dishes for a real boost of flavour.

You must start with good, unblemished, fresh mushrooms. Slice them thinly – but not too thinly. In most cases, that means 2–4mm thick. Then lay them on a rack – a cake cooling rack or grill rack is ideal – and put them in a warm place where air can circulate freely around them. A warm windowsill is perfect, or the top of an Aga, or a *very* low oven, with the door left slightly ajar. Commercial dryers are also available – though hardly necessary for most small-scale foragers.

Another technique, useful if you don't have a rack or you have lots of mushrooms to dry, is to thread the slices on to string, ideally with a piece of cardboard between each mushroom, and hang them over an Aga or radiator.

Speed is crucial – you must dry your mushrooms before they get any chance to spoil. However, it's also important not to toast them. The ideal drying temperature is 45–55°C, no higher, and you should expect the mushrooms to take five or six hours to dry properly. Good ventilation is essential or the mushrooms will spoil quickly and the unmistakable smell of elderly trainers will start to fill the air.

Once dried, store your mushrooms in clean, dry jars with sealable lids and keep for up to a year.

To rehydrate mushrooms, soak for 15 minutes in warm water. The soaking water, which becomes a sort of light mushroom stock, can be added to dishes too. If your mushrooms were gritty, rinse them once reconstituted, and pass the soaking liquid through a paper coffee filter to get rid of any debris, before using it in a dish.

Freezing

You can freeze any mushroom. Very young ones freeze reasonably well raw, without any preparation, apart from basic cleaning. Once defrosted, you can use them just as you would fresh fungi. Slice and cook more mature specimens before freezing. Follow the basic sautéing technique used for mushrooms on toast (p.184) – without the garlic, as this can taste unpleasant after freezing – then let the mushrooms cool completely. Divide into portions and freeze in small bags or containers. After defrosting, revive them with a few minutes in a hot frying pan and then serve as they are, or incorporate in any recipe that uses sautéed mushrooms.

Mushrooms don't keep well for very long in the freezer, so use them within three months if you can, and certainly don't keep them for longer than six.

If you've had a good haul of mushrooms, but are unable to stow and stash them, make the wild mushroom soup on p.204, and freeze that instead.

Pickling

Pickling works best with whole small mushrooms such as Fairy Ring Champignons or very firm mushrooms such as button Field Mushrooms or firm young Ceps. This clever technique involves lightly pickling, or 'sterilising' the mushrooms, first with salt, then with vinegar, then preserving them in oil for safe keeping. Done well, they are delicious to eat straight from their jar of oil.

Clean your mushrooms and remove the stalks if they are tough. Cut them into fairly small pieces or, if they're small, leave them whole.

Put the mushrooms in a bowl and sprinkle liberally with fine-grained sea salt until all surfaces are covered. Leave for 1–2 hours, then pour off the accumulated liquid. Sprinkle on a fresh layer of salt and leave for a further 1–2 hours. Pour off the liquid again, then rinse the mushrooms under a cold, running tap to get rid of all the salt. Do it quickly so they don't have time to reabsorb any water.

Bring a pan of cider vinegar to a simmer (enough to cover the mushrooms). Drop them in and blanch for 2 minutes, then remove from the heat. Leave in the vinegar for at least 2 hours, and up to 24 for really big ones, such as whole Ceps. The longer they pickle, the longer you can keep them – but the more vinegary they taste.

Sterilise jam jars by washing them in hot, soapy water, rinsing and leaving to dry in a very low oven – or by putting them through a dishwasher cycle. Drain off the vinegar and transfer the mushrooms to the jars. Pour on enough oil to cover. Walnut oil is best in terms of flavour, but it only keeps a month or so. Sunflower or olive oil lasts longer. Give the jars a few firm knocks on the work surface to get rid of air bubbles and seal with lids. Label and keep in a cool, dry place, for up to six months.

The End

Useful addresses & further reading

It is quite impossible to have too many books on fungi but if you buy just one more you could do no better than *Mushrooms* by Roger Phillips (MacMillan, 2006). Also extremely helpful is Roger's website (www.rogersmushrooms.com), which is a stunning collection of photographs nicely laid out.

While there are many specialist and often impenetrable texts on individual genera, there are few books in print that make any attempt to cover the whole range of the larger fungi. If, however, you are prepared to take out a second mortgage it is really, really worthwhile getting hold of all six volumes (at around £80 each!) of *The Fungi of Switzerland*. Do not be put off by the mention of Switzerland, nearly all of the fungi in this vast work are found in the UK. The photographs are excellent and the descriptions technical but perfect. It is available from Richmond Publishing in Slough.

The venerable society devoted to the study of fungi, the British Mycological Society, is open to professional and amateur mycologists alike. It organises several forays each year, some of which are residential. It also publishes a number of journals ranging from the learned *Mycological Research* (which sports scientific papers with snappy titles such as 'Variability in Ribosomal DNA Genic and Spacer Regions in Phytophthora Infestans Isolates from Scottish Cocoa Plantations') through to the more digestible *Field Mycology* which has articles of actual use to the average mushroom hunter. Its address is British Mycological Society, The Wolfson Wing, Jodrell Laboratory, Royal Botanic Gardens, Kew, Surrey, TW9 3AB. The website address is www.britmycolsoc.org.uk.

Armchair mushroom hunters can obtain some of the species in this book from Smithy Mushrooms at www.smithymushrooms.co.uk. If you have ever thought of planting a Truffle tree do get in touch with Truffle UK at www.truffle-uk.co.uk.

There is nothing quite like going out with an expert to extend your knowledge of the fungi and many fungus forays are run each autumn by local societies and organisations, led by local experts. Fungus forays are among the many other day courses run at the River Cottage HQ on the Dorset/Devon border. If you would like to join me on one of these do contact us at www.rivercottage.net.

My own website is www.mushroomhunting.co.uk.

Acknowledgements

Writing is usually considered to be a very solitary enterprise, but I have found that in writing a book such as this one, it is not necessarily so. I have spent a great deal of time talking on the telephone to friends and reaping the benefit of their extensive knowledge. So it is a great pleasure to be able to thank them for their undue patience in helping me in my endeavour.

First I must thank Dr Peter Roberts and Gordon Dickson for their unstinting support. These are people of whom I can say, without the slightest hint of false modesty, know vastly more about the fungi than I will ever know, though I do believe that I am better looking than either of them. My good friend Dr John Cockerill has saved me considerable embarrassment by correcting some of my medical howlers in the section on poisonous fungi. It is gratifying to know that his years spent studying toxicology were not entirely wasted.

Alan Outen has kindly contributed photographs of fungi that proved too elusive for me and his general advice has been invaluable. The entries on the Boletus species would have been that much the poorer were it not for the support of King Bolete himself, Alan Hills.

I would also like to thank Dr Brian Spooner for his advice; Peter Chandler for his inspirational championing of maggots; Nigel Hadden-Paton for sharing his passion for Truffles. Also Tim Brodie-James from Natural England, Jim White and Bryan Edwards.

The team at River Cottage headquarters have put together a wonderful recipe section. The credit for this is due to Nikki Duffy, the River Cottage food editor, Gill and Dan and everyone else in the kitchen, and to Helen Stiles for organising the photoshoots. Also Colin Campbell for his superb food photography.

I have had enormous encouragement from the eternally patient editorial team at Bloomsbury, so much gratitude is due to Richard Atkinson, Erica Jarnes and Natalie Hunt, and to Emma Callery, the copy editor, for all her work. Also to Will Webb for his sterling work with the layout.

Many thanks are due to Gordon Wise for his invaluable guidance. I am immensely grateful for the enthusiastic support I have received from Rob Love and Antony Topping and hope that Rob now has the mushroom book he has always wanted.

Of course, this book would not have been possible without Hugh. So, quite simply, thank you Hugh.

Index